THE WORD
BEHIND BARS AND
THE PARADOX
OF EXILE

THE WORD BEHIND BARS AND THE PARADOX OF EXILE

Edited by Kofi Anyidoho

With a Foreword by Jane I. Guyer

Northwestern University Press

Evanston, Illinois

Northwestern University Press
Evanston, Illinois 60208-4210

Copyright © 1997 by Northwestern University Press.
Published 1997. All rights reserved.
Printed in the United States of America

ISBN 0-8101-1392-9 (cloth)
ISBN 0-8101-1393-7 (paper)

Library of Congress Cataloging-in-Publication Data

The word behind bars and the paradox of exile / edited by Kofi
Anyidoho ; with a foreword by Jane I. Guyer.
    p. cm.
Includes bibliographical references.
ISBN 0-8101-1392-9 (cloth : alk. paper). — ISBN 0-8101-1393-7
(paper : alk. paper)
    1. African literature (English)—History and criticism—Congresses.
    2. Prisoners' writings, African (English)—History and criticism—Congresses.
    3. Exiles' writings, African (English)—History and criticism—Congresses.
    4. Political prisoners—Africa—Literary collections.   5. Prisoners' writings,
African (English)   6. Exiles' writings, African (English)   7. Prisons—Africa—
Literary collections.   8. Prisoners in literature—Congresses.   9. Prisons in
literature—Congresses.   10. Exiles in literature—Congresses.
I. Anyidoho, Kofi.
PR9340.A515W67   1997
820.9'920692—dc21   97-16003
                                                                     CIP

Contents

ACKNOWLEDGMENTS

I acknowledge with gratitude the various roles played by the following in making possible the 1994–95 Institute program and the publication of this work: the governing board of the Institute, for offering me appointment as preceptor and for approving my original proposal defining the field of inquiry for the year; David William Cohen, former Institute secretary and former director of the Program of African Studies (PAS) at Northwestern University, for helping to shape my initial proposal into a comprehensive program document; Sandra L. Richards, former acting director of PAS and interim Institute secretary, for working with me on my initial proposal for the workshop on Prison and Exile; Jane Guyer and Akbar Virmani, director and assistant director of PAS respectively, for the many long hours and careful planning that went into finalizing arrangements for the workshop; to Roseann Mark, department assistant and publications manager at PAS, for her energy, dedication, and excellent sense of humor in handling the many logistical and technical details of both the workshop and the preparation of the manuscript for publication; Adam West, program assistant, and Karyn Hernandez, financial manager, for their invaluable support during the workshop and throughout my stay with the Institute; to my daughter, Nana Akua Anyidoho, for transcribing Dennis Brutus's plenary address for me to edit; Northwestern University Press director Nicholas Weir-Williams, editor-in-chief Susan Harris, and the rest of the NU Press staff for their encouragement and guidance in the preparation of the manuscript and the actual production of this book; and finally, to the various contributors to this volume and other participants in the Prison and Exile workshop, for responding so kindly to our invitation and for working hard to meet our rather unreasonable deadlines.

Foreword

The place of writers, at home and in exile, acutely reflects social and political conditions. Writers' fates provide direct testimony to those conditions, and their capacity to write makes accessible an experience that they share with many others who are less artistically endowed. Unique and yet part of a larger reality, writers assume a particular responsibility as deprived yet privileged witnesses: they are voices warning against the downward spirals they can already see, but they are also heralds of the future, raising a rallying cry in search of new directions. Under the circumstances, exile may be not only a bitter personal fate but also the writer's best opportunity to contribute to a collective future.

This mutual reference between the individual writer and the public that inspires and reads the written work points up the logic of combining works on both prison and exile in this book: where does the personal continue to be grounded and in which collectivity? How is persecution by "one's own people" to be framed and made meaningful?

The workshop held at Northwestern University in November 1994 brought together a group of African writers that included many who suffered imprisonment in their home countries and/or exile abroad. They came from many different places and had been victimized for various reasons. For some this was a first attempt to write about their experience and to compare it with that of others from the same continent. This collection represents their invocations—in prose, poetry, and drama—of the many-faceted role of "witness" assumed by the writer whom world events have chosen, with or without consent.

The present papers are graphic, eloquent, and thought-provoking. They are varied—as they should be. While some authors choose to describe prison, others—such as Célestin Monga—address the general condition of the population, trying to find modes of expression and communication that can flow around political barriers. There is the problem of language, and a solution in graphics; there is the reality of political outrage coupled with political simplicity; there is the multiplicity of crosscurrents within African polities, and of communities seeking a surer footing on what seems to be an increasingly slippery slope of viability in a changed world. The value of this collection lies both in the expressiveness of the papers and in the varied terms with which the authors try to provide coherence to their experience and to some kind of vision for the future. With such an important topic, such strong contributions, and an unusually interesting format, this book promises a unique approach to the recent African version of what is both an old story from political ages past and a dreaded horizon for a destabilized Africa in the immediate future.

Jane I. Guyer

INTRODUCTION

Prison as Exile/Exile as Prison
Circumstance, Metaphor, and a Paradox of Modern African Literatures

Kofi Anyidoho

> & this is the pain & the glory, said I:
> that, after bidding Africa goodbye,
> we still cannot leave her behind, said I:
>
> That even when we know her love has waned
> we can never stop her odors clinging on
> — Okinba Launko

In these lines from his poem "A Birthday Card," Nigerian drama-tist, poet, and critic Femi Osofisan, writing under the pseudo-nym Okinba Launko,[1] captures for us probably the most recur-rent paradox in modern African literatures: the writer's persistent attachment to a home/land which history has often denied and contemporary reality is constantly transforming into quicksand; a land reputed to be among the best endowed in both human and material resources, and yet much better known for its prover-bial conditions of poverty; Africa, the birthplace of humanity and of human civilization, now strangely transformed into expand-ing graveyards and battlefields for the enactment of some of the world's worst human tragedies. This is the Africa of the intellec-tual and creative writer's hope and despair, the Africa of the glory of vanished civilizations and of the pain of mass populations set adrift in a world falling apart and yet full of many possibilities. At the root of this paradox, it may be argued, has been oppression in its many forms, oppression that imposes severe constraints on the creative, productive potential of the land and its peoples.

The 1994-95 program of the Institute for Advanced Study and Research in the African Humanities at Northwestern University was dedicated to the theme "Powers of Expression and Expression of Power: Cultural Production under Constraint."[2] As part of the overall focus on cultural production under constraint, the Institute organized a special workshop under the theme "The Word Behind Bars and the Paradox of Exile." The workshop, which took place on November 11-12, 1994, at the Program of African Studies, examined various issues related to intellectual and artistic production under conditions of imprisonment and exile. Bringing writers, journalists, and human rights activists together with research scholars and advanced graduate students, the workshop addressed, on the one hand, such issues as the physical, psychological, material, and spiritual constraints imposed by the state; strategies for producing and circulating work in spite of such conditions; and the implications of imprisonment for subsequent production. On the other hand, the workshop focused on issues related to the complex and paradoxical location of exile as a liberating space and as a prison of sorts.

Some presenters sought to identify characteristic features of discourses produced under conditions of imprisonment and exile, particularly strategies of resistance and subterfuge adopted by imprisoned and/or exiled persons. Others posed questions concerning the public that responds to the writer's/scholar's work within the context of its own complex negotiations of coercive state authority or assumed plurality of ideological and other positions. How, for example, does a particular public decode or read politics into an artistic work? To what extent does it regard art as a space comparable to the civic arena in a less oppressive regime; that is, how does artistic production offer a more "protected" forum for the debate of ideas of sociopolitical consequence? Or, how do geographically distant publics decipher the writer's often subtle strategies of critique and resistance? In a situation of potential political instability, how does a critic—particularly one far removed from local conditions—write honestly without endangering the life of her/his subject?

Another area of the workshop's inquiry centered on the challenges that the genres of prison and exile literature pose to critical methodologies currently deployed in Europe and the United

States. Such literature reproblematizes our consideration of the conditions enabling social and political resistance, and argues for a reexamination of the epistemological grounds from which theory arises.

In the particular instance of exile, workshop participants focused on the consequences of exile on production; the reinvention of identity—both personal and national—attendant upon exile; and the exile's impact on those who remain "at home." Somali writer Nurudin Farah suggests that the artist in exile is often simply one of the most visible members of an entire community. His assertion provokes considerations of how exile functions as an implicit critique of the nation-state, or how claims of authority and tradition are negotiated in the anguished ambiguity of an embryonic diaspora community.

The focus on prison and exile as two sides of the experience of oppression was almost inevitable, considering that intellectuals and creative artists who insist on fighting oppression often end up in prison, that those who manage to survive prison often end up in exile. Those we invited, almost all of whom were generous enough to respond to our call, were gifted and brave individuals who had been personally engaged in the fight against oppression; many had personally suffered imprisonment as a result and were now living in exile, far away from the land and the people to whose cause they had dedicated their lives, for whose sake they had suffered so much personal misery.[3] We knew it was a blessing to have their commitment to participate in the workshop, but we had not anticipated experiencing the rare privilege of having all these unusually gifted individuals in one place, at the same time, testifying to shared experiences that were at once revealing and elevating to the spirit, and yet so profoundly disturbing. "These stories that we are telling are very serious stories. They are stories that sometimes refuse to be told. They are stories which you discuss with people close to you. These are frightening testimonies . . . these personal stories. . . ." Such were the preliminary warnings with which Micere Githae Mugo opened her presentation. And as she went on to argue and demonstrate how "exile can negatively affect creativity," her voice rose and fell in tones that were part confessional, part conspiratorial, and which ultimately celebrated an irrepressible spirit of resistance that endured in spite of all costs to personal safety and comfort, in spite of the tragedy of death and separation. In turn, those who had spoken before or were to speak after her told similar tales of individual and shared agonies, but invariably concluded on a hopeful note as they spoke of an end, however temporary, to individual dictatorships they had known, and as they underscored the promise, however tentative, of new beginnings for themselves as well as for their societies.

But why would these writers and others like them risk the oppressor's wrath? The participants in this workshop tell us that through silence and inaction, a whole community becomes implicated in the terrors of oppression. "The man dies in all who keep silence in the face of tyranny," Wole Soyinka tells us in his now classic prison memoir, *The Man Died*.[4] Listening to our speakers' stories, one could not help but conclude that they knew or should have known what fate awaited them, yet they did not look away. Many of them could have fled immediately, and yet they chose to stay and resist for as long as it would take. Dennis Brutus was finally compelled to take a one-way exit permit into a lifelong exile, after having been "shot in the back, the bullet exiting through his chest," and after serving "eighteen months imprisonment on the notorious Robben Island."[5] Jack Mapanje, Célestin Monga, and Micere Mugo resisted the "easy option" of exile until finally each one paid the ultimate price for fighting against oppression on the side of truth: imprisonment without charge, without trial. We discover from each one's personal testimony that the most difficult fight of all turns out to be the one waged in prison; but having passed beyond prison and into exile, the battle suddenly takes on unexpected complications, for it now must be fought in unfamiliar territory, where far too many factors come into play. In exile, the very nature of oppression and the identity of the oppressor are harder to define, and therefore more difficult to confront.

Anyone who reads Mapanje's "Censoring the African Poem: Personal Reflections," a piece originally delivered in 1986 at the Second African Writers' Conference in Stockholm, cannot but wonder whether he did the right thing by returning to Malawi after so openly condemning the censorship system in his country. Perhaps it came as no surprise that barely a year later he was detained without charge, without trial. Mapanje argues that "censorship ultimately protects African leadership against truth." He further urges that "the situation has become so serious now that writers, scholars, and others," in their role as defenders of truth, "must take stern measures to counteract this development. I suggest that writers must use as much subtlety and imagination to fight censorship as they do to fight injustice and exploitation . . . in their works."[6]

Against the backdrop of this sketch, the artist begins to emerge through the metaphor of *Santrofi Anoma*—the artist as *Santrofi Anoma*. *Santrofi Anoma* may be translated as "the dilemma bird of Akan mythology." Endowed with mysterious treasures of the mind and voice, Santrofi is both a blessing and a curse. Santrofi is a blessing for the clarity of its vision and for the transforming beauty and power of its gift of song. But Santrofi is also a curse for its irritating and irrepressible urge to expose the unsavory side of society. That is why it is often said that the hunter who carries Santrofi home also brings misfortune home, but the hunter who abandons Santrofi in the wilderness leaves behind a rare treasure. Society is blind without Santrofi's visionary guidance, but it stands forever condemned by Santrofi's persistent accusations of improper conduct.

This probably explains society's ambivalent attitude toward the artist as Santrofi Anoma. It would appear, however, that such ambivalence need not translate into hostility toward the artist, as we find certain contexts in the past where institutionalized safeguards have tended to assure for the artist in Africa a free space for critically assessing public and private conduct.

In a particularly lucid moment in *Anthills of the Savannah*, Chinua Achebe offers a most compelling view of life as struggle, pointing out the importance of the role that each of us can play according to our various talents and skills:

> The sounding of the battle-drum is important; the fierce waging of the war itself important; and the telling of the story afterwards— each is important in its own way. I tell you there is not one of them we could do without. But if you ask me which of them takes the eagle-feather I will say boldly: the story. . . . Why? Because it is only the story that can continue beyond the war and the warrior. It is the story that outlives the sound of war-drums and the exploits of brave fighters. It is the story, not the others, that saves our progeny from blundering like blind beggars into the spikes of the cactus fence. The story is our escort; without it, we are blind.[7]

Often we may not like the story the artist reenacts for us, but we need not blame the artist for the unpleasantness of the tale, especially if it happens to be the truth. People who turn away from the path of truth soon run into a dead end. And, as the poet Kwadwo Opoku-Agyemang puts it, "History does not repeat itself. / It merely quotes us / when we have not been wise enough."[8] In an attempt to keep track of history's ruthless logic, one writer offers a brief but memorable portrait of the artist as *Santrofi Anoma:*

> I have been a witness to and a chronicler of my time. One cannot live outside one's time, even if one projects oneself into times future or past. Attempting to see beneath the surface is what I strive to do. I want to be an oracle, a knower of hidden things, the knower of the other side of things; not a conventional oracle who foresees doom, but the oracle of good tidings, the oracle who alerts his people against taking a course that leads to doom. The things we need to do to overturn current hardships are there for us to seize upon. One finger has to point out those things that need to be done. That's the sort of poet I would like to be known as. The poet should be an oracle and a healer. All the more reason that our vision should be one of hope: for restoration of the good we have lost, for attainment of a state of well-being. Only hope can save us.[9]

Remarkably, these very strong words of hope come from an African poet, Tanure Ojaide of Nigeria, who now lives in and writes from what has often been termed "self-imposed exile" in the United States. Exile as a characteristic dilemma of the modern world is a recurring theme in contemporary literary and cultural studies. Andrew Gurr, for instance, sees exile as "the normal role for the modern creative writer," a role in which the writer functions both as "a lone traveler in the countries of the mind" and as a symbol of a displaced and alienated community:

> Exile as the essential characteristic of the modern writer anticipates the loss by the community as a whole of identity, a sense of history, a sense of home. . . . Homelessness, and its corollary loneliness, are beginning to be recognized in the technologically advanced societies as the chronic and deplorable condition of society at large.[10]

There is an almost celebrative tone to Gurr's study as he examines the impact of exile on the works of Katherine Mansfield, V. S. Naipaul, and Ngugi wa Thiong'o. But, as he himself notes, the true exile is no ordinary traveler who "leave[s] home with the intention of acquiring the superiority of the international traveler. . . . The exile leaves on an impulse to escape, not to enjoy travel." At the time of the publication of his work, Gurr's description of Ngugi as an exile may have surprised many readers, since, as he puts it, Ngugi had not "taken flight into physical exile. . . . Physically he can live with his people, [but] culturally he is set apart by the alienating pressures of a Western education and a Western language." [11] Clearly, then, what is being argued here is a case of exile as metaphor. Aliko Songolo's essay in this volume offers considerable elaboration on this dimension of the exile experience.

An even earlier work, significantly titled *Exile and Tradition,* treats what editor Rowland Smith describes as a "basic obsession with the differences between indigenous reality and the imposed values of Africa's white conquerors." [12] Several of the contributors to the volume are themselves practicing African writers, among them Chinua Achebe, Kofi Awoonor, and Wole Soyinka. Each of these three has since then known exile in its true and most problematic form, not merely as a metaphor for cultural alienation, but as "a physically and psychologically oppressive reality imposed by circumstances beyond the writer's control." [13]

Something of the truly complex nature of exile as a characteristic dilemma of our world emerges in the more recent work, *Women's Writing in Exile.*[14] Angela Ingram opens her introduction with a prefatory quote from Joseph Brodsky's essay "The Condition We Call Exile" that usefully illuminates probably the most paradoxical aspect of exile for the contemporary African writer:

> If one would assign the life of an exiled writer a genre, it would have to be tragicomedy. Because of his previous incarnation, he is capable of appreciating the social and material advantages of democracy far more intensely than its natives are. Yet for precisely the same reason (whose byproduct is the linguistic barrier) he finds himself totally unable to play a meaningful role in his new society. The democracy into which he has arrived provides him with physical safety but renders him socially insignificant. And the lack of significance is what no writer, exile or not, can take.[15]

One of the contributors to *Exile and Tradition* provides a highly comprehensive description of "the condition we call exile" as far as the African writer/intellectual is concerned. In his essay "Senghor, or the Song of Exile," Max Dorsinville sums up

> the multiple forms of exile for Senghor and for all colonized people: the exile of the colonized man educated in a colonial context; the exile of the colonized man in the metropolis; the psychic exile of the colonized man wherever he may be; the exile of being black in the world; the exile of the artist; the exile of being in the world of modernity.[16]

Another very critical dimension of exile for the African writer is briefly stated by Dorsinville: "A literature in the language of the colonizer is situated precisely at the crossroads. One path leads to exile; the other to the native land."[17] In the case of Léopold Senghor, "the artist-prodigal son," this observation on language is of special relevance and significance. In Senghor's own poetry as well as in his prose, we find some of the most poignant statements of the contradictions, the complexities, and above all the paradoxes of exile. The "pointlessness" of the exiled artist's best efforts, simultaneous with the pain of separation and what Brodsky terms "a sense of insignificance," come through in Senghor's poem "For Jazz Orchestra":

> During the abysmal night in our mother, do you
>   remember, we played at drowning?
> The peace of the cotton trees and the brows of her
>   Champion hovered over her hope.
>
> Since then, like a man chasing the smoke of a dream
>   I have followed my unquiet quest
> To the sands of the levant to the Point of the South
>   among the peoples of the green sea
> And the Peoples beyond the seas. And the distant
>   shell in your dreams was me.[18]

Of Senghor and other African writers whose exile experience has often been seen as giving birth to "romantic nostalgia" as a characteristic feature of their work, it may be said that the circumstances of their lives as well as of their countries have a great deal to do with what emerges as the essential ingredients of their special kind of exile. Today, however, we may have to pay more attention to those for whom exile is more than a metaphor, for whom exile is a choice imposed by forces of oppression that leave little or no option for flight. The testimonies of exile outlined in the life stories of several of the contributors to this volume should lead us to the rather sad conclusion that however much we may celebrate exile as a kind of "liberated space," we cannot easily ignore the many ways in which exile can become a prison of sorts, especially for the African artist seeking close communion with those for whom his or her creativity is likely to have the greatest relevance and usefulness. This realization must inform our critical approach to a new kind of African diaspora—a consequence of the mass migration from Africa in the last few decades—consisting of those who have now permanently relocated to other parts of the world.

In his 1991 assessment, Onyekachi Wambu estimates that "the Non-European population of the EEC is about 16 million, of whom six million are African-descended peoples."[19] An even more comprehensive picture of the African diaspora in Europe emerges in the March 4-10, 1991, issue of *West Africa* magazine, with its special collection of reports on "Africans Abroad." The reports address, among other things, Africans in France, Britain, and America, as well as the special case of the new Afro-Soviet diaspora. An editorial comment on the reports further suggests:

> Africans travel and live abroad for all kinds of reasons. Many are students or would-be students; together with ex-students, this is perhaps the largest group. There are refugees from all over the continent who are displaced by persecution for their political, religious, or ideological beliefs. Some, from South Africa, just happened to have the "wrong skin color at the wrong place." But there are also a large number of African professionals—doctors, teachers, engineers, journalists, accountants, and the like—who have chosen to live and work outside the continent for all kinds of reasons.[20]

We see some of these reasons for ourselves in Ama Ata Aidoo's *Our Sister Killjoy*, where we meet various groups of African exiles, many of them professional students enrolled in courses that never end, all finding justification for their prolonged stay outside the continent. Perhaps the most remarkable case is that of a medical scientist who claims he has become the last word in gastric disorders and insists that the kind of well-equipped laboratory he requires would consume the entire national budget of the Ministry of Health in his unnamed African country. So we are supposed to understand why he cannot go home. But we are told that his mother, back at home, is probably dying of some unknown internal disease.[21]

The simple truth is that many of the new generation of Africans in exile, especially the so-called African Europeans, are mainly economic refugees who have been "compelled" by ruthless postcolonial conditions to seek refuge in various parts of Europe and North America. We must also note the special case of highly skilled professionals, some of whom could argue that their emigration from Africa has more to do with a lack of professional support, since several African countries are unable to afford the expensive equipment and other resources these professionals require to carry out their career obligations with any measure of satisfaction.

While lamenting the spurious justifications many Africans of the new diaspora advance in their own defense, we must also give special consideration to one of the most frequently cited reasons for the exodus of African intellectuals: political persecution. An appallingly large number of African intellectuals, writers among them, have had to go into exile because of their determination to speak the truth about the injustices of their society. We may recall Peter Abraham's assertion in *Tell Freedom* that, in order to be personally alive, free, and able to tell the truth about the urgent need for freedom in South Africa, he had no choice but to flee into exile. South Africa happens to have been an extreme example in the continent's recent history. Until recently, the majority of South African intellectuals and writers have had to spend their entire adult lives in exile. Dennis Brutus and Keorapetse Kgositsile, two key contributors to our "Prison and Exile" workshop, provide very revealing testimonies of the particular circumstances of the exiled South African under apartheid rule. To South Africa we must add the more recent cases of Malawi, Kenya, and Cameroon, as represented in the workshop by Jack Mapanje, Micere Mugo, and Célestin Monga, respectively.

PRISON AS EXILE

For many, real exile begins when one is no longer able to be part of one's social, political, cultural, and economic reality. And for the intellectual or writer at home who would not submit to a kind of death by silence, there is the other, often more devastating kind of "exile within": prison. "I am only a stammerer who tries to find articulate speech in scribbled words," says Ngugi rather modestly. "Pen and paper have so far been my only offensive and defensive weapons against those who would like to drown human speech in a pool of fear—or blood."[22]

A document issued in February 1995 by the International PEN Writers in Prison Committee expresses alarm at "the increasing number of violent attacks in several countries in Africa," attacks specifically targeting writers and journalists. The report notes that "at least 25 writers and journalists were killed in Africa in 1993, around a third of the world total of writers killed for that year."[23]

Despite these distressing statistics, it is important for us to note that, in a way, writers and journalists are not only a minority but also quite often a privileged group, the chosen few for whom PEN International and other organizations and individuals are prepared to raise a voice of protest. The prison diaries of Soyinka, Ngugi, Awoonor, and others draw our attention to the many others for whom no one raises a voice, for whom no father will pay a lawyer or bribe the security functionaries to pursue the possibility of eventual release. As Ngugi observes, "Most of those who had said 'No' to the culture of fear and silence had ended dying untimely deaths, buried alive in desert places, or left on hillsides for the hyena's midnight feasts."[24] And for vivid but painful insights into those prison populations of which the human rights groups often know very little, we may turn to Don Mattera's personal account in *Memory Is the Weapon*.[25] Here we are confronted with the raw brutality of prison as a place where the inmate's life is constantly at risk. Here the laws of decency are suspended. It is no place for the weak, for it is where bullies rule by violence with the full connivance of the state and the law.

Regrettable as the conditions of exile might be for the writers personally and for the society at large, we may still argue that, in a very important sense, even exile can be very productive as a form of intellectual exodus. Of course, there are those unable to handle the pressures of exile: some commit slow suicide simply by drinking themselves to death. But for others, life in exile becomes an important instrument of combat, wielded in defense of those they have left behind at home. We can say that Dennis Brutus, Ngugi wa Thiong'o, Mongo Beti, and many others in exile have been significantly effective in their fight against oppression in South Africa, Kenya, and Cameroon. By devoting their lives in exile to mobilizing international opinion against the repressive regimes they left behind, they have carried the struggle much farther than they otherwise could have done back home, where all of them would most certainly be languishing in jail. In any case, even from exile, their careers as writers in defense of social justice continue to have significant impact on the struggle at home. Micere Mugo raised this key issue in her presentation. Her account shows how a stubborn refusal to leave home despite unrelenting persecution can be not only counterproductive but also suicidal. The impact of Ngugi's last novel, *Matigari,* illustrates this point. Its publication in the original Gikuyu caused much unease among the security agencies in Kenya:

> The novel was published in the Gikuyu-language original in October 1986. By January 1987, intelligence reports had it that peasants in central Kenya were whispering and talking about a man called Matigari who was roaming the whole country making demands about truth and justice. There were orders for his immediate arrest, but the police discovered that Matigari was only a fictional character in a book of the same name. In February 1987, the police raided all the book shops and seized every copy of the novel.[26]

Ultimately, we will have to reconsider our standard response to the so-called brain drain, however we may define it. It is important to recognize the impossibility, and indeed the undesirability, of having all Africans and all people of African descent return to and permanently settle on the continent. To be sure, the forcible demographic shifts that African peoples have undergone historically were painful and are regrettable in many ways; but it is pointless to hope for the reversal of a situation that historical circumstances and contemporary geopolitical and economic realities have clearly made permanent. On the contrary, we should begin to develop a more positive attitude toward the growing phenomenon of a global African community. Indeed, the examples of other peoples of the world should teach us that historical and geographical dispersal is not necessarily an unsalvageable disaster. It is unimaginable that

Europe would have emerged from its "Dark Ages" except through its enterprise in discovery, expansion, and empire, although we must question the manner in which Europeans moved out into the wider world, in particular the violence with which they imposed their will and rule on others. Today we witness the Japanese, the Chinese, the Koreans, and other Asian peoples embarking on their own age of discovery, expansion, and empire.

These and similar examples must begin to reshape attitudes and responses to the fragmented reality of the African population in the contemporary world. It is tempting to continue stressing the fundamental difference between the historical experience of African people and that of other groups in the manner of their respective dispersals. Wambu, for one, articulates the difference as

> the impossibility of ignoring the tragic events of the slave trade. . . . Contrast this with the other great migrations of the last 1000 years or so by Europeans, Chinese, and Indians which have so transformed the world. These have, on the whole, been voluntary. . . . Even when, like the Boers and the Quakers, such migrants were under enormous pressure to leave because of religious persecution, they went forward to their new dispensation with a language and culture intact, as well as with a continuing notion of themselves as Europeans.
>
> The migration of the African diaspora remains unique as a world phenomenon. Despite the fact that we can marvel today at the sometimes exciting and vibrant civilizations constructed by these same Africans over the last 700 years in the Americas, . . . we always come back to stressing the discontinuities of their experience. These include the brutal and forceful severing of old emotional and cultural links; the devastating psychological damage that ensued as a result; and the feeling this evokes in us as being a world people more sinned against than sinning, more victim than aggressor.[27]

The fundamental difference—the historical phenomena—Wambu delineates is indeed valid; however, this experience must be measured against the equally relevant experience of the massive numbers of African people who have moved and continue to leave the continent for reasons other than the trans-Atlantic or trans-Saharan slave trade. Further, we must recognize that our present global realities render such movement almost inevitable, even if regrettable. Our concern, then, should be to undertake a serious exploration of how Africans can create mechanisms through which the continent as well the diaspora can profit from the new skills and resources African-heritage people all around the globe have acquired through their dispersal. A new and positive image of Africa in the global community will, of course, be a source of strength for diaspora Africans. This in fact was how Europe developed itself and in so doing gave much pride and power to Europeans all over the world. We see that various Asian countries have also managed to take off by capitalizing on their global dispersal. So far, Africa seems to be the one major region of the world that has yet to reap the full benefits of its diaspora experience.

It may be argued that the economic, social, and political prospects of the majority of diaspora Africans are so bleak or uncertain that they cannot be expected, realistically, to make any meaningful contribution to what is going on back home. Valid though this argument may be, it fails to explain why even those who are not so disadvantaged are often unable and/or unwilling to reconnect with the continent in ways that could begin to enhance the quality of life for those left behind. Perhaps there is a need for a change of attitudes. But too often we find that the colonial residue and the pressures of global economic and political manipulation have contributed to the failure of the continent, especially its leadership, to find and support the means of systematically absorbing returning skills and resources into carefully planned programs of meaningful development.

In this regard, we need to cultivate new understandings and a more radical awareness of Pan-Africanism. These days, many of us dismiss Pan-Africanism as an irrelevant, even a regressive, tendency. However, not only does Pan-Africanism continue to be relevant, it seems to be our only guarantee against the helplessness and hopelessness besetting African people throughout the world. We need to revisit Marcus Garvey and see how much difference it would have made if his bid for establishing a global network for African business entrepreneurship had been allowed to take off. We miss the real significance of the Garvey phenomenon when we simplify it into an impossible dream of returning African people to Africa. Garvey's "back to Africa" agenda was much more sophisticated than many of us tend to believe. At least the colonial powers of his day understood the ultimate implications of his dream; otherwise they would not have banned his movement's publications and declared him persona non grata in practically every country on the continent. The following call to diaspora Africans is very much a restatement of that old rallying cry: "The struggle to keep open and develop channels of communication with Africa will be one of the biggest challenges to face the African diaspora in the twenty-first century."[28]

As this century comes to a close with desperation firmly rooted among African people worldwide, we find that several of our leading thinkers and visionaries are beginning to refocus our attention on the abandoned agenda of early twentieth-century African nationalism. Nowhere is this vision more insistent than in the works of our creative writers. From the continent as well as from the diaspora, we see a new generation of literary works that explore ways to rebuild bridges and restore broken bonds, thereby opening up avenues for a mutually beneficial interchange of ideas, skills, and resources. This relationship must not be seen simply as the continent reaping the fruits of its enormous contributions to the wealth of other nations through the intellectual and physical labor of its dispersed people: for the diaspora needs the homeland as much as the homeland needs the diaspora.

Speaking elsewhere on behalf of the African Literature Association, Abena Busia, one of the key participants in our "Prison and Exile" workshop and a contributor to this volume, reminds us that the continent remains an inescapable point of reference as well as a continued source of renewal for the global African community:

> For some of us, Africa is indeed home. For others she is a metaphor for home. For all of us, Africa is a vocation and an avocation. . . . And we have with us this week, for the first time in our twenty-year history, over twenty African writers whose works we read, study, teach, laugh with, quarrel with, and above all share. We are missionaries in a little caring world, but we don't stop. There is no *one* new life. Only many lives renewed and it is our writers who make our world an exciting place.
>
> They remind us that the distance from Africa Square at 125th Street and Lenox is not so far after all from Bukom Square, if you have walked through both places. We live in shared cultural spaces. And though not identical, we can trace the ties from Africa through

Afro-America to the popular culture of the Americas, back here to Africa through food, dress, music, dance, and the shifting language which is the substance of our lives. . . . it is not our individualities that keep us whole, but our whole that keeps us.[29]

It is this Pan-African dimension of the global experience of exile that is captured most eloquently for us in the contributions of both Abena Busia and Nourbese Philip. For both of them, the need to overcome displacement through a repossession of language is not only urgent but an absolute precondition for dealing with the primary business of self-definition and creativity in a world devastated by a history of dispossession. Busia's contribution, "Preface to *Testimonies of Exile:* On Territories, Tied Tongues, and Translations," provides invaluable insights into her collection of poems.[30] And Philip's essay, "Earth and Sound: The Place of Poetry," is a powerful commentary on her two seminal works, *She Tries Her Tongue; Her Silence Softly Breaks* and *Looking for Livingstone: An Odyssey of Silence*[31] — two works that constitute "a highly complex exploration of the nature of the relation of language to power and gender and racial identity."[32]

At the time of the "Prison and Exile" workshop, one of the major participants, Ola Rotimi, had just arrived in the United States from Nigeria, then overshadowed by a looming national crisis which was prompting many intellectuals and writers — Ken Saro-Wiwa and Nobel Laureate Wole Soyinka among them — to raise a brave voice of dissent. Soyinka has since become persona non grata in Nigeria and is condemned to live in exile. Saro-Wiwa and others have since paid the ultimate price of death by hanging — this despite a storm of protest and urgent appeals from all over the world. There is no better closing statement for an introduction to this volume than Ken Saro-Wiwa's closing statement to the military-appointed tribunal that sentenced him to death:

My Lord, we all stand before history. I am a man of peace, of ideas. Appalled by the denigrating poverty of my people who live on a richly endowed land, distressed by their political marginalization and economic strangulation, angered by the devastation of their land, their ultimate heritage, anxious to preserve their right to life and to a decent living, and determined to usher to this country as a whole a fair and just democratic system which protects everyone and every ethnic group and gives us all a valid claim to human civilization, I have devoted my intellectual and material resources, my very life, to a cause in which I have total belief and from which I cannot be blackmailed or intimidated. I have no doubt at all about the ultimate success of my cause, no matter the trials and tribulations which I and those who believe with me may encounter on our journey. Nor imprisonment nor death can stop our ultimate victory. . . . I predict that the scene here will be played and replayed by generations yet unborn. Some have already cast themselves in the role of villains, some are tragic victims, some still have a chance to redeem themselves. The choice is for each individual.[33]

Of Orality and Memory in Prison and Exile

(A Personal Note on How to Survive the Chaos of Incarceration)

Jack Mapanje

ON CAMPAIGNING FOR INCARCERATED WRITERS TODAY

I have one excuse for telling my story. It is the only gift I offer in exchange for your successful campaign for my freedom. Allow me, therefore, to start with a word about the pleasures of campaigning for incarcerated writers, in case you assumed there were none. Let me declare at the outset that there is no need for this workshop to send another petition to Banda demanding immediate liberty for political prisoners in Malawi. All the political prisoners who have been choking Malawi's prisons these three decades have been freed. I am here. It worked. Thank you. Besides, Banda is out of a job as President for Life. He came in a poor third and last in Malawi's May 1994 presidential elections. The new democratically elected government of Malawi is now confronted with the bizarre matter of what to do with Banda, his henchpersons, and the wealth they have amassed, largely illegitimately, these thirty years of their autocratic rule. And if you cannot at least smile about your having contributed, however obliquely, to the fall of a notorious dictator in your campaign for our liberty, then it is difficult to imagine what you will smile about.

First, then, let me put on record the noble energies you spent for my release. I note with appreciation that some of you traveled from one conference to another talking about my plight. Some of you were lobbying your governments or their representatives in order to remind our stubborn octogenarian about my continued imprisonment. Some of you sent postcards, letters, faxes, books, and magazines. Some of you wrote articles, poems, books, or chapters of books and dedicated these to me. Some of you offered precious prayers for my freedom. Even now, three and a half years after my release, everywhere I travel I am constantly reminded of the campaigns you mounted for my release. I am overwhelmed by the warmth of your generosity. Your efforts inspired me and the political prisoners in Mikuyu and other prisons in Malawi to struggle against great odds in order to survive our imprisonment.

Technically, however, most of your priceless labor never reached its target. We only heard about your campaigns through the underground communication system we had established in prison. I was not allowed to get the letters and messages that you sent. They were confiscated by the various Malawi authorities before they could reach Mikuyu Prison. But, as I was to discover immediately after my release, your letters, faxes, telegrams, articles, poems, petitions, books, journals, magazines, and verbal messages were not sent in vain. They reached Malawi's central sorting post office in great numbers. They became a nuisance to the dictator and his infamous bureaucracy. Dictators do not want to be bothered. They hate petitions. That is probably why I am here today.

When I was in Norway recently, I remembered the time you spent warring for my release, and it is in the form of a parable that I would like to share that memory with you. I record this story because it is based on fact, not fiction, and in gratitude to those who are never mentioned in our campaigns.

PARABLE OF MY RENAULT 4 DRIVER

It's like the story of any driver
In my part of the fourth world

There's a knock on the door
He's heard I've purchased a fifth-hand Renault 4

The guy next door has just got his license through him
He proudly displays the credential that's done the trick

The fellow must worry about anything he touches
But six months later, I get my own driving license too

Then the real bargaining begins
Do I seriously want to see him begging at the market?

The best way to celebrate my first-attempt driving license
Is to get him a job among my friends or colleagues

He makes no effort to conceal the intended blackmail
He believes I have enough clout

I casually suggest the police station
We part company in rather inconsonant smiles;

A year later, his vehicle is policing roadblocks
Our story is sealed in mutual grins

Until recently, exactly sixteen years later,
I am madly trying to send a message to England

From the post office of his rural district
Where they exiled my wife at their hospital

(To punish her for my sins —
She now enjoys feeding the border fugitives

At the weekends particularly,
Sharing with the malnourished fugitive babies

Those priceless vitamins
She often brought to my prison cells.)

On the phone I accentuate each point
With my now familiar chorus

"Yes, three years, seven months, sixteen days
I have been released unconditionally . . ."

But a booming voice behind me jolts
My British Council telephone conversation

"You are the most dangerous man I've had to deal with!"
I duck, to confirm it's not another arrest;

My Renault 4 driver's tale then unfolds:
After the police, he went to the post office

Where he's had the enviable duty
Of sorting out all my protest mail

"Bags upon bags arriving from the world each day
Where on earth did you get these friends?"

He apologizes to my wife,
He could not even greet her when I was still in

For fear of recrimination;
"But those bags upon bags—

Some we sent to your headmaster,
Some to the Special Branch,

Others to the Secretary to the President and Cabinet;
A few books and magazines

We managed to derail to your wife here"
But he mustn't talk too much,

He must be off, wishing us well.
Today, from another corner of the globe

When this Stavanger pub in Norway recounts
And Bergen Philharmonic Orchestra underscores

The extent of the war of my liberation
The parable of the driver of my Renault 4 still muddles.

So, if you believed that dictators were never bothered by signatures from workshops and conferences of this kind, you are wrong. And your letters, petitions, books, messages, and wishes do not need to reach the writer you are fighting for. They do not need to be received by the prisoner in question. Their very arrival at some office in the country concerned is an effective statement that will not be ignored by dictators or their bureaucracies, however much they might appear to disregard them at first.

Today, I suggest that we should not stop at the successful story of the fight for my liberty. I implore participants of this workshop to be more vigilant on behalf of other writers who are still imprisoned in other parts of the world. It is the paradox of our times that as one problem gets resolved in one part of the globe, another begins elsewhere. The writer's life on the African continent and throughout the world is still threatened. I gather Wole Soyinka, who received the Rotterdam Poetry Award in 1988 on my behalf when I was in prison, has just had his Nigerian passport as well as his United Nations passport confiscated by the Nigerian military government. Another Nigerian writer, Ken Saro-Wiwa, who has been in and out of prison for his views and his writings, has also been recently imprisoned in Nigeria. The Bangladeshi writer Taslima Nasrin and several Asian writers and freedom activists are being threatened with death or imprisonment. In Britain, Salman Rushdie is still under death-threat for his writings and his beliefs. The list could be extended. The point that needs stressing is that there are lots of writers under death-threats or in prison. These still need our prayers, warm thoughts, and petitions.

MEMORY AND PRISON WRITING

I want to talk briefly about my prison experiences. I want to demonstrate principally how certain aspects of orality were fundamental to my survival in prison. I want to suggest particularly the central role that selected configurations of memory played in my survival and what part they continue to play in the reconstruction of my prison experiences now that I am free. But talking about prison experiences before an audience that includes writers who have been imprisoned for nobler causes and for longer periods and have already written about their own experiences—this is humbling. My prison experiences differ from those that some of you have recorded, mainly in their locational detail. Indeed the literature on prison writing and incarceration generally is so vast that one wonders whether anything new can be said today. When I share with you the memory of specific features of orality and indicate how they helped me repair the physical and psychological chaos brought about by three and a half years of incarceration in Banda's prison, it is not because I present you anything new. I boast only one or two rather personal anecdotes.

My reconstitution of the memories of my imprisonment will be disjointed. Any reconstruction of events after a relatively long lapse of time must be fraught with immeasurable shortcomings. Our memories of them fade. Important episodes lose their sharp edge. Facts slip. Gaps within events yawn. The totality of the events themselves takes on remarkable fuzziness. Besides, the world under which we recast the experiences is so turbulent and often so unpredictable that our perspective on even the most painful experiences changes, at times reducing their relevance to vacuity. Above all, there are images of incarceration which one does not intend to relive or share with one's audience. Some stories of humiliation can be too painful to be repeated. They are better left alone. When the decision to exhume and relive them through verse, prose, drama, paint, or speech is finally made, other practical problems surface. One is whether we want to present them as fact, fiction, or a combination of both; the other is what we are actually reconstructing in either case. In prison the line between the two is often nonexistent.

Writings that have recorded prison experiences throughout the world divide generally into three rather loose groups: those written in prisons where the writers had access to libraries and were allowed some form of reading and writing; those written by prisoners where no library existed and where no writing and reading, even of government propaganda, were allowed; and the gray area in between where, if the libraries existed, they contained such vulgar propaganda that it was not worth reading. In very broad terms, Mikuyu Prison belonged to the second category. Not only were we not allowed to work, but no books, no newspapers, no writing was allowed. We had no access to news even from the government-controlled radio and newspapers. No writing materials were permitted. No chalk with which to teach one another was sanctioned. Today I cannot show off that I have come out of Mikuyu with another academic or professional qualification. Thus, when Dennis Brutus and the African Network at Evanston, where this workshop takes place, honored me recently with the magnificent Kwanzaa Honors List Special Award Certificate to crown my prison graduation, the irony of my situation was brought home more poignantly. The only doctorate degree I could boast having achieved at Mikuyu in three and a half years was what was stored in my memory and will probably remain forever locked up there.

However, from the time I entered Mikuyu Prison, I decided that I would covertly sabotage every rule possible. The decision was made very early. The indignity of my public arrest at the Gymkhana Club, my being paraded handcuffed on the way to my office in Chancellor College, the violent search in my office and at home before my children and my ailing mother, followed by the humiliation of my being stripped naked on entry into Mikuyu Prison—these and many other forms of insult to my humanity and intelligence could not be left to chance. As a matter of fact, now that I was in prison, I had found better reasons to fight the repressive regime, fighting I had hitherto done largely through my verse. Moreover, Banda's famous declaration that when he arrested a dissident he would send him or her to prison where he or she would rot, rot, and rot, was too challenging not to be demonstrably disputed.

If I could avoid it, I would not use conventional methods of protest. It was preached to me, after the first night I was confined, that there were to be no hunger or other strikes, no jumping over prison fences, no breaking of this or that prison rule. But I swore to my ancestors that I would watch the environment first and strike when the time was ripe. What I required was patience and time. And we had both in abundance here, particularly because we did not know when we would be released, if we were going to be released at all. We first chose to fight for issues whose relevance to everyone was not in question. The first person I made friends with, Brown James, whom I had known only by name outside because he used to run a controversial discussion program on the local radio, had already been hatching different kinds of insurrection at Mikuyu Prison with the support of other inmates. The gentle revolt Brown and others were engaged in fitted my ideas precisely. It was discreet but devastating.

Some revolutions start like a joke. One day Brown's wife decided to bring cooked food from home when she came to visit him. She knew that this was not allowed. She chose to come when one of the kinder guard-commanders controlled a shift of largely kinder warders. The food was obviously so well cooked that even the warders and the officers coveted it. They probably never tasted that kind of food at home. The officers and warders who sat at visits controlling discussions between inmates and their visitors told Brown's wife to take the food back home because it was not allowed here. She refused, whereupon Brown came to her rescue. He took off his prison shirt and showed the officers and guards the gray spots, ringworms, and red pimples covering his skin and face. "This is because of your food. Do you people want me to die here? Tell my wife that the Special Branch has instructed you to kill me. Tell her!" he shouted.

His wife had already started sobbing at the sight of Brown's spotted skin. Taking up her husband's cue she declared, "Give me back my plates and pots. Take the curry rice and the chicken. Stuff it! And I will tell the authorities you did not allow my husband the food which could have cured his skin disease! I got permission from the Special Branch to bring this food!" She had not, but she knew that they would tremble at the mention of the Special Branch. Everybody feared the Special Branch. When the officer in charge upstairs heard the voice of the distressed woman downstairs, he quickly ran down to the visitors' room to inquire what was happening. The food was allowed in. Brown naturally left several tablets of Lifebuoy and Sunlight soap, some pineapples, bananas, cabbages, and oranges in the office. If the officers needed it, they could have it. The rest he took inside the cell where everybody had a feast that day. The following month she brought cooked food again. There was no fight. Then the next. Soon all visitors began bringing whatever cooked food they could afford to their relatives in prison.

Other battles were won in a similar manner. At the end of my three years, the first clinical officer was allowed into Mikuyu Prison to examine our health and give us treatment. Flip-flops, which were not allowed when prisoners entered Mikuyu, could be worn. Visitors could bring to Mikuyu their own Bibles and pamphlets on Bible commentaries as well as hymns from their various churches. One inmate, Ian Mbale, even had the courage to jump over the prison fence of Mikuyu Prison to prove that the security at this invincible prison could be conquered. The escape was the subtlest in the history of Mikuyu. The search for Mbale that followed was conducted in the manner of animal hunting of long ago. Police and prison officers with bloodhounds, guns, and clubs combed the bushes around Mikuyu Prison in rows. Ian Mbale was to be brought back dead. He had brought to shame the invulnerability of Malawi's top-security prison. Meanwhile the police had arrested Mbale's parents, his sister and her husband, and other relatives who might otherwise help Mbale in case he arrived at their door to seek refuge. And instructions were issued that any officer who saw, arrested, clubbed, or shot dead Mbale was to have instant promotion.

But the gods were with Mbale. After three days he was re-arrested by school children at a Catholic primary school not far from Mikuyu. He fell into a ditch as he ran away from the school —the children had thought him a thief. Although the prison and police officers nearly killed Mbale when he was delivered to them by the school, the damage to the reputation of police and prison security had been done as Mbale had intended. It is not surprising then that when some of these political prisoners were released, it was their simple, perhaps parochial but deadly strategies that had worked—like the famous "open letters" that were distributed clandestinely throughout the country during the 1992 campaign for the referendum for multiparty democracy and the 1994 general elections, both of which eventually dealt a deadly blow to our obstinate dictator.

One other example might not be out of order. After I was moved from my isolation cell to the general cells that slept about twenty-five prisoners, we were shocked one night to receive two illiterate detainees from Zomba Central Prison. The detainees were both village businessmen. The older had been running several small shops and the younger had owned several small farms. The crime committed by the younger, Laurenti Phiri, who was also epileptic, was particularly astonishing for those of us who were accustomed to expecting "rebels" entering Mikuyu Prison to come largely from the urban areas of Malawi.

Everyone who had money in Banda's Malawi went into the tobacco-farming business. The owner of the farm divided his or her farm into acres. He or she then employed tenants, men and women, as well as families to grow tobacco on given acres. The farm owner provided the crop, the equipment, the fertilizer, and food to the tenants he or she employed in return for the tenants' labor and the crop which they sold to him or her after the harvest. The farm owner in turn sold the tobacco at higher international prices at auction in the nearest city. The conditions of employment on the farms differed from one employer to another. Laurenti Phiri could not read or write. His accounting was done by his wife, his effective manager, who was literate. Laurenti's crime was that he paid his tenants better prices for their tobacco, he gave them more maize, more salt, more and better beans to live on than did, for example, the South African and Zimbabwean white managers who manned Banda's tobacco farms.

One day during tobacco harvest, however, Laurenti's manager bought tobacco which the tenants had bought from Banda's tenants. Banda's tenants naturally wanted to sell their tobacco to the highest bidder. Laurenti was one. The police bundled up Laurenti and dumped him in a local prison. They took him to court for having embezzled the tobacco from the farm of His Excellency the Life President. Laurenti lost the case and paid a K500 fine. He was released. But a week later the Special Branch came to pick him up from home, dumped him in Zomba Central Prison first, then transferred him to Mikuyu Prison. Both were sordid national prisons. There was no reason for the action that the Special Branch had taken, but no explanation was required. After we heard this story, our welcome of the two was warmer than usual. Some of us were ashamed of ourselves. We wished we had committed a crime against our dictator which was as virtuous as this.

When Laurenti settled down to the boredom of Mikuyu and saw that most of us occupied our time reading the Bible, he felt the urge to learn reading and writing. He said he felt stupid because his wife could read and write and he could not. Those of us who were literate therefore got together and tried to help Laurenti. As chalk was not permitted, we decided to steal chloroquine tablets from our own stocks and started scratching letters of the alphabet on the walls and floors for him to repeat. Then we moved on to a combination of consonants and vowels until he was able to read and write simple words. Soon he was able to read the Chichewa (the national language) translation of the Bible. Before he was released after two years at Mikuyu, Laurenti was able to write his first letter to his wife. He insisted that I read it although it was private. Tears ran down my cheeks as I read his delicate sentiments and noted that he no longer needed us to write his letters home or to the Special Branch pleading for his release.

But our teaching had been conducted in secrecy. No marks of chloroquine were supposed to be left on walls and floors. The risk we took was enormous but worth it. We were helped by other inmates who acted as sentries to give us the appropriate cues when the warders were coming or when there was some other danger. If we had been found teaching Laurenti, we would have been summarily thrown into the punishment cell. Perhaps we would have been beaten up without mercy. We would have lost our right to medical treatment for abusing the use of chloroquine. But we were satisfied that Laurenti's second and subsequent letters were written by him under the supervision of the warders, who had by now forgotten that he had walked inside Mikuyu walls and entered the prison's gate-book page with ink on thumb as his signature. With gentle care it is easy to break the resolute walls of dictators.

At Mikuyu we were not allowed to write letters to our relatives and friends except under supervision. And having written the letter, you sent it to the officer in charge of the prison to read and clear. He decided when it could be sent to the chief superintendent of prisons to read and vet. The chief superintendent's office would then send it to the Special Branch, who would send it to the head of detainees to read, vet, and eventually post. By the time the letter reached its destination, it would be some six months or more. And sometimes if you were lucky enough to be released early, your letter would reach home long after your release. As can be imagined, the procedure for writing and sending letters home was so tedious that it was not worth writing, which must have been the obvious point. No letters bound for Europe or outside the country were officially allowed, whether they were written under supervision or not. One did not even begin to contemplate writing any.

Furthermore, no books, no newspapers, no pens were allowed in Mikuyu. If they found you with a pen, paper, a book—even the well-known police magazine—they punished you severely. They roughed you up and took you to the punishment cell, sometimes referred to as the dark room, where you were stripped naked, clamped with leg irons and handcuffs, and tied to the stocks (iron bars stuck firmly to a cement floor). They poured two or three buckets of cold water on you. They locked the door and left you there for three days without water and food. Only memory saved you from death, the memory of events that had led to the punishment cell; the memory of the scars that would be left by leg irons and handcuffs; the memory of the stiff joints to be suffered and cracked bones healed; the memory of justice once known or once imagined. For three days you remembered, invented, and re-invented the stories your parents had told you, or you had told each other, or you had read.

Two Postcards and a Bit that Slipped Past the Tight Special Branch

One day the officer in charge (OC) of Mikuyu Prison summoned me to his office. Being brought to his office was always a frightful experience. My head started racing with visions of what prison rules I might have broken to deserve an invitation to the OC's office. Surely, they had not discovered the note that I had smuggled out to David and Pat at the university. Noriega, our wonder-warder-courier, could not have been so reckless. He was not known to be. I was nervous. And when I reached the OC's office, accompanied by the guard-commander in charge of the day's shift, I was not encouraged by the rhetorical question that ensued: "You have lots of friends outside this country, haven't you?" The question was too loaded to be answered flippantly. I concealed my irritation by choosing to remain silent until he had turned it into a statement to which I could respond properly.

I had learned quite early that the only rights I had as a political prisoner were the right to silence and the right to prostrate myself before warders or officers chanting, *I am sorry Sir, I am sorry Sir, I am sorry Bwana,* even when I was not responsible for whatever was supposed to have been amiss, even when I was not sorry. Merely to claim the right to your hostility often landed you in punishment cells. I did not want that. I loved life. I chose silence. He smiled the smile of a pig, a pig pleading not to be chosen for slaughter that I once saw in Mpokonyola village where my uncle kept a pigsty. The last time the OC wore that weird smile was when he invited me to help him with a letter of promotion for one of his senior members of staff. Could I read the letter he had drafted to recommend the promotion of one of his members of staff? Could I advise him on the most effective phraseology so that the fellow could be promoted? I accepted the invitation because I anticipated a catch. There was none. That was months ago. Could the blackmail be coming now?

What was I going to be cajoled into today? "Do not worry. I am

not sending you to the punishment cell. You have not done anything wrong to deserve that yet. I have received these postcards
from Europe. They are addressed to you. I thought you might like
to see and read them." He passed the postcards on to me. The first
came from Holland, a typical tourist postcard. *Groeten uit Holland,* it read. Someone whose signature I was not meant to decipher
had sent me greetings. The address was inadequate. I wondered
why, of all the postcards that must have been sent to me and never
reached me, this one chose to arrive. It has since been the subject
of a poem titled "To the Unknown Dutch Postcard Sender." The
second came from a certain Celia Leak in London whom I have
since traced.

But the picture of some spotless men selling Dutch cheeses from
oval-shaped trays, the picture of men selling clogs on stalls, the
picture of a mother and daughter sharing yellow and red tulips on
a well-trimmed green lawn, and of a family of four strolling along
some Dutch avenue and more—the postcard was cheerfully colorful. And the white and red roses on Celia Leak's seasonal greeting
card were quite bright. I felt a sense of exhilaration at this first encounter with the beauty of the commercial reality that I had left
behind and that had never really excited me. I had never been to
Holland. The white and red roses invoked the rural British landscape that once felt alien when I was a student. Today, however,
these colors contrasted sharply with the monotony of the gray
walls and brown bricks of my prison cell. "Well, I thought you
should see them. I will now keep these in your file until your release
when you can take them as souvenirs," he said. That was the second time anyone in authority mentioned the word "release" before
me. It was first mentioned casually on the night of my arrival as the
guard-commander stripped me naked to give me prison clothes to
wear. I was told then not to worry, as people had been known to
be released within days of their arrival at Mikuyu. That was about
a year ago. I wondered why he could not see how cruel it was to
tantalize me with release when I was meant to rot in prison.

When I went back to the cell, I was surrounded by anxious
faces bombarding me with questions I could not answer. I felt uncomfortable. My heart continued to pace as if I were still at the
OC's. I felt like a detainee briefly released and brought back into
prison full of stories from outside. The postcards had given me

tremendous energy, though at first not very much cheer. They had dispelled our despair and given us courage, hope, and reason to continue to live, fighting on. People's faces brightened up when they realized that someone somewhere cared. The cards had such a mysterious impact on our dull and disconsolate lives that it was difficult to encapsulate the exact feeling in words. That evening after lockup there was pandemonium in cell D4. As we reviewed the incidents of the day, everyone was agreed that the postcards were the most important event of the day. Almost everybody was ecstatic about the reasons behind the OC's action. Mail from outside the country was not allowed to be shown to prisoners, especially by officers in charge of prisons. "What exactly did the OC say about the cards?" I was asked more than once. When I concluded that he would keep the postcards in my file until my release when I could take them as souvenirs, most of the inmates believed that I had been taken to the office to be told about my release, not to be shown postcards from Europe. Every statement I attributed to the OC was minutely dissected, and it all led to the inexorable "release!"

As the night wore on, the detainees' speculation became more bizarre. Two inmates were locked in an argument. We had to stop them before the argument could erupt into a fight. It was now that I understood that people in prisons can be so desperate that they would do anything and believe anything when a ray of hope for freedom should appear. "People are fighting for us outside. I knew it. I dreamed it. We will soon be released!" someone suddenly shouted in the corner. I laughed and loudly addressed my question to the whole cell, "Are we still talking about the postcards, people? Let's go to sleep." But the assumptions that were made and the conclusions arrived at in the interpretation of "the postcard affair" became more stunning. The commotion continued until the night warder patrolling outside the prison walls struck the wall of our cell three times with the butt of his gun and told us to shut up.

The following morning, one man who hardly ever talked to me took me aside and told me about the dream he had had that night. He very quickly narrated the crime he was thought to have committed against Banda. Another confided in me the story of his family. He requested that when I was released, which, according to the events of the previous day, would be soon, I would tell his wife where his wealth had been hidden so that she could get it to feed the children. Others sent me messages for their wives and children. "When you get out of here, fight for us too," said yet others. They sought other sources to prove or disprove the truth of my story. Unfortunately, the guard-commander who was in charge of the shift and had been at attention as I read the postcards in the OC's office was too hostile to give confirmation of these stories. I wept at the indignity of it all. To think that these were once respectable men who had been reduced to such a state! I wept for their desperate search for freedom. Watching political prisoners fumbling for fresh air, for peace of mind, for liberty was not funny.

If the OC was seeking another favor from me, he had obviously decided to wait. If he was trying to tell me about the human rights campaigns mounted outside the country against our dictator on behalf of the political prisoners in Malawi, he must have changed his mind. Perhaps he too feared being reported to the Special Branch by the cruel guard-commander who was in charge of the shift that day and who watched me read the postcards. Everyone feared him. He was reported to have killed a prisoner at Catcher Prison in Blander with his bare hands, but the Young Pioneer paramilitaries (under whom he had trained and for whom he was still secretly at work even in this prison) are said to have protected him from prosecution. He was believed to be very well connected. I was to remain in prison for another two and a half years before release.

Unlearning the Oral Culture to Survive Exile

Today, after release and now living in exile, the mechanisms for reliving these experiences are virtually nonexistent. These events quickly reduce to mere disjunctive memories that seek to be effaced. No environment, not even another prison environment such as a "retreat," is readily available that would adequately help to recapture the precious moments of one's incarceration. And in exile, where the business of survival looms large, those silences, those temporal gaps, those blank spaces that I knew in prison are too elusive.

It is difficult to recapture the art of just sitting because you are denied work; the art of sitting without reading because the only book you are allowed is the Bible (at first only three Bibles for ninety prisoners); the art of sitting without thinking or saying anything; the art of watching the blank wall expecting to get nothing; the art of counting and recounting the bricks; the art of standing at the door of one's cell after lockup, counting the number of wagtails hanging on one's leg; the art of sleeping on the wire gauze that covers the courtyard; the art of fighting over a glimpse of the moon that passes in some direction for only one week in a month; the art of watching cockroaches; the art of listening to the monotony of the music of mosquitoes or the croaking of frogs outside; the art of speaking to the person in the other cell by hitting the wall first and then speaking through it afterward; the art of lying on your cement floor-bed on blanket rags, knees up, facing the ceiling, hands crossing the chest, watching the cobwebs, with nothing in particular to dream about; the art of musing about scorpions as they disappear into crevices; the art of avoiding the stinking bat shit that pours like rice down the ceiling; the art of adopting a half-remembered and imposed oral culture; the art of rejecting the printed and read culture of a lifetime: all these need special strengths of memory to exploit in their composition.

To survive imprisonment, the negative features of prison existence—such as the overreliance on oral culture; the numerous repressive rules; the warders' notorious daily searches in our clothes, on our bodies, and on wall cracks and crevices for pens, pencils, paper, needles, and razors which do not exist—all these and others had to be turned into something positive. I found that the stories I had learned from childhood, stories I had taught from or done research into, were central to my survival in prison. Mother used to tell us stories at the fireside when we were young. For a very long time I had been engaged in research in orature at the University of Malawi. I used to analyze with students and colleagues the features of oral composition and the performances of those verbal artists who had relied on memory for their livelihood. We had studied how repetitions of whole chunks of structures were patterned. We had examined varying syllable, tonal, and other patterns. We had noted how different concepts, choruses, themes, and rhythms were incorporated in varying degrees in songs and tales. We had found the songs of women pounding or grinding grain to make their work light; the fishermen's songs; songs from drunks;

songs from hunters; riddles, proverbs, and folktales—all were fascinating and created a world of their own. Most of them were crisp and short. Their stories had elaborate similes, symbols, and systems of characterization interspersed by choruses that punctuated each new movement or rhythm. As we groped for a theoretical framework for analyzing diverse categories of orature, we, perhaps unconsciously, began to question the very essence of the written word and began to understand how verbal artists relied on memory for their profession. The oral culture that I had become accustomed to helped me tremendously in accepting, albeit unwillingly, the new prison culture that did not allow books. As the only book that we were allowed to read (the Bible) was also based in orality, my situation was simplified somewhat.

I found that pragmatics, my field of study in linguistics, could be exploited to advantage. When my turn to read the Bible arrived, I often looked for those stories whose meaning involved deductions. I needed to keep the logical faculty of my mind alive in a world which was surrounded by the illogicalities of boots, clanging keys, locks, and the endless banging of prison doors and gates. The biblical parables were particularly mentally stimulating. Often I wrote out in my mind a varied (even contradictory) set of suppositions, interpretations, meanings, and deductions of the parables I read. When I was moved from the isolation cell, I had the opportunity to join the others in prayer every morning and every evening. Because priests and church ministers were not allowed in Mikuyu, we preached to each other. The services and the choir practices that preceded our sermons were a serious matter. Sometimes I would give an academic sermon based on specific stories of the Bible to some imaginary audience. I remember making a critical study of the interpretation of Samson's Riddle using Relevance Theory. But these "papers" were "written" in the head. I often had lively arguments with the other inmates regarding the different interpretations of the riddle and the parable. This helped to reinvigorate the mind.

The other memory of academic life that helped my survival was the Writers' Group which I had cofounded and once directed at the University of Malawi. The memory of incidents depicted in specific poems and stories that I had read or taught from was particularly crucial. I recalled Wole Soyinka's "Conversation at Night with a Cockroach" in *A Shuttle in the Crypt;* I remembered Dennis Brutus's *Letters to Martha* and Ngugi wa Thiong'o's *Detained: A Writer's Diary;* Breyten Breytebach's *True Confessions of an Albino Terrorist;* and works by others who wrote stories, poems, and letters, or sent their messages from prisons on toilet paper and through other tortuous means. I found this tradition in extensive operation at Mikuyu Prison. The very fact that there had been writers in Africa and elsewhere who had gone through the horrors I was going through (and, in some instances, worse) was sufficient to sustain me, however temporarily.

Clearly, the memory of the lives of fellow inmates would enhance one's determination to live on. The experiences of other prisoners not only gave me food for thought about my own situation, but sharing our memories of the worlds that we had left behind strengthened our resolve to survive. We wanted to go back to the world to do better. The inmates who had been near me had more stories to tell: stories of previous releases that had passed them by and how empty they felt when they were left behind, alone; stories of the drunkenness of warders; stories of their exploits during their youth; stories of their various women; stories of the homosexuality that used to be rampant here and how releases had eliminated it; stories of the contributions they had made to the country's politics and social development; above all, stories of their experience with Banda when he arrived in Malawi after forty years abroad. What was particularly surprising was that we seemed not to mind even those stories that we all knew were not true. Sometimes we spun yarns that were patently too fantastic to be true. It was inexplicable how intently we still listened to them. It was as if we were bent on challenging the distinction we often made outside prison between truth and falsehood, fact and fiction, reason and irrationality, and so on.

The strongest memory for any married prisoner, though, must be the memory of one's spouse and children. Recalling what my family, relatives, and friends might be doing at specific times of my silences; recalling what they might expect me to do given a terrifying prison situation; admonishing myself with the voice of my wife, my child, a friend, was common medicine for survival. The memory of the mentors I knew and admired, even the memory of the enemy, the torturer, was invoked. One of the earliest pieces

I wrote in my mind and stored in my memory captures the fears I had for my friends and relatives, and speculates on what foes might have been saying immediately after my arrest. The poem is called "Fears from Mikuyu Cells for Our Loves."

TALK TO SURVIVE INCARCERATION WITHOUT TRIAL OR CHARGE

A favorite strategy to which humans consciously or unconsciously revert in order to survive the extremely stressful blankness of their lives in prison is talk. In order to survive my prison, I talked to myself, to my God, to my (real or imagined) torturer, to my wife, my friend, my child. I talked to the mosquito, the flea, the gecko, or the cockroach on the wall. When I was alone in my isolation cell particularly, I used to quarrel with Banda or whomever I chose to be my enemy. We used to argue vigorously. And all the time I insisted on winning the argument or quarrel. This helped me comprehend Wole Soyinka's method of writing his poems so that the persona's voice would address a creature like the cockroach, as exemplified by the poems in *A Shuttle in the Crypt*. I understood Dennis Brutus's voices or that of his persona that were meant as an address largely to his sister-in-law in his *Letters to Martha* and other works. One must talk to something.

My poems were written and stored in my head. I reverted to oral forms of composition. First, I chose a topic like Valium and considered its effect on political prisoners in Mikuyu. Then I took specific aspects of its use or abuse by detainees or by myself in prison. I strung these in some order. What was composed was then stored in memory until paper was available or until it was recovered from memory after release. Free narrative verse came naturally because of the talking mode which I adopted. Each poem had a voice which talked to or addressed the self, an imaginary or specific thing, person, or audience. How this was done can be demonstrated by considering how ideas, images, or themes are strung together to produce, for instance, the following extended simile or symbol from the Yoruba oral tradition. In print the folk tale is given the title "You Can Fool Others, But Can You Fool Yourself?":

For years they lived very happily together, but their *happiness* was built on *a lie* like the *road* that is *constructed on swampy ground*. And *lies* are like *bats*. As long as they are *kept in the dark, they elude everybody* silently and swiftly. But when *exposed to the light* of day, *they hang stupid and defenseless* for *anybody to see and pick up,* and they appear *the ugliest of creatures on earth*.[1]

Note especially how abstract notions are compared to concrete items. Happiness and lies are compared to the road and bats which are in turn compared to light, darkness, and ugliness. Clearly, the final symbol to be strung out of this configuration will be stored in memory most easily, partly because of its brevity.

Where one has not been tried or charged, manipulation of talk as a strategy for survival is particularly significant. Because I had not been taken to court, I knew that I needed to argue my point, my case, my matter, with some character. Because inmates could not be trusted until after sometime, I conducted monologues with myself, Banda, his henchpersons, and others. I needed to discuss those profound or trivial matters of state, family, finance, and friendship which I had left behind unresolved or unfinished. Because singing was allowed, I sang, alone at first when I was in the isolation cell, and later, when I was promoted to the general cells, with others in a choir. Often even the OC used to come to hear us sing. We did not mind them hearing what was de facto our crying to God. But we were not so naive. The officers' and warders' attendance at our choirs would be used to relax one or another prison rule at the time the prison authorities least expected. All in all, the rules of survival under subhuman prison conditions conflate into one: use your memory to create an alternative world which you can enter and exit on your own terms, unencumbered.

However, all forms of survival in prison are contingent upon the prisoner's decision to want to survive. The first decision I made when I was brought to prison was that I was going to survive. I decided that I was not going to allow the dictator and his repressive apparatus to win. Fortunately, I arrived at Mikuyu Prison when most prisoners were convinced that Banda's dictatorship was cracking irreparably. I found everyone intent on wanting to beat the system. We all assumed that the methods that would beat the prison system would liberate the country from Banda's repression. In prisons where nobody knew if and when anybody was going to be released, the temptation to give up on life and accept inevitable death was immense. But we decided that we were not going to succumb to that temptation—for the sake of our families and friends, for our own sakes. Almost everyone assumed that his life was more precious than Banda's. And the inmates used every trick in the book to get their way. We pampered stupid warders and officers into believing that they were great. We made them feel as important as Banda. The principal idea was that one had to appear to be serious as one did this. This was precisely how the people of Malawi hoodwinked Banda into believing that they really thought he was their savior, their Ngwazi, the greatest one! Only Banda believed this. The truth about Mikuyu Prison is that it was a microcosm of the country. Everything that happened in Mikuyu happened in the country in one form or another, and vice versa. Fights intermingled with friendships, hatreds with loves, generosity with meanness.

The other aspect of life in Malawi to give us strength was the frantic disinformation about political prisoners that had become the tradition throughout the country. The Malawian intelligence had learned its disinformation tricks from apartheid South Africa. This is how it operated: a story would be started by some warder who obviously hated you for whatever reason, and who knew that you were ill; the story found its way outside the prison and then came back to you in prison to shock you into submission. I was supposed to have died of cholera or malaria or AIDS in prison. The stories were meant to demoralize my wife and children, relatives, colleagues, and friends. They were also meant to prepare people for the event of my actual death, natural or created. But when you made up your mind not to die, stories of this sort gave you the will to persevere. *I will shock those who want me dead by coming out of here alive!* would be the natural defiance in reaction to such stories.

Imprisonment is no laughing matter, however short or long. Yet, paradoxically, if one does not learn fast how to adopt laughter as one's major posture for survival, handling imprisonment could become hazardous. So I laughed at myself. I laughed at the notorious warders. I laughed at my torturer. We all laughed at each other's stories without malice. The inmates who had been in Mikuyu longer had always claimed that those who laughed about their own situation in prison lived longest. Even the memory that one once used to laugh was enough to cheer one up. But there was one important caveat: one must remain able to distinguish, with as much honesty as one could muster, laughter from madness, reality from fantasy, truth from fiction. This involved a certain amount of recognition (the existence of which was quickly provided by the circumstance), for instance, that laughing very loudly, alone, could be the beginning of fatal madness; it could also be the expression of therapeutic hysteria; at other times it could be an excessively destructive form of self-justification. The biggest problem was getting the right balance between hilarity and solemnity, fact and fiction, sanity and insanity, truth and falsehood.

The Living Ghost of Dictators, Racists, and Others in Exile

Today, in this exile, I am having to unlearn the oral culture and relearn the written one. And it has not been plain sailing to start reading again after four years of absence, particularly after the world has so drastically changed: the Berlin Wall has crumbled; the Cold War is over; Nelson Mandela is the president of South Africa; even the politics of my own country have moved on. I must literally catch up with the world. However avid a reader one might be, catching up with the changed world and being expected to tell one's own story demand more than mere memory. It is not easy to relearn the culture of the written word.

Besides, my release had taken the university registrar and his chairman of university council by surprise. They had not made the subtle plans against my rejoining the university that I expected. When I reported my release and wish to return to the university, the registrar was shocked to see that I had indeed been released, that I had been cleared to work in the university or with whomever needed my services. He was particularly amazed to hear that I could travel abroad without his or the university's fighting for my clearance. He was not enthusiastic about my reentry into academia. He had apparently been told by the chairman of the university council to ask me to reapply for my post, although I had not been sacked. When I reapplied, just to prove a point, it took the university registrar more than two months just to acknowledge receipt of my letter of reapplication. And for that I had to effectively threaten him that I was going on leave for the United Kingdom anyway. It should have been clear to anybody in my situation that I had to look for work elsewhere. Other Malawian academics before me had followed a similar pattern. Most of them had not been taken back. Why did I expect to be treated differently? As I had to create my own space and bring my family to some sort of normal life, I left. The Poetry Society and Irana Trust in London (bless them!) got my family and myself one-way air tickets.

But exile brings its own problems. Writing from exile does not necessarily mean writing from some cozy environment far from one's home. Leading the life of an exile has not always been a happy affair. My family and I live in one of the friendliest parts of England, North Yorkshire. But even here, as European refugees mingle with African exiles who mingle with other foreigners, and as local unemployment figures rise, it is not unusual to find tempers among the locals rising and racism manifesting itself in a myriad of unsubtle ways. The struggle to survive often drives to the background certain important battles against racism in Britain that one ought to fight. Sometimes, however, an event such as "moving house" might unconsciously help to reconstruct exile experiences that one might have desired to disregard. The dilemma of wanting to tell or not to tell another prison story in exile and the temptation to equate exile with prison might be resolved within the lines below, which endeavor to capture three and a half years of our stay in England. Perhaps seeking a more somber mood would have been unrealistic.

CHRONICLE OF OUR RHYMING EXILE
(Or the delights of another alien louse)

Now that Walmgate Removals are finally here,
Our neighbors are greeting us without fear

Fervently tendering their pretty belated offers,
Confounded that we've not yet seen the harbors

Of splendid Whitby or the marvelous beaches
Of Scarborough or the Yorkshire moor birches

Which scroll in green, red & brown like spotted
Canvas spread out on sand dunes, gingerly dotted.

When we first landed here, their children (who,
Like their parents, needed to see foreigners too,

As they were downright racists, perhaps taking
After their ancestors), laughed loudly, spitting

Without ambiguity, milling about our front hedge
Menacingly, throwing their eggs even at the edge

Of our bedroom window; Judy's temper snaps,
"How dare Yorkshire do this to such poor chaps

Rescued from the jaws of the African crocodile?"
"I only wish they offered us the eggs their bile

Wastes on our walls!" Lunda restlessly jokes;
Lika merely sulks, mending his bicycle spokes;

Mercy bites her lips, frantically mopping our
Kitchen floor, "Time for such rituals to glower

Is here, my children, hold on!" she says firmly
"*Mea maxima culpa,*" [2] I must concur solemnly.

Our true friends at Newton Terrace, Nether
& Upper Poppleton, Clementhorpe & other

Places are painfully nonplussed. But the eggs
Splatter on, until Mercy's ultimate faith pegs

On Father Austin O'Neal & his potent prayer:
Then one Police Constable Bailey's wily care

Dries the spittle from the dire crowds of lads.
Besides, our youthful landlady's colorful wads

Of a wedding we recently had the pleasure
To attend, constrains us within the treasure

Of her dad's amiable smile until Nancy Reed
Across the back garden hedge sees the need

For the children to share her cuppa, afterwards
Always waving or popping over with her cards

& a bunch of flowers for each child's birthday
(She'd meticulously kept in her diary someway).

And Mercy sends her my little book of verse
For the squalor of prison wagtails to converse

With her at Christmas (what of her electric
Mower across the hedge to speed up our metric

Chores, sprucing up the lawn, tidying our trim);
Until Amanda Webb's house is full to the brim

When the children's friends start sleeping over
& the Maxwell's chancy wink stops to hover.

Today, as Mrs. Tiddy's property's up for sale
& New Year braces the hostile Pennines gale

& we must move on, the neighbors have begun
Pouring their pearls of overtures for their fun;

They wonder why we could not get a Council
House, why don't we just squat, even fake ill,

As we know we cannot get a Council House
Unless we are doleful like some idle grouse

(With blankets & pillows actually on the curb
Of Seventh Avenue), that's the sanctioned herb

Which officially testifies we are neither lying
Nor solely meaning to jump the long undying

Queue; but even that won't guarantee a house
For "Such a family of five! God, that mouse

Breeds!" And tomorrow as I run my creative
Rounds across the ashen Pennines so evasive,

Tomorrow, after my spirited ration of Express
Regional Railways, where trolleys forever depress

Appetites for sandwiches & coffee, I'll span these
Nipping snow slopes of County Durham to freeze

Me through the smoggy red roses of Lancashire
(Punctuated by Chorley cakes & tea or the shire

Vernacular, staff jokes of Frankland, Wakefield,
& Garth prisons), I'll sample gusts of Sheffield

Charcoal, blasts of Leeds & sodden Manchester
Before Liverpool's fog lingers in peeling plaster;

For tomorrow, I resolve to be ticket holder 1059
Summoned to desk 17 to submit my official line

Why I must not be deported by Lunar House,
Croydon: the delights of another alien louse.

One Tentative Conclusion on the Literature of Incarceration

As I recast these snippets of my experience of prison and exile, it is tempting to string together several statements about the nature of the literature of incarceration and how writers try to contain the chaos of incarceration through their art, hoping in the process to restore, at least at the psychological level, their emasculated dignity and that of their community. There are two types of literature of incarceration: first, there is the literature of factual or semifactual experiences written about or within the constrictions of the prison, the concentration camp, or isolation chambers where the writer was incarcerated. This type of literature is principally (auto)biographical. It is restorative in nature. The writer is engaged in the restitution of self-respect, which had been violated physically and psychologically by the barbarism of the writer's prison environment. Clearly, the writer who composes from the solitary confinement of a prison or a detention camp is not as free as one who writes from confinement with other inmates, detainees, or hostages. The stresses and compulsions of the life they lead and the world they recreate may be different. The principles operative in the creation of the work, however, remain the same.

The second form of the literature of incarceration is the product of one who may not have personally been imprisoned, taken hostage, or experienced the holocaust. In this case, the writer feels the duty to reconstruct the justice, the honor, the hope, the integrity, and the identity of his or her oppressed peoples. In broad terms, this type of literature subsumes the work of those writers who, covertly or overtly, primarily battle for the restitution of human dignity which was lost, for instance, through the imposition of political institutions such as slavery, colonialism, apartheid, or dictatorship. Even if the writer's motivation is purely restorative or therapeutic, the product of what is reconstructed—the novels, poems, plays, paintings, songs, autobiographies, or memoirs written about these experiences—must be judged according to their success or failure as works of art. Most postcolonial, diaspora, and exile writing is a subset of this literature; it is noble; it is meant to restitute a sense of justice and dignity among the oppressed peoples of the world. These works are based on the same concepts of incarceration and exile as those of authors who have been incarcerated or exiled, but they are to be judged more completely as works of art rather than as strategies for survival, as testimony.

One cardinal feature defining the literature of incarceration is its exploitation of orality and memory. Both types of literature exploit specifically the writer's memory; that is, recall of oral/aural features becomes a major strategy in their reconstruction. Memory is used here in its broadest possible sense to include libraries or archives of books, paintings, newspapers, and magazines from which the writer constructs his or her material. Memory also subsumes the mental states under which writers reconstruct the fractured identities they depict in their works. And orality includes specific oral and aural features operational in the process of reconstruction. Whether the final images or symbols that writers reconstitute are remembered, because the writer experienced them, or imagined, because the writer studied their various forms, does not seem to matter. What matters is the extent to which the artifacts represent the incidence and reality of incarceration, in fact or fiction. I believe there may be untold wealth in the stories of the reclamation of our fractured identities through the restoration of our dignity and the reconstitution of our memories of incarceration.

Containing Cockroaches
(Memories of Incarceration Reconstructed in Exile)

Jack Mapanje

prologue

The following dawn, I woke up to the reality of
Thumping boots, jangling keys & streaks of golden
Sun; my bones, muscles & joints—my new plight

Stiff: "The most dangerous rebels start out here;
They may then be moved to other minor prisons
Or perhaps promoted to the general cells inside;

Even the country's legendary statesmen landed
Here first after lockup; I commanded the guards
To chain them to the stocks in the cell you slept in

Last night. (Have you ever heard notables crying
Like naughty children?) The next day the dissidents
Were released, although the Special Branch who

Freed them refused to enter their names & signatures
In Mikuyu Gate Book 43; that's when we suspected
There was something suspicious about their liberation;

So when we heard the rude radio pronouncement
About their intention to cross the border at Mwanza
& their accident there, guards on duty that day came

To bear out the Gate Book 43 inscriptions of those
Special Branch who had discharged their eminence—
But, truly, men have been released within days here."

The guard-commander had strictly meant the story
To chill me into submission after the first day of my
Arrival; he wanted no hunger strikes; no jumping

Over prison fences; no protest, no nonsense here;
He invoked my university mentors, the country's
Awesome demagogues & others who had felt his

Sheffield handcuffs grip & blister without blinking.
I embrace only his tale of the Gate Book signatures
& names in case someone found it funny some day.

I

The limelight:
The fundamental transgression of our despotic times is to be in the limelight; and to think or do anything on your own terms is its perfect embodiment. When I returned home after about four years of my studies in London, I expected to be arrested. I had not committed any crime against anybody or against my country. You did not need to commit a crime to be arrested. Being in the limelight was sufficient. I had been dangerously in the limelight. I therefore expected to be arrested and detained on April 1, 1983, at Chileka Airport in Blantyre upon my arrival from London. Not because I was guilty. You did not have to be guilty to be arrested and detained. In these hopeless times even laughing at the blank space might land you in prison. "Why is he laughing so loudly? Who is he laughing at?" These loaded questions, implicating that you were laughing at the system or someone in authority, were common. Everything was a statement, a punishable statement. Your very presence was a statement.

Publishing a book of poems outside the country is worse. It only needed someone in some authority to consider your poem, your book, your thoughts and ideas subversive, rebellious, or merely radical, for you to be in trouble. And everyone was incredibly generous. Warmth emanated from every corner. They warned you when you were going below the belt. But my return home was just another Fool's Day. Nothing happened. No arrest. No detention or imprisonment, despite the stories I had been told when I was in London about how subversive my poems had been.

I had had some inkling of the extraordinary influence my slim volume of poems, *Of Chameleons and Gods,* published in London in 1981, was having particularly among the civil servants in Capital Hill offices in Lilongwe. Some who had clearly not read the poems invented their own quotations and made me responsible for their origin. Others linked up lines of one poem to the lines of another to exercise their faculties of interpretation of the contemporary politics of Malawi. The result was blamed on me. I could do nothing to stop them. At any rate, I realized that their faculties of deduction and interpretation, which had been paralyzed for so long, needed exercise. I had come to understand the truth I had always feared: the interpretation of an artifact after its publication was outside the artist's control. I suspected that my poems might have been causing some stir among some authorities. Unexpected questions, like "So, what's this we hear that you are into good books then?" came far too frequently not to unnerve. I knew that my book of verse was waiting for its time to be banned or withdrawn from circulation. I knew I would be arrested. I did not know when. "They wait for you to hatch then they take you in, you know, like chickens!" everybody said intimately. And like everybody I could have left the country. They encouraged you to go into exile. I did not want exile. I was already living in exile in my own country as it was! Why look for another? I wanted to die and be buried at home. I did not see anything wrong with being that romantic. Our ancestors started it. And by what right could some people lay a more legitimate claim to citizenship than yours, especially when you too were born there? Some of these cockroaches were not even born in Malawi!

The censorship board was cautious about banning my book outright. They refused to ban it. It would have made me an instant hero. They did not want other heroes here. One hero was enough: His Excellency the Life President of the Republic of Malawi, the Ngwazi Dr. Hastings Kamuzu Banda, the lion of Malawi, the father and founder of the nation. No other person mattered. But perhaps for the first time, and I gather on recommendation of the principal of Chancellor College, the censorship board had invited academics to read and report on my book. "We'll get his colleagues, his friends, and his ex-students to ban him," someone apparently said cynically. The list of readers included one British professor of English teaching in the university, several Malawian lecturers, and the university's alumni working throughout the country. These readers had promptly sent their reports to the censors. Luckily, a colleague, brother, and friend had stumbled on the reports. He photocopied and sent them to me in London so I could sample the type of official response I was likely to encounter. One report summed up how the officials were going to react: "These poems poke at the raw wounds of the nation." They decided neither to ban nor not to ban the book. Keeping the book on a shelf in one's living room was neither acceptable nor unacceptable. That was more painful than banning. Meanwhile, the fifty or so copies still held by the university bookshop in Zomba were bought off by the Special Branch, only to be thrown into a pit latrine, as I was later to learn. Those that were in the central bookshop in Blantyre were either impounded, ordered to be returned to the United Kingdom publishers, or merely withdrawn from the shelves.

Instead of being daunted, however, I wrote a letter to the chief censoring officer to explain why the poems were only another batch that would not destabilize the "peace and calm and law and order" prevailing in Malawi! There was nothing rebellious about them. And having been largely influenced by our oral traditions, as she would discover after reading them, the pieces tried to preserve something of our culture, however unsuccessful the exercise might have been. What did she, in her considered opinion, think? "Should I bring copies of the book when I return to the university?" In reply she asked why I had not sent the poems in manuscript to the censorship board in Malawi first, before giving them to Heinemann in London to publish. I laughed. I wondered why nobody had warned me about that. Months later, the managing director of Dzuka Publishing Company, Malawi's de facto official publishing house, wrote to ask if I could give them permission to buy the rights to publish the bulk of the volume. He wanted a Malawian version of my poems, he said. He was sure that I would appreciate that Malawian readers deserved to enjoy my work. He did not indicate which poems he would exclude. It was patent, however, that the book had increased my conspicuousness.

In addition, I had coedited with Angus Calder and Cosmo

Pieterse an anthology of contemporary African poems that was published by Heinemann UK before I returned home. This was based on the 1981 BBC Poetry Competition for Africa, for which we were judges. Part of our duties as judges of the competition was to explain for listeners of the BBC World Service for Africa what type of poems we chose and why. These programs were heard by ordinary Malawian listeners as well as by government informers. They were probably recorded in Special Branch files. I had also coauthored with Landeg White an anthology of oral poetry from Africa which was published by Longmans in the United Kingdom. "This is too much," said one friend when I showed him the three books I had had published in the United Kingdom while I was doing my doctorate degree. My fears were encapsulated by the loaded question I was asked by an unknown police officer at Chileka Airport on my return: "Have you decided to come back, then? What happened to the BBC jobs we used to hear about?" I expected to be arrested.

Everybody expected to be arrested, everybody who was in the limelight. If you did not anticipate arrest, you were one of them or you lied to yourself or you were a foreigner. If you were a foreigner, you expected to be deported. And no special qualities were needed. Whether you were an adventurer, worked for yourself, or worked for others, you were in the limelight. No village or town, however remote, no profession or trade was safe from the limelight. You did not have to perform any feats to be in the limelight for your arrest or deportation. And when an expatriate was deported or a local decided to go into exile or was detained without charge or trial, nobody asked why. Everybody either knew or could speculate why. The late James Stuart, professor and head of the Department of English, used to cite Russian experiences, particularly Akhmatova's cry quoted in Nadezhda Mandelstam's *Hope against Hope:* "It's time you understood that people were arrested *for nothing!*"

If you tried to do anything for the good of the country, you were looked at with suspicion. Only they knew what was best for the country. If you did not want to be involved in the compulsory yearly Youth Week Development Projects—if only because you thought you were no longer a youth—they were astonished. If you declined the invitation to the national independence celebrations, they inquired what alternative revolutionary celebration you intended to hatch instead. However much you might have loved the country, you were not given the opportunity to genuinely live there. Professor Stuart's own endeavors to settle in Malawi (after receiving his exit visa from apartheid South Africa) were thwarted by an inexplicable early deportation. The lists of those who had been either deported or detained without trial multiplied with each independence anniversary celebrated.

They did not want you to travel widely either, even as part of your profession. Various barriers were set up. One of them was the thing they called "official clearance." You could not publish, attend a conference, travel, do research, or anything else without official clearance. The joke went, "You cannot pee without official clearance, here!" My being invited to become external examiner in the Universities of Swaziland, Zimbabwe, and Botswana naturally shocked them. In a country where journalists were heavily censored, they feared that I would tell outside journalists, Malawian exiles, and others what was happening in Malawi. The country's image would be tarnished by such stories. The International Monetary Fund [IMF], as a result, would not lend Malawi the money we so much needed. Someone must have loathed me in spite of my decision to reduce my verse writing and concentrate on merely teaching linguistics instead. Sam Mchombo and I decided to focus our energies on the creation of what was to be known later as the Linguistics Association for Southern African Development Coordinating Conference (SADCC) Universities (LASU). With the help of the Swedish Agency for Research and Development Cooperation (SAREC), UNESCO, and the German and British governments, we initiated the association for the coordination of teaching and research in African and European languages and linguistics in African universities south of the Sahara.

We were amazed that we had problems in getting the authorities to open the first international conference of the Linguistics Association. We had got all the participating international delegates cleared to come to Zomba to attend the conference. They were not communists. They did not include in their CVs any papers or books they might have published on Marxism. We had warned them not to. The minister of education who was to inaugurate the conference was not available. His permanent secretary could not come. Our British vice-chancellor conveniently went on his tour of West African universities after we had implored him to exploit the rather original idea embedded in the concept of the regional academic association. The principal of Chancellor College opened the international conference largely because it was hosted in his college, although he must have enjoyed the publicity he received afterward in the local papers and on the radio. Unfortunately for me, I was elected chairperson for LASU at the association's first meeting, putting me further in the limelight. LASU would become another organization which would give me the opportunity to travel outside the country.

Other connections with the outside world had been established. I was chairperson of the Africa region for the Commonwealth Poetry Prize for a year. This gave me the opportunity to travel to one African city and to London, where regional and international committees or chairpersons could meet. I attended a workshop on Bantu linguistics held at Butare in Rwanda, and the first Zimbabwe International Book Fair in Harare. These were followed by the invitation from the Indian Council for Cultural Relations to participate in the Valmiki World Poetry Festival held in New Delhi and Bhopal. The international conferences, seminars, and workshops to which I was invited multiplied. What might have been doubly disagreeable to the authorities was that although the university or government had to provide clearance for the conferences, they did not have to pay. I was in the limelight but out of their control.

Within Malawi itself I performed duties which put me in the limelight. I was head of the Department of English and editor of the *Journal of the Humanities* which I helped initiate; a member of the University Senate and the Academic Planning Committee; chairman of the School Certificate (O-level) English Syllabus Committee; a member of the National Examinations Council; a member of the board of governors of the Malawi Broadcasting Corporation. The duties that put me in the limelight were numerous. Yet instead of being grateful that whatever I published or did would put the university and the country on the world's literary or linguistic map, those who exercised Banda's authority were scornful of my efforts. "What does he want to become, His Excellency the Life President?" was the common question, intended to domesticate the inventiveness of those who tried to improve the nation's lot.

Other countries took pride in the achievements of their citizens; indeed their citizens were encouraged to achieve. Not in Banda's Malawi. Here anything that made you conspicuous was abhorred. Anything you accomplished on your own terms threatened the image of His Excellency the Life President or the image of the country. Nobody explained how. Banda's henchpersons particularly detested anyone who performed wonders (however minor) on his or her own initiative. Everything was to be done in the name of and in gratitude to His Excellency the Life President. Whatever you did had to be likewise acknowledged to His Excellency the Life President without whom you could not have done it. Banda was the alpha and omega of life in Malawi. If you disagreed with him or any of his supporters, however mildly or constructively, or if you proposed alternatives to a given problem, you were not safe; these were the cancerous traces of a "rebel" who needed to be uprooted from the "peaceful" society being created by His Excellency the Life President.

To be a rebel was the ultimate crime. Banda used to say that those who were rebels, if caught, would be sent to prison where "they would rot, rot, and rot." Everybody in the towns and the villages was asked to watch out for rebels and report them to the nearest police station or nearest Malawi Congress Party office. No boundaries between rebel and nonrebel were drawn. No explanation was given why rebels could not be taken even to the traditional courts, which Banda had specially created. You expected to be arrested and dumped in prison to die. Nobody fought for you. Your relatives dared not lift a finger for your release; they feared to join you wherever you were. The so-called civilized international community dared not upset the dictator. You expected arrest, feeling helpless, totally dejected, alone. Only the memory of some affable justice lingered to sustain you.

2

The arrest,
when it came, felt like some stupid ancestral saying come true. An idle fragment of colonial superstition, probably invented by

the British, says "when Friday falls on payday or payday falls on Friday, the world grinds to a halt and begins to spin in the opposite direction!" The locals held on to this belief long after the colonials had left the political arena, although nobody really believed such incredulities ever happened. Today is Friday. Payday. Anthony Nazombe and I have just had fish and chips for lunch at Gymkhana Club, Zomba. We are washing it down with our respective Sheffield and London pub experiences and joking about the papier-mâché Queen Victoria, who used to arbitrate over the golf, tennis, and football trophies in the bars of Gymkhana Clubs once upon a time. Where has she been moved to? Who dared move that precious symbol?

We are rudely interrupted.

"Is there a person by the name of Dr. Mapanje here?"

We look at each other. Silence. The man is in civilian clothes. He is wearing a dark blue blazer. He had walked quietly towards our table. Having checked in vain for whatever he wanted in the other bars of the club, the man comes back to survey our bar overlooking the ex-colonial cricket pitch, now occasionally used for independence celebrations football. Except for the two of us, the barman, and one soldier drinking in the corner, this bar is also empty. The man comes our way again, repeats his question more loudly. Perhaps he is chagrined by our silence. We are amused. Still silence. He walks towards the Golfers' Bar next door.

My children at home are waiting for me for lunch. I do not know why I was so irresponsible as to have been persuaded to come here for fish and chips with Anthony, a poet, friend, and colleague, when my lunch was waiting for me at home. Why did I not tell the children they should not wait for me? I hope they had a lovely time at the lake at Uncle Cuthbert's. They had brought my favorite fish, Judith had said on the phone. How thoughtful of them. The man comes back and more anxiously interrupts us again.

"Mapanje here?"

"Don't you know him?"

I decide to spare him more breath.

"Are you Dr. Mapanje, the head of the Department of English, Chancellor College, University of Malawi?" he resolutely says.

"Supposing I was?"

"Well, there's a man in the Golfers' Bar next door. He would like to see you."

"Man, down here, it is the monkey that follows the mountain, not the other way round. What about where you have come from?" I answer with ease.

He snaps back, "My friend, this is no time for proverbs. You must see the man waiting for you there!"

He points where I have to go. He is clearly hurt. But where has he come from? His face is new in these parts. Another one of the Special Branch to scare us into submission, perhaps? We won't be cowed. We get up.

My heart jumps when I see in the Golfers' Bar the Eastern Division commissioner of police. Everybody recognizes him. Few know his name. He is spruced up in full commissioner gear. The bar is desolate; the high stools around it and the wooden chairs that have lost their cushions since goodness-knows-when are forlorn, scattered all over, as if there had been a chair-throwing fight the previous night; the stench of stale beer hangs uncomfortably in the air; the dart board is firmly shut. Why is nobody here today? No drunk on payday at lunch hour in the Golfers' Bar? I wonder. . . . The commissioner suggests we step outside. Anthony nervously follows behind us, stops at the club's gate, and watches me hobble toward the car park. Only my car and the police Pajero brood in the dusty car park. The commissioner stops near his Pajero and asks another question.

"Are you Dr. Mapanje, head of the English Department at Chancellor College, University of Malawi?"

"Yes."

"We have been directed by His Excellency the Life President to arrest you."

"But His Excellency does not know me, and I do not know him except as the chancellor of the university and the Life President!"

The police commissioner is obviously not listening to my protestations.

"Have you got the handcuffs?"

"Yes, sir!" the junior constable quickly answers, shrugging to attention. He takes the handcuffs from the right-hand pocket of his dark blue blazer. I should have known. His hands feel scabrous as the iron of his handcuffs clumps tightly around my wrists. He forcefully elbows me into the Pajero, which dispatches down the university road at a speed reminiscent of British colonial armed vehicles during the 1959 emergency in the country's fight for independence. My car is still parked at the Gymkhana Club. They have taken my car keys. I am glad I have finished paying the loan for the car. When we reach the university, I am turgidly nudged up the stairs to my office. I feel like an escaped criminal rearrested. When you are still handcuffed, limping up any steps is not easy. And whoever invented handcuffs had a contorted mind. Did they hang him for this massive crime against humanity?

The office of the head of the Department of English is full of new books which have just been donated by Ntchima Trust (one of the organizations which first started growing tea here) based in York, England and the British Council office in London. There is a crisis at hand: these books are intended to beat IMF directives that have imposed fees on university students. Our courses in English literature and literature in English are in danger of not being taken by students because they have no money to buy the texts. (The government has patently found an impeccable excuse for killing the literature section of the department: IMF structural readjustment directives. When did literature departments begin to be regarded as subversive?) So I thought I should appeal for assistance from friends. This is the result. But such gestures are not appreciated here. And when the search begins, the Special Branch belligerently throw the fresh-smelling books all over the floor, deliberately trampling the delicate pages with their boots. The commissioner shouts.

"What type of office is this? How do you work in here? Where does one put his feet? How can you clutter the floor with books, books, nothing but books? Is this the office of the head of the department? What do you head in such a place?" The commissioner nearly chokes in the barrage of his own rhetorical questions.

Out of the blue, I hear myself saying:

"If you've heard that there's a head of the Department of English and you are looking for his office, this is it! Tell me what you are looking for amid this sumptuous confusion of fresh books, and I will get it for you."

Silence.

The search continues. The commissioner trips over a heap of woodwork in the corner of the office, left here by the maintenance section of the university. They are putting up shelves for the books. Drawers bang. Books fall from the wobbly shelves. The fresh smell of the new books they are topsy-turning is overpowering. Obviously, they do not find what they want. I do not know what they want. They do not give anyone the impression that they are looking for anything professional or academic. After some thirty minutes, the searching party divides. Two remain behind to continue searching my office; the other two with their commissioner must take me to my house for more search. What are they looking for? Again, it's not funny being pushed down the stairs handcuffed. The messengers, the cleaners, and the people walking about in corridors look away when I look at them. This is the culture of deception we have learned to live with.

We cross Kamuzu Highway past the little wooden Mulungusi bridge, up the dirt road, turn into 11 Mulungusi Avenue where my house is located. I notice the jacarandas exceptionally purple and flowers from the flames-of-the-forests remarkably red. At home, my mother, who is in her seventies, almost faints when she sees me brought in handcuffed. She had not seen this done to any of her children or her relatives during the colonial period. And now, after independence, what is she seeing? Words fail her. She wants to ask. She does not know who. I feel like Jesus watching Mary watching Jesus. My children are too stunned to move. They are trembling with fear. They do not understand the handcuffs. They do not understand anything. Nobody understands anything. Nothing is explained to anybody. The search starts in the living room. They pull books from the shelves and scatter them all over the living room. They do not seem to find what they want. I do not know what they want. Nobody understands what's going on. They throw down the records and the newspapers. The children's bedroom and my mother's bedroom are searched with impunity. They take me to our bedroom. They viciously overturn our double bed, throwing on the floor the blankets, the bed sheets, and the pillows. Drawers and wardrobes bang. Blood rushes to my face. This thing is getting on my nerves. It is probably meant to. Hold on. I must stop all this nonsense. I am still handcuffed. Man, suggest something positive—anything to distract their attention.

"If you are looking for our passports, the drawer you've just banged closed more than five times now has them!"

One of them looks at me with utter disgust.

Control your temper now; things could get worse! Shush!

They have found Legson Kayira's *The Detainee*. This novel is banned here because the author is a Malawian living in exile in England, and the subject of the novel is subversive by our standards. I keep this book in the bedroom in order to protect the public from it. It is on its way to the National Archives, to which all banned books must eventually be surrendered by heads of department. Surely, nobody in his right mind could accuse me of being an irresolute head of department on that account. But then I suppose nobody is in his right mind at this moment in time. As for Stephen Gray, who brought this novel, he must have been too naive to realize the effect of his kind gesture. Nobody has any reason to bring in banned books from South Africa or anywhere else in order to introduce themselves and their widowed father to this warm heart of Africa. Unless it is prearranged. Poets especially have no excuse; they must know the principles that apply in the countries they visit. Otherwise it will not help the cause of democracy and freedom that poetry is forever fighting for in these parts. Poets should not be obsessed principally with the solution of their personal or political problems! But wait, Gray has nothing to do with this. Why are we shouting at the wrong man? This may not be what they are looking for anyway!

It is clear that the Special Branch men do not like to be told where things are when they are searching the premises of rebels, especially when they do find my passport and my wife's. He passes them on to his mate. I know that they know that I know that this is not what they are looking for. I do not know what they are looking for. I wonder if they really know what they are supposed to be looking for. He flicks through the pages of my passport all the same. The passport has not been to any communist or socialist country. That would have been the most unpardonable contravention of the four cornerstones (peace and calm, law and order) upon which this nation is said to be founded. One of them answers my thoughts with a look of contempt. My suggestion has worked better than the cuff-restrained physical punch I had intended. I have won. But you could not beat His Excellency the Life President's officers for long.

They must therefore reassert their authority lost at my suggestion. Wardrobes and drawers bang louder. Trays where I put photocopied articles are upside down. The dozen or so articles I wanted to use to finish my linguistics paper ("The Ghost of Temporal Distance," which I had presented in draft at the Harare SADCC Linguistics Conference two weeks before) are scattered all over the bedroom. They are intentionally trampling on them. The other fellow has found other papers—explosive papers, if he understands their impact on the mind. They link the Tanzanian socialist program with South Africa's African National Congress [ANC] struggle against apartheid. Malawi is the first independent African country to have cozy diplomatic relations with apartheid South Africa, despite the apparent universal boycott of South Africa. Any enemy of apartheid South Africa is therefore an enemy of Banda's Malawi. I got this publicity material with ANC tapes from Stockholm at the Second African Writers' Conference. And the stuff, especially the music, is good—no need to apologize for it. The first shows his find to the second. They shrug their shoulders. Praise the Lord! It's not what they are looking for. I do not know what they are looking for. They throw the ANC paraphernalia on the floor and keep the novel, which they pass on to the commissioner who is just coming in to join them. He had temporarily gone home on his way from my office. This arrest has destroyed the leave he was supposed to have started today, the commissioner moans, as he takes the novel and looks earnestly at my passport and only incidentally at my wife's.

I now remember my wife in Lilongwe, three hundred miles away, taking a course in community nursing. She insisted on this course not just to add to her general nursing and midwifery qualifications, but because she had no time to read anything on nursing while she worked. The poor woman is overworked and needs a break, for goodness' sake! I cannot imagine what she will go through when I am gone. Next week she writes her hospital finals. Lord, what have I done to her life? What have I done to the lives of these children? I wonder where they will take me. Now that the commissioner is here, the Special Branch create more chaos out of the peace of the house. They unambiguously intend to impress their boss by creating more clutter in my house. Their flagrant chicanery angers my mother, my children, and my niece even more. But they are too frozen to act or move. If this army of innocent people had known how best to unleash their blow against these men, they would not have hesitated. The police have still not found what they are looking for. Nobody seems to know what they are looking for. Mother's choking fury finally bursts out.

"How can you people scatter this peaceful house? What has my son done? Why don't you take me instead? Leave my son alone. I am the one who is already dead. Kill me instead, you insensitive men!" she fumes.

I am worried about her temper which I have seen for the first time. I am proud of her. But I fear for her blood pressure.

The reply to the verbal blow she has so nobly struck comes as tumbling chairs and more flying books. Classical records are spinning on the smooth floor like the wooden tops of my childhood years ago. The Special Branch put their boots on anything that appears precious, especially the records. I remember Felix Mnthali, my teacher and colleague, now teaching in the University of Botswana. When they arrested him they accused him of having been in possession of subversive material: classical records by some Russian composer! I begin to comprehend what he might have gone through. Papers rustle. Pandemonium reigns. Now the Special Branch are locked in a nasty quarrel with my five-and-a-half-year-old son. He says they should not have carelessly thrown his toy police van, which I had brought him from Harare in Zimbabwe recently. They are so flustered by my mother's pleas and my son's fury that they must shout, perhaps to prompt their commissioner into action.

"If you two do not stop your nonsense, we'll take you too!"

"Why don't you try that? You have no shame, look at them!"

My son challenges them, pulling his face. The commissioner of police must come to their rescue. He orders that we leave for Blantyre, where the "higher authorities" at Southern Region Police Headquarters are waiting for us. Having gone through this indignity, there is nothing wrong with seeking more. Beg, man, beg before you leave; they might listen.

"Mr. Commissioner, could you kindly do me a favor?"

"What?"

"In my left shirt pocket here, there is money for water and electricity bills which I must give these children. Could you take it out for me and pass it on to my niece or my sister-in-law there, please? Also I need to write several checks with which the children can buy food for themselves and their granny and to pay the workers. Could you . . . ?"

No words are uttered in reply. He peremptorily points at the constable to unlock my handcuffs to enable me to perform for myself the tasks I have asked for. Another kind of victory?

As I am about to get in the Pajero again outside the house, Anthony and Steve Chimombo (friend and previous head of department) arrive. Anthony must have broken the sprinting record of a lifetime to have brought another member of the department here with such speed.

Steve, rather agitated and clearly daunted by the Special Branch presence starts, "What's the matter? What's happened?"

I do not need permission to talk to them. I just find myself drawing closer to them as I hear myself whispering: "I am being arrested. They are taking me to Blantyre to see the 'higher authorities.' Please, do not do anything stupid; no protests; no boycotts of classes. We all know what those bring. Keep the ship afloat, the fire glowing—for my sake and especially for the sake of the students for whom we are in business; they must not suffer unduly. I will be back soon. Do not worry. It's only another passing phase, this, soon to be forgotten."

I avoid a final glance at my abandoned children and my mother. I do not know what they are going through. Their mother is not here. I do not know how long it will take for her to know about the arrest. I have some notion of how our world will soon reject and ostracize them. The children wave at me. They will probably be orphans today. My hand falters. I cannot see my eyes. We are off.

Father Patrick O'Malley, another colleague in the Department of English, to whom Anthony must have run from the Gymkhana Club and probably not found, drives in as our Pajero disappears into the distance. Stuck between two plainclothes officers, I have no time to wave him goodbye. At the Oilcom petrol station we must refuel and pick up a guy whose physical features and English accent are South African. I overhear the conversation between him and the commissioner.

"Is it him?"

He looks in the mirror and answers, "Yes."

I take the cue. I did not do my linguistics for nothing, I pride myself. Perhaps it was those South African whites I threw out of the Harare conference? My thoughts are interrupted by a cassette of South African requiem hymns that the commissioner puts on at full blast. I am totally demoralized. My feet start knocking. I remember Aaron Gadama, Dick Matenje, Twaibu Sangala, and David Chiwanga—senior statesmen who were murdered four years ago. I feel I am going in their direction. Why do they blast this vehicle with church hymns, for goodness sake? I am devastated, totally. It's some forty-two miles to Blantyre. It takes us exactly thirty minutes. On the rough tarmac which has not been resurfaced these thirty years of our Republican status. I do not remember anyone taking thirty minutes to travel between the Mulungusi part of Zomba township and the Southern Region Police Headquarters in Blantyre.

3

The waiting room

at the Southern Region Police Headquarters is on the first floor. It is no more than three paces by three. Three soft chairs surround the rectangular stool in the middle. I am given one in the corner. I look out for listening devices. No microphones are visible from here. In this oppressive confinement I am left alone. The walls are blank. On the stool are magazines which I will not touch. I do not want to react to anything here. Someone is watching you. In these sophisticated times, you can never tell who is charging you and trying you by remote control. I will sit quietly like a nice little boy. That's how they want us to be anyway. I am waiting patiently for something to happen. Nothing happens.

Ubiquitous, a portrait of His Excellency the Life President is on the wall. I recall the story of another portrait of the Life President:

My college principal had summoned me to his office. Lecturers from my department had been drinking themselves stupid again. This time it was not at the Gymkhana Club. It was in the lounge at the Government Hostel (G. H.). Obviously sloshed to the bone, one of them got up and started shouting at H. E.'s portrait, calling him an illiterate whore, accusing him of holding the nation's health to ransom with his fake medical vouchers from Edinburgh University: "You are a disgrace to humanity. And don't ever think you'll not be held accountable to the nation's plight and shame one day!"

If the portrait had not been out of reach, my principal says, the lecturer would have gored His Excellency's eyes! Failure to appreciate that anyone could have extended this catalog of our ruler's wrongs against his own people ad nauseam is written all over my principal's countenance. But he is getting more serious. Question: "How many times must a principal appeal to his head of department to control his staff, especially in such public places?"

No answer.

Of course I had frequented the Government Hostel. Everybody did. The principal himself patronized the place, for goodness' sake! It was the nearest resort for anyone wanting to temporarily drown his sorrows. We all knew that it was not safe to drink at the G. H. Parliamentarians and other government officials always stayed at the G. H. whenever they had business in Zomba. In fact, although the country's capital had moved, the parliament remains in Zomba. The Government Print, which handles all the business of state, was still intact there. That the move of the capital had been, by and large, a tactical matter, was a truism beyond dispute. Besides, everybody knew that the G. H. was infested with other frightful swarms of cockroaches that were almost impossible to contain. Bats landed and flew away to the rhythm of lights going out or coming on, pouring kilos of their stinking ricelike shit in our beer. Everybody went there nonetheless. Answer: "What nook is safe for anything without subtle harassment in this country?"

A university lecturer who had been badly distraught was clubbed to death at the G. H. This was partly because he was considered to have come from a rebel family. The authority's definitive pretext was that he had hung himself by the bed sheets at night. His body was taken home the same day under police escort. The primary attraction of the G. H. was that at least you heard about, even saw, the latest wife-swapping and other stories there.

Yet I was not there that night. That much was a fact. Dare I then say to my principal: "I am sorry, Mr. Principal, I was not there that night"? Dare I ask my principal which member of staff he had been informed about so that we, together, could apprehend him before things got out of hand? It was our diplomat who works in New York who had watched the "H. E. at the G. H." saga. And we must thank him for his thoughtfulness in telling us that we must warn our staff about the matter. What if the ambassador were a foreigner? What image of the relationship between university staff, the president, and the country would he or she have taken home? I had often wondered how low our diplomats had really sunk under our despotic rule. That day the matter had come home to roost. The hilarity of the affair was that the lecturer concerned had come from the Department of Psychology, not from the Department of English, as the principal had assumed. Obviously, I had not bothered to inform my boss about the truth of the matter when I found out.

Today, as H. E.'s portrait keeps vigil over the police headquarters waiting room, the spiritless walls fail to stimulate even stories of such tedium. Only death is exciting to think about. The death of the celebrated gang of four this country shamelessly accidentalized in broad daylight four years ago begins contesting my mind again: Who actually killed them? Where exactly? What crime could they have committed, careful as they had been throughout the years not to rock the boat? How could we have been so callous, killing our own people in cold blood? I wonder where they are. Where do dead people go? I will probably join those martyrs today. Yes, perhaps we'll meet. Gazing at these walls does not provoke any discernible positive sentiment. Silence.

It's nearing seven at night. Nasty things happen at night. Across the stream that divides this industrial area from the townships that squat below Soche Mountain yonder, there is a bridge which I watched being built. I was a young man living with my cousin's family at Matenje village, near Queen Elizabeth Central Hospital. We used to hear troubled Congress Party Land Rovers whining down the Soche township road, past the bridge, on their way to feed Shire River crocodiles with political dissenters. It was always at night. And when I saw this police headquarters going up, did I ever imagine I would be looking at its blank walls today? Why am I wringing my hands now? I must be getting anxious. This is called restlessness. No, perhaps I am just unstrung. Or feeling a little iffy. I hear doors squeaking and gates banging. It's probably in my head. I hear shuffling feet. Are those boots? The heart jumps. This is it. I must sit still. Someone peeps into my waiting room. I remember a snake retracting its head into its hole after discovering danger outside. A cramp on my thigh as I try to stretch my leg. Loosen, stupid muscle; will you twitch first then? Well, go on! But for how long have I been sitting here?

"Come this way!" a nameless voice shouts at me.

My knees knock. This is it. I rise. I must sheepishly follow.

4

The interrogation
is farcical. At 7:30 P.M., it is getting late even for the officers who must have better business at hand on a Friday. I have to be hurriedly ushered into the large bare room where the imposing oval-shaped mahogany table is flanked by eight commissioners of police with their inspector general at the head. All is quiet. I bite my teeth. I don't like it. When did they arrive here? There must have been some brisk business in town. If it's about me, it must be very serious indeed. Perhaps these are the people we were waiting for. How did they travel here in a country where the airplane is reserved for only the Life President? The ubiquitous portrait of His Excellency the Life President above the inspector general's chair ominously mediates the grim proceedings. Despite the agony of waiting for more than four hours in a dismal waiting room, it is a relief to see some movement at last, however macabre its direction was eventually going to be. If I must go, it had better be now. Let's get it over with.

The ammunition which the Special Branch had abducted from my bedroom are the passports and a banned novel. If there is justice, I will easily handle this court of commissioners, the tradition of no provision of defense lawyers notwithstanding. Alas, the vindication which I had been carefully preparing since my arrest at 1:35 this Friday afternoon does not materialize. Anything planned on your own terms here is always repulsed. Endeavoring to frustrate whatever imaginative schemes you might hoard is the policy they vigorously pursue. I had expected the interrogation to be a more protracted and tortuous affair. But, technically, there is no inquisition. It's too brief, too abrupt. I cannot even begin to defend myself!

The inspector general of police starts.

"I went to see His Excellency the Life President at 11:30 this morning. H. E. has directed me to arrest you and detain you. Since it is a directive from above, we must tell you that we cannot investigate your case. It would be questioning the wisdom of the Life President. I have called upon these commissioners, therefore, to find out if there is anything in our files about you. There is nothing. They all say they do not know you. So we thought we should ask you to tell us why we should detain you. Who are you? Why should we detain you? What have you done to each other at the university?"

I am flabbergasted. I have not misheard. What have we done to each other at the university? My mind is blank. I am nervous. First, who is going to believe that I am really a nobody when matters have reached this far? Second, someone at the university has reported me to the Life President. Although anyone could have done it, the options must narrow down from the country's population of ten million to the handful who have easy access to the state house. In the context of the university, these must whittle down to a nephew and his uncle. These officers genuinely want the tale from me. But watch. How could H. E.'s commissioners not know? How could H. E.'s and the country's eyes and ears instantaneously not see and not hear? Pray. I look again at H. E.'s portrait on the wall and notice the rebuke on the octogenarian's youthful face. An uncomfortable silence reigns. I not only refuse to talk but I cannot see on what I should waste my breath. Silence.

The inspector general does not like silence. He continues.

"Tell us where you come from and where you grew up, that is, where you went to school."

That's better. All the commissioners suddenly look at me at once. I choose to dwell on the innocent parts of the "rebel" district where I was born. The East Bank, as the locals call that part of Mangochi district where I was born, is as explosive as the Middle East after which it was named. There are no more desperadoes left there. The first son of the land who would have toppled this tyrannical police state, if his foolish exiled friends in Mbwani had not betrayed him, had been mysteriously killed by "CIA's sugar disease" in the exile of California, as everyone claimed. The other two dissidents were publicly hanged. The nation only "sobbed in its stomach," as some people said, unable to protest in any substantive way, for years having been terrified into abandonment and resignation. The list of victims in the East Bank alone—those accidental-ized by crocodiles, lions, cars, even by timid hyenas, largely from police cells and Young Pioneer bases—runs into the thousands.

A friend told me the story of a well-known retired assistant commissioner of police (who now boasts the most successful to-bacco farm in the district, second only to the farms run by the Greeks who decided to settle here goodness-knows-since-when): the retired police officer apparently shoots dead the rebellious vil-lage men, women, and children in the name of the party and gov-ernment; he loads them on the back of his small truck, covers them with canvas, and does his drinking rounds from bar to bar. When fights cunningly instigated by him break out in the drinking bars, as reconciliation he invites the combatants to come out and take a fish each from his catch at the back of his truck. When they see the reeking bodies, they run for their lives, never to enter the bars again. Besides, it is a well-known story that after the abor-tive rebellion led by Masauko Chipembere, the little population of more than three hundred men, women, and children of CheMoto village was severely trounced for surreptitiously supporting the re-volt. Except for a woman who was too old to travel, everybody in the village was rounded up, packed into police and army vans, and thrown into Maula Prison some three hundred miles away. Most of them died there. Their houses and grain stores were burned down or confiscated by the Congress Party's invincible Young Pio-neer paramilitary.

The open secrets that helped to subjugate the whole district and sustain the heinous tyrant are abundant. Would I have had the nerve to want to become another martyr, at this late hour? No way. I must mention Mangochi as my home of birth without too much enthusiasm. I decide to answer the commissioners' sudden effrontery by emphasizing Chikwawa District as the home where I grew up. There are very few well-known dissidents who have fought this government there. It is a trick we have all learned to invoke in time of trouble. Cowardice, really. But what the hell!

"When my late uncle Mr. Frederick Siyabu left Mangochi in the early thirties, he came to settle in Blantyre beside Soche Mountain. He was one of the earliest founders of St. Columbus Scottish Pres-byterian Church, near Kwacha International Conference Center. He married a woman who came from the Lower Shire. With her he eventually left Blantyre for Chikwawa District and settled at Mpokonyola village on the East Bank of Shire River, about three miles immediately to the left after descending the Shire Highlands mountain ranges. He established himself in a lucrative business as a traditional herbalist who was well known throughout the district and beyond. It is my uncle who sent me to school when we moved from Mangochi District to Chikwawa in the fifties. Afterwards he became the traditional court chairman at Chikwawa District; and he was in fact one of the first treasurers of the Malawi Congress Party Branch for the Lower Shire valley in the late fifties. My uncle sent my late brother and me to school at Chikwawa Catholic Primary School. I then went to Zomba Catholic Secondary School, Soche Hill College, Chancellor College, University of London, first at the Institute of Education and then the University College . . ."

The inspector general interrupts.

"So you, too, grew up in Chikwawa District? By the way, do you commissioners know that I was first posted as police constable at Chikwawa District Headquarters?"

The sudden unanimous "no"-chorus, like officers' boots called suddenly to attention, mingles with the noise of shifting chairs. Another interrogation complete. Another directive is issued: I am to be kept in one of the best prisons until it pleases H. E. to have me released; a prison which has no lice, no fleas, where cockroaches can easily be contained. I detect a tinge of pity. I do not believe anything about policemen and policewomen. But today, something tells me these are telling me some sort of truth. I do not believe it. I do not believe that I am going to prison. Actually going to prison. Me. To get there we have to go back to Zomba where I was arrested. That's where there is a prison with less lice and where cockroaches might be contained, says the commissioner who brought me here.

But wait. A gentle tap of a hand on my shoulder. What now? The heart races. Before I know what is happening, I am yet again shoved into another room next door where there's a replica of the inspector general's oval-shaped table, only smaller, and H. E.'s portrait still glares menacingly at the head of the table.

"I am the head of Special Branch. I report direct to him," he points to the portrait. "I thought we should have a brief chat before they take you to prison. What church do you go to? I mean, what religion do you belong to?"

"Roman Catholic."

"So do I. Tell me everything so that I can present your case to H. E. in your favor. Everything you might have withheld or omitted when you were talking to the inspector general. I know you wanted to say something personal in there. This is your chance. Have no fear; trust me, a fellow Catholic!"

I am getting impatient with this familiar type of dishonesty. I remember a rat I cornered once when I was young. It began running in circles, in vain. It was the last rat I killed. It looked pathetic.

"Look, as I said, I never talked to any rebel at the Harare Linguistics Conference." (I suddenly see flash past, in my mind's eye, Peter weeping for Jesus beside the glowing fire, instead of weeping for himself.) "And as I said in my verbal report to my principal, it was the most successful conference we ever organized. It was brilliantly opened by Zimbabwe's minister for higher education, Dr. Mutumbuka, which was followed by a wonderful address from the university's vice-chancellor, Professor Walter Kamba. It was very well attended. We even had six intruders from several South African universities who, after posing as tourists, decided to show up themselves because the conference was so good, they said. We decided to throw these gate-crashers out. Their South African colleagues who had had the courtesy to contact the local organizing committee in advance had been accepted as full participants, academic boycott of apartheid South African universities notwithstanding.

"And all our lecturers presented papers which became superb reference points for the rest of the conference. They did our university and this country proud. Granted, there was a quarrel among members of the local committee of the Linguistics Association which I chair; but this domestic matter was resolved amicably. At any rate, it had nothing to do with tarnishing the image of H. E. or of this country in any way. As for the rest, I am sure your vigilant staff know that I am not a member of any dissident party fighting this government from outside."

I do not know how much of what I have just said he understands. I don't think he is listening. My armpits are sweating profusely. I have been pushed too far into this most brusque defense. I do not like being pushed.

"As I say, I will do everything in my power to get you out of this. Meanwhile, you had better pray three Hail Mary's everyday."

Some characters time their jokes!

5

The way to prison
is circuitous. The Eastern Division commissioner who arrested me makes the point less enigmatically than the head of Special Branch, who had just interrogated me unannounced. Since it is getting on to 8:30, we must first have dinner at the house of his friend on the other side of this twin city. Trundled into another blue-gray Land Rover, I am snug between the two officers who had so boisterously ransacked my office and my house. Their perspiration now stinks, as if they had been jogging, then did not have a bath because of a sudden call to duty. I do not know exactly where we are going. I do not understand how H. E. could have done this to me. How anyone could have done this to anyone? Did H. E. really know me? Did he even care? What of the humble contribution I have made these years to the development of education in this country? All that down the drain? I do not understand.

Three occasions stand out when I have had anything to do with H. E.: First, at Mtendere Secondary School, where the headmaster Brother Dosties from Canada gave me the duty, exactly twenty years ago today, of forming a special school choir that was to sing H. E.'s praises. H. E. was visiting Chinkhu and the rural precincts of Dedza district, which he had not visited since he took over the reins of power from the British. The school had to present the head of state with something in the form of a dance or performance. I remember soliciting the music expertise of a priest friend at nearby Mtendere Junior Seminary. We pinched the church tune of a well-known hymn and replaced the pious key words with heretical and banal ones to recount how H. E. had developed Malawi beyond recognition since he came back from England. We listed distinctively the lake shore road, the university, and the move of the country's capital to the central region from which the President had come. Everybody performed these tricks ad nauseam, often adulterating the structures of good traditional songs. Sometimes I wondered why Banda never got tired of hearing these transparent lies. It was the first public lie I had ever cobbled together in praise of my President. When Mtendere Secondary School Choir eventually got to the platform, however, we only got honorable mention, and H. E. was not allowed to hear the praises of my school choir, despite their sweltering in the oppressive sun for more than five hours — another form of plagiarism not worth the effort. I smiled at my folly and swore never to forgive myself for this. Having come from the wrong district and the wrong region, perhaps I should have known better.

Second, I remember feeling exceptionally jubilant and triumphant on graduation day, when Vice-Chancellor Dr. Ian Michael called out my name first. I remember shaking the President's hand firmly to receive the B.A. with distinction that I had achieved! I suddenly discovered how brittle the man felt. I wanted to tug at his hand to see if he could have withstood my wrestling on Lake Malawi sand, if I had had the opportunity.

Third, I remembered those "noble" duties the staff in the English Department especially performed. H. E. always insisted that every member of parliament pass proficiency tests in spoken and written English before entering parliament, and these tests were to be prepared by the Department of English and administered by university staff throughout the country with the department's supervision. I felt sharp exhilaration principally when some arrogant, fat-necked, illiterate Malawi Congress Party politician tripped over the l's and r's when forced to read sentences that staff had subtly constructed so that words like "read" and "lead" were not too far removed from each other! The absurd duties that His Excellency made us perform were manifold. And I believed I was performing these duties superbly, considering our eccentric circumstances. Why is he arresting me now? Was that solemn robe of university respectability we wore on national occasions another huge lie?

It is probably the most fascinating paradox of our despotic times that some lies had to wait for my arrest to be fully appreciated. Take the late revelation of the lie at the house of the friend of our commissioner of police. I had all along naively held the view that no serious relationship could ever be cultivated, let alone thrive, between locals and the Asian or the European community beyond the commercial, the marital, or the academic. Today I walked into some Malawian-born Asian's residence that threatened to belong to a true friend of His Excellency the Life President's commissioner of police. Four dazzling floodlights situated in strategic corners to protect the mansion from armed robbery are reinforced with two police hounds that bark their blood-curdling welcome, making even the sweet night-smell of the white jasmine at the gate seem suspicious. Could this be the gate to the torture chambers I had heard about, where, after confessing their lies for survival, people were killed nonetheless, bundled into sacks, then dropped into the River Shire in Chikwawa? Did I misconstrue the inspector general when he said he had spent his first years as a constable in Chikwawa? Was that perhaps part of their coded communication? Are we really going for dinner in this mansion? Could this be it? The last hour?

Here, the commissioner must treat us to another classic lie. He introduces his nervous juniors as his friends and me as a colleague to whom they are giving a lift en route to the famous university. (The ambiguity on the last two words is clearly intended by the commissioner). The trouble with lies is that they never stop. Our commissioner's must extend to his friend's rough handshake, accompanied by his Dracula-toothed smile. It must continue to the commissioner's friend's wife, whose sly genuflections and well-practiced traditional greetings naturally follow her extemporaneous gesticulation to servants to make the table ready. Another lie of an interjection. In her capacity as sister-in-law she must protest. The commissioner had promised to arrive at 7:30, when her dinner was still steaming. By coming to dinner this late, did he intend to put her cooking to shame in the presence of his university friends? But she understands how busy commissioners can be. He is absolved.

The lie sickens its way through the curried rice in hot chicken sauce—all of which would have been very tasty otherwise; it slips through the persistent ChiSena tonal patterns, now showing, which his friend's wife must have acquired during her childhood in Mozambique and found impossible to shake off; until it finally dawns on me that through this noncommercialized exchange in an almost perfect dialect of the national language, through these inexplicable bows and counterbows of apparent politeness, I might be treading in the "torture" chambers of highly protected and extremely volatile mandrax, *chamba,* and cannabis territory otherwise nicknamed "Renamo."[1] After nine hours in dingy custody, who would not need a toilet at this point?

6

Sometimes dialogue with the self
is more uplifting than communication with thousands. It is part of the distancing game we always play, particularly in times of stress when humans are seeking survival. I confer with myself: "There is a certain peculiar ambivalence about the disbursement of power in our despotic times. Commissioners and their officers live in a world which is inaccessible. Their actions defy logical definition and spatial and temporal location. On the one hand, they appear unwilling to do what they are ordered to do. They seem unhappy to do their interrogations, for example, especially for cases which they claim do not emanate from them. You wonder whether they are bothered about how matters of life and death are eventually concluded, particularly when officers claim that they are not consulted first. They are answerable to no one for their behavior because the so-called authorities prosper from the same incompetence.

"On the other hand, those in power present themselves as totally committed to the duties they are told to perform. They display tendencies for inexorable enjoyment of whatever brutalities they are asked to inflict on the innocent, be it mental or physical. It is as if they did this in order to avenge themselves for the financial and other inequalities imposed on them by society. At this level power does not seem to be the exclusive domain of the dictator nor his acolytes. For instance, although His Excellency depends on his commissioners to imprison people, the right to suggest who gets imprisoned often rests in his concubines (should he prefer these to wives) and their relatives whose final word in reality counts more than yours or that of the ordinary citizen. And the courts cannot be invoked. They are irrelevant. The tyrant is the final judge; his word law and everything that goes with it."

"Yes, but why they don't give up, or revolt, or simply say no, amazes me. Why do the police in other countries respect human life and human rights? How do other people survive without being police people?"

"Did you ever say no in the university or wherever you worked for your dictator? Can't you see how trapped these people must be? How scared? Exactly like you? It's easy to be dismissive."

"Now hear this, my friend: victim I am; defend these cockroaches I might consider; but scared I definitely am not! What wrong have I done to be scared?"

"Let's change the subject before we tell more lies or these cockroaches overhear."

"Fine. Do you think it was the Young Pioneer intelligence or the army intelligence that reported me to the state house? Or shall we keep our original nephew-uncle assumption, which is perhaps one of the many most plausible?"

"It could have been anybody; even Bill, your boss's brother. Did you hear he was in Harare at the time of the conference? He might have twisted the story of your going to Harare on sabbatical next year to his brother. He might have got the story of the successful interview for your sabbatical from your very friend who is on your committee or was in your delegation, saying you're running away to Zimbabwe next year under the pretext of sabbatical leave—that would be enough to get you where you are!"

"We still believe in a conspiracy theory, eh? Anyway, why does H. E. need all these informers and intelligences? Besides his police, army, and Young Pioneer informers and intelligence, there are those from South Africa, Israel, Britain, America, and others—for such a small country? Where does he get the money to pay for all these? What does the West see in this egotistical, evil, and fragile man?"

"Have you heard of money from mandrax toppling healthy nations? That's probably where he gets his money and from the rural poor who contribute whatever they have to him and the civil service or yourselves! As for the West and H. E., you underestimate the power of the bond created between the colonial student and the country that educates him. But now you know what to do if you really want to overthrow this government . . ."

"You have not been watching the interrogation, then; why

would anyone be so crazy as to contemplate government overthrow here?"

"Anyway, if you should consider ousting this government in future, you now know when to do it. All the police commissioners gather together in one part of the country where there's a trivial event like you. What you can do is take the rest of the country while they are sleeping, as it were. Palaver finish! Why don't your dissident friends outside see this, if they are really serious about liberating this country from the beast?"

"Look, I think you don't understand. These clowns know what's going on outside and inside this country. They know where real opposition is. Thinking of toppling this government reminds one of that stupid saying about fucking yourself with your finger when the sexual urge is great. Rebellions have failed more than twice before."

"We are into vulgar sayings again, are we? I thought those just got us into this state today. Do we know where we are going? Why can't you learn from your mother's or your son's civil and dignified protest? Yours doesn't stand up to theirs. It comes in a poor fourth. And anyway, you too have been brainwashed into thinking that this government is invincible. I disagree. You may not have tried out other options."

"What options? There are no options. Yatuta, Silombera, Kanada, Chipembere, Muwalo, and others have all been here. Forget it. Change the subject. Let's talk about what's intriguing about oppressors. For instance, why do dictators and their henchpersons never seem to suffer any shame? I mean, did they really have to handcuff me in public this afternoon, then parade me to my office in everybody's full view—secretaries, messengers, cleaners, the lot! They must enjoy these things, don't you think? How do they invent these sadomasochistic tendencies?"

"But sadomasochistic tendencies is what they are paid for, don't you understand? And that's where your strength might be in future. I mean, you might have gained the people's sympathy when the Special Branch were pushing you about in public. And they might have lost their honor. That same general public are probably talking about you now. They are probably saying to each other by their paraffin tin-can lamps, 'Did you see how they pushed him about? Did they need to do that? Those beasts!' "

"But I am not the first one. And anyway, that won't help us today, not even after we are gone, wherever we are going. Where am I going? Where is this? Have we gone past Chiradzulu Mountain yet, do you think?"

"We have only just left the outskirts of town, man, bound for Zomba."

"Which prison do you think they will dump me in? Zomba Central Prison, Domasi Prison, Mpyupyu Prison, or the notorious Mikuyu Prison?"

"I don't know. It will be a prison whatever its status, don't you think? Away from your beloved wife and children, away from your mother. I think those kids have probably not had their lunch up to now. Did you see your children and your mum when you arrived in handcuffs? Can you imagine the state they are in now? And when your wife gets the news. Your fault. Irresponsible. Agreed?"

"Yes, even in Latin: *mea maxima culpa*—I have sinned gravely! By the way, did you hear and see what I heard and saw?"

"No."

"I reckon that Gymkhana Club public arrest was a mixed blessing. I saw three Special Branch Land Rovers. One was hiding on Mulungusi Avenue near Blaise Machila's house; the second, on the G. H. and C. C. A. P. Primary School junction; the third, on the road to St. Luke's Hospital near the last petrol station. If I had ventured out today, my friend, I'd probably have been a dead man, another one accidentalized. Don't you think?"

"We haven't finished yet; I wouldn't bank on this rough drive. We could be going anywhere!"

"Don't you think I got at them in the office, though? Remember the commissioner agitated about the heaps and heaps of fresh-smelling books donated to the department by Rosalind and by Lizzy? 'Is this the head of department's office? Where can one begin to search? What do you head?' he whined."

"Yes, but your answer was a bit daft. How dare you say to people whose venom you are aware of, 'If you've heard that there's a Department of English in this University, if you are looking for his office, this is it! Ask the secretary next door!' And you actually shout to Lyscar, showing her your handcuffed hands?"

"What's left of me, my friend? Look."

"Still, no excuse for being careless. There might still be some hope. Who knows?"

"My communication with Lyscar was discreet, though. Grant us that, for heaven's sake. Pure professional, it was. And did you note how shrewd she was after seeing me? No emotion. No tears. Instead she asks firmly: 'Did you call, sir?' "

"Yes, but who rescued you from your stutter, 'Help these gentlemen, if they should need er, er, er, any, any, any information about me!' You nearly broke down before her!"

"I disarmed them all the same, don't you agree?"

"Okay. But did it cross your mind that she might have already been tipped off about your arrest? She could even have been planted in your department from the word go. You can't be sure. Do you remember she made one of those long-distance calls in her Zambian language again as you gave her your Stockholm conference paper to keep in your confidential file?"

"We are continuing to accuse our closest friends of betrayal then, are we? Not very funny, what dictators get us to do! But hold on to your Land Rover rails, man! Is this Mbulumbuzi? And what are we doing swaying from left to right here? What's the matter? Listen! The commissioner in the front seat is speaking. Listen!"

"Driver, stop that bastard in front of us! That's no driving! Overtake that truck! Stop in front, quick!"

"He does not want us to overtake, sir. Driving left then right— probably drunk, sir!"

"Steady, driver, now!"

"He's turning to the bottle store, sir."

"Follow him. When he stops, take his car keys at once, you hear? Stupid night drivers!

" 'Eastern Division commissioner of police. Give us your keys! Careless driving! What, you're drunk too! Quick, open the bonnet! That should do it! The nephew of what?' "

"He says, 'Regional police commissioner's nephew,' sir!"

"Driver, get off at the next police station; take another constable and come back here to tow this car to Namadzi Police Station, okay?"

"Yes, sir!"

"I can't stand stinking fools causing unnecessary accidents on our roads! I will drive to Zomba from Namadzi myself, okay?"

"Yes, sir!"

For once I had feared that my time had come. I kept watching the two officers on my sides as the shouting was going on. Perhaps all this was deliberate. Perhaps this was how the nation's celebrated gang of four—Gadama, Matenje, Sangala, and Chiwanga—were accidentalized. My spine is cold, my throat dry, and legs numb. I hold on. Try to think. Cheer up.

I remember the accident I was involved in years ago. My ANC friend and external examiner in our department Lewis Nkosi had come from the University of Zambia. In spite of his being a famous exiled writer, distinguished critic, and a tireless, vociferous fighter against apartheid—and with the tact of Steve Chimombo, the head of the department then, mixed with some remarkable oversight on the part of national security—he was allowed to examine for three years in the only country in Africa which had diplomatic relations with apartheid South Africa. I was dropping off Nkosi at the G. H.; we were getting whimsical about the ease with which one could dupe dictators, reminding each other about our old drinking times at the Rising Sun on Tottenham Court Road and at the Marlborough Arms off Gower Street in London, when suddenly an oncoming police van speeding down the steep from the G. H. gave us full floodlights. I panicked, quickly swung to the left to avoid head-on collision; into the ditch I went, then into a tree—crash! My red Daihatsu was seriously damaged but not written off. It had to be towed to safety and stored at the Zomba Police Station that night. We were both fine, but Christ, was it horrific!

We have stopped at the Eastern Division Police Headquarters to "inquire where the prison with reduced lice and cockroaches might be," says the commissioner. It's getting well after midnight when the gates of Mikuyu Prison finally open. I walk upstairs to an office three paces by three. I am stripped absolutely naked. I look ugly. The body shivers, muscles twitch. They have taken off my tweed jacket, the cardigan which I had hoped to turn into a night blanket, my shoes, shirt, trousers, and underwear. They shove these into my handbag. They insist on taking the money I have and holding it for me. For safekeeping until my release, which could be tomorrow, the warder jokes. I do not understand. They also have to search my backside to find out if I have stuffed any proscribed material there. Could I do them the favor of bending, please? I feel very small. It's cold but I am wet all over. Yet I am assured that these precautions have to be taken in order to protect me. I must understand. I do not understand. To protect me from myself? I am unable to laugh. I wonder if I will ever understand these jokers. My cold skin is suddenly covered in a rash as if I were beginning to suffer from long-maturing malaria or terrible pneumonia. The warder opens a cupboard on the wall and takes out clothes for me to wear.

I recognize their cream-white. Prisoners, who often dig on both sides of the highways and put up white-painted poles carrying national flags as part of the independence celebrations each year, usually wear these. I slip into my new prisoner's pocketless garments made from cream-white cheap cloth. In the villages this cloth is normally used to wrap the dead. The resemblances to my present situation are too close to speculate on. We must go down the steps again back to the cells outside, which I did not see on our way here. I struggle to walk back down the steps without shoes. But like everybody, I will have to get accustomed to walking on bare feet here. I am told this is the rule in most prisons in this country. We learned this from the colonial times, he claims. After more than twenty years with shoes on except in bed, the bare feet feel numb. The sand on the steps and outside pricks. I am shoved into a damp three-by-two-pace stuffy cell. My feet stick to the pungent urine on the floor. The cement floor is cold. He throws two stinking rags of scruffy blankets at me as he switches the lights on for the night. Apparently this will protect me from poisonous creeping night creatures. A holed bucket for the night is in the corner. I understand why the floor sticks. The keys jangle as he locks both my door and the courtyard gate from outside. I sit down in the glaring light, shorn of everything on earth save memory. I reconstruct why I think I am here.

Exile and Creativity
A Prolonged Writer's Block

Micere Githae Mugo

STAGE DIRECTIONS

The subtitle of the following drama is: How the pangs of exile caused my prolonged writer's block — a reflective autobiographical narrative, not an apologia. *Read on.*

When I originally agreed to make a presentation on the above subject, the task had seemed straightforward. I had planned to conduct some library research focusing on any work that explored the exile experience, analyze the emerging perspectives through contrast and comparison, revamp my findings with some personal illustrations, draw up lessons to be learned, and thus neatly conclude my assignment. On sitting down to attack my agenda, however, I found the task to be more demanding than I had anticipated. In the first place, the undertaking refused to be just another academic exercise. The notion of referencing, footnoting, and abstracting an experience that insisted on being narrated from the heart began to register as another form of intellectual posturing. I was in a dilemma as to how to go about my task.

Finally, amid my agonizing and introspection, I was seized by a compelling urge to address my audience simply and directly in a personal, conversational manner. The experience of a woman writer, also a single parent, faced with the challenges of exile under unique circumstances, demanded that this story be told through empowering discourse. A big load dropped off my shoulders. I was ready to run. But then another problem emerged.

Having developed such intimacy with the subject matter — under exploration since 1982, the year I left Kenya to go into exile — my effort to distance myself from deeply felt experiences proved to be another futile academic endeavor. This time, defiance against the kind of theorizing that equates involvement with irrationality and noninvolvement with objectivity took fast care of that problem. After all, what is so objective or rational about the unfeeling composure of the cold murderer who puts a knife through a victim's throat without wincing? That is the scientific style in which the A-bomb was dropped on Hiroshima and Nagasaki, no? Calculated, callous, precise objectivity. On the other hand, what is irrational about telling a tragic story with feeling and even tears? Does being human mean surrendering intellectual capacity? That particular problem was also thus solved.

But there was yet another problem to wrestle with. In demonstrating how harrowing, draining, eroding, and imaginatively vacuuming the exile experience can be and has been, I might be perceived as writing an apologia for my creative barrenness during the initial period of this nightmare. After all, many writers, including the famous Karl Marx, have not only written volumes while in exile but actually composed great literature on toilet paper smuggled out of prison cells. All that is needed is discipline—period. Well, as might be put in extended, reversed, hackneyed terms: not all birds are made of the same feather. Apologia or protest, the compelling story must be told.

But who was going to assume the narrative voice? I considered trying a first-person narrator all through to provide the needed immediacy and dramatic embodiment, but the story sounded individualistic, if not actually egocentric. I tried a distanced analytical tone, through the eyes of an omniscient narrator, but the intended distancing injected awkwardness and fictitiousness into unyielding hard facts. A factual, descriptive essay then suggested itself— an attractive option, but its immanent trimness would require maneuvering and contriving to contain zigzagging ends. This might in turn transform the whole discourse into an abstraction of life and pain.

The harder I tried to imaginatively capture the voice of an omniscient narrator, the more it failed to breathe life into the living person of the real woman at the heart of the story—a story rejecting fictionalization, for the narrative was, has been, and is a part of one's continuing history. It is one's tomorrow.

Ultimately, the story chose to unfold itself at the crossroads of collective narrative, dramatized dialogue, true anecdote, generalized observations, and autobiographical discourse. It begins with reflection on the conditions that led to exile, showing the move as an imposed course of action and not an open, voluntary choice. The exile experience is indeed depicted as a rough journey which is exacting not just for the key traveler but also for the traveler's immediate family and for the children in particular. Illustrations, anecdotes, and firsthand testimony are frequently brought in for authentication of the experiences explored, providing a personal touch to the narrative. The primary objective of the piece is to draw attention to the unique and adverse ways in which exile affects the creativity of some writers—in this case, a professional woman, political activist, and single head of a household. The obstacles outlined, the story closes with a celebration of the triumph of the human will over forces of oppression, as those exiled for their opposition to the abuse of human rights relentlessly struggle on for justice and freedom.

Let us begin with the question of what leads to exile while posing another related one: whether or not going into exile can be considered a voluntary choice. These questions cannot be addressed in isolation from a larger concern, that of the writer's role in society, including duty to the homeland. This, then, constitutes our point of departure.

First, a classification regarding writers: in the African context, writers tend to be members of the privileged elite, the products of a colonial education which, in most cases, trained them to view themselves as a unique breed of people, occupying an elevated presence in relation to the rest of the colonized population. Lured by the image of the Bohemian artist of the Western liberal tradition, African writers came to view themselves as even more special than the group of specials that their colonial masters had created of them. Okello Oculi, the Ugandan poet and political scientist, once referred to them as "spoilt children." The neocolonial state plays upon this spoiled-child syndrome, offering privileges here and there, volunteering assured patronage, in an attempt to coerce the recipients into collaboration. Those accepting the bribes have a good life, taking appointments as cabinet ministers by the patronizing neocolonial regimes or by accepting lucrative directorships where they can make a quick buck, and so the alluring offers roll on. Those who reject the blackmail are severely punished for daring to prohibit the violation of their consciences. Others try to abstain from casting the decisive ballot, lying low, and either remain mute or speak in paradoxes: this way they save their necks while not quite throwing conscience to the wind, like the collaborators. We will come back to these groups momentarily.

At this juncture, it is important to underline the fact that these initial observations point to the fact that writers cannot be lumped together as a cohesive group of people. Indeed, it is mandatory that we further scrutinize the above broad categorizations, using a class analysis in order to accurately place writers within the general production process.

As members of the intelligentsia, writers represent three main strands: conservatives, liberals, and revolutionaries. Given that under neocolonialism members of the ruling elite (whether military or civilian) essentially represent the interests of imperialism at the expense of the economically deprived masses, the above ideological positions assume telling significance. In sanctioning and servicing proimperialist neocolonial states, reactionary writers ultimately become promoters of antipeople practices, reinforcing the oppressive systems and structures at the root of the people's dehumanization. Often these writers reduce their writing into apologia for the systems of injustice that they live under. Indeed, in many cases, such writers have not only raised the volume of the choruses of state praise-singers and parroting chanters but also joined the ruling parties of the oppressive regimes, often operating as their active agents. A number have even been known to write treatises on state philosophies, unfounded as some of these philosophies are, no more than mere footsteps on sinking sand.

Liberal writers assume a middle position, choosing to be neither hot nor cold (as the Bible would say). They are more anxious to make it in their personal careers than to struggle for the collective emancipation of their societies. Hiding behind compromise and pragmatism, they run away from decisive action by refusing to use writing as intervention to change the oppressive reality around them. In the final analysis, they end up chasing the proverbial rat (of Chinua Achebe's Ibo proverbial evocation) even as the house is perishing in flames of consuming fire. Another tactic used by these writers is to engage in either mysticism or enigmatism, thus keeping their readers mesmerized and confused by what they write.

This way they free themselves from the responsibility of conscientizing their audience in preparation for transforming the suffocating reality around them.

The third major category of writers within the neocolonial state is represented by the revolutionary artist. This artist's creative energies are devoted to affirming human dignity and creating a world in which each and every human being finds possibilities for utmost self-realization within a nurturing, validating collective environment. Revolutionary or progressive writers take sides with individuals and groups who are denied a voice in naming themselves and the world around them by the violation or suffocation of their imagination, as well as through exclusion from the production process. Using their writing as a vehicle for the affirmation of humanity and life in general, such writers are dedicated to creating the visions of hope and limitless possibility to which human beings can and will reach out, if given the opportunity.

All three types of writers exist side by side in African neocolonial states. However, the ranks of the third category have yielded the most would-be victims of imprisonment and torture, even though in some of the most repressive regimes a writer does not have to engage in any serious revolutionary activity to be targeted for harassment. The simple act of speaking out and breaking the terror of silence imposed by such states is enough of a "crime." Indeed, most writers under neocolonial dictatorships find their creativity censored, stifled, and targeted for vicious attack by the system. Through the use of terror, the offending systems go all out to impose silence in yet another effort to close another channel for raising the consciousness of the people. This is particularly so when the artistic works reach the oppressed as their primary audience.

Thus a lot of writers have landed in detention, in prison (usually on trumped-up charges), or have been subjected to police harassment or army brutality—or all of these and more—for denouncing the gross abuse of rights and individual liberties that is characteristic of our neocolonial existence. Where writers have not actually been locked up, they have been kept under the kind of censorship and surveillance that makes "freedom" under oppressive environments a farce. These writers have remained "inmates" in the larger prison of society, metaphorically living behind bars and inside the barbed wire of suffocating repressive institutions that seek to fetter their imagination and lock up their creativity.

In a situation like that of neocolonial Kenya, from which this writer departed to go into exile, the symbolism of this larger prison is real, painful, and torturous. Writers have either been detained without trial or served prison terms on planted evidence, and walked out into "freedom" (usually following a lot of local and international pressure) only to find themselves joining the armies of the unemployed for years—this, in spite of their badly needed professional skills which no African country can afford to waste. Beyond this, constant surveillance of the writers, their families, and friends by state security forces and their agents is such that, hyperbolically speaking, the aggressors know when their victims turn in bed at night or even go to the toilet in the assumed privacy of their own homes. Deliberate attempts are made to create a sense of fear all around, to permeate the air with suspicion, while enforcing abandonment and alienation from the communities in which the writers live, including circles of loved ones. Obviously, all these measures are aimed at breaking the victims and turning them into neurotic psychological wrecks who are so intimidated by their insecurity that they are pressured to surrender their consciences, agreeing to become parrots for the repressive regime.

It is to the credit of these writers that they have resisted such persecution, refused to be silenced, and continued not just to denounce injustice but to reaffirm, through activism, their commitment to the people's struggle for human dignity. However, in some cases the tyrannical practices outlined above have caused untold suffering to the targeted writers and their families. They have at times succeeded in destroying the lives of the individuals affected, breaking circles of friendship and even rupturing cemented family relationships. When immediate families are targeted the experience has been extremely painful. The violation of children's psyches is particularly frightening as the oppressive police-states try to criminalize the parent. I remember my elder daughter, then about three years of age, viciously attacking the security officers who had come to arrest me. She tried to bite them when they pushed me around, treating me like a criminal. That image still tears a mother's heart. Other children have, of course, witnessed much worse.

Given the foregoing, it becomes clear that for the writer under the siege of state terror, going into exile is not a voluntary choice. The term "self-imposed" exile is not only a contradiction in terms but a perversion of reality. Why impose exile on oneself? It is as illogical as suggesting that an innocent human being would opt for a prison sentence and then check into a jail, just for the fun of it. No normal human beings have ever been known to engage in this kind of crazy behavior. However, when conditions such as those described above are imposed on a writer, living at home translates into a more acute form of exile, and one has no option other than to leave. In the first place, remaining at home is a risk to one's life. Second, it is a sadistic version of self-supervised extended arrest. Third, it is psychological self-deportation, even as one is seen to be living among other free people.

On the question of self-exile, I experience some of the most agonizing moments in my own exile when I am subjected to sermons, usually from collaborators of neocolonial Kenya's repressive regime, blaming me for having left the country. Some of them would even go to the extreme of accusing me of imagined persecution, vouching that nothing would really have happened had I stayed. The very thought that a woman—who holds one of the highest jobs in the academic world, has a comfortable home, and is the mother (and custodial parent) of two young girls aged seven and five—would suddenly wake up, pack a few bags, abandon her home and job, and flee into exile is more than ludicrous; it is an act of insanity. Yet, of all the problems and ailments I might have suffered, insanity has never been one of them.

Another time, a woman who visited me in exile and who knew where and how I lived at home simply burst into tears when she walked into my flat. I could not tell whether it was the sight of the bare, faded, aged furnishings of my simple university flat that touched a soft part of her heart, but she just broke down on me. You see, official government propaganda spreads false tales of how those who go into exile do so in order to live in luxury in foreign countries. The propaganda even mischievously implies that the exiles are in the paid employ of "foreign masters," usually imaginary "communists." But let us return to what I have termed "psychological deportation" or "mental exile."

The targeted writer can be subjected to this whether at home or in exile. For instance, propaganda in government-controlled media disseminates thuggish-looking photographs of those under attack, enforcing images of criminalization and brutalization. Someone once sent me one such photograph from Kenya and it was truly dramatic: in it my mouth was wide open, as if I were either madly screaming at someone or getting ready to cannibalize a victim. In yet another, my eyes were sleepy and drooping as if I were high on drugs or as though I had hit the bottle rather hard. No wonder someone who had never met me before—who had only seen photographs of me in government-controlled media—stared at me open-mouthed upon being introduced to me. He was truly in shock and all he could ask was: "Are you really *the* Micere Mugo?" This man obviously expected to meet some creature with horns! This subtle criminalization is yet another form of dehumanization. It has a profoundly negative effect on a public who have access to little, if anything, outside government-controlled media. Indeed, some of the photographs of exiled colleagues are so scary that, if the individuals depicted were not known personally, a casual glimpse would have provoked the urge to turn around and run in the opposite direction! The terror of repressive media registers with sobering impact.

The argument, then, is that exile is not a normal choice; rather, it is a step in the victim's refusal to become a martyr or an adventurer in a situation where state terror is the rule of law. It is a dignified attempt to retain control of one's imagination as it is threatened with invasion and silencing: a determination not to have one's conscience buried under persecution and terror. It is a refusal to allow the human being in oneself to die under the treachery of negative silence. Above all, it is a calculated retreat from a bombarded war zone and surrounded battlefront, not a permanent withdrawal from, or abandonment of, a continuing struggle. Indeed, the progressive exiled writer uses displacement to create new networks of resistance away from home, joining with other internationalist struggles against injustice, oppression, and dehumanization.

However, every serious struggle has its costs and casualties. The progressive exiled writer lives through the experience of exile at a cost which is particularly heavy at the imaginative, psychological, and emotional levels. Let us illustrate this observation by tracing the bumpy path of the exile from the moment of exit onward, with special emphasis on the crisis immediately following going out into the unknown.

The most harrowing feeling to come with exile is extreme anger. All kinds of provocative and torturous questions plague the mind: what right does anyone have to force me to leave the home that I love as my birthright, to go into exile? Why should my tormentors remain behind, continuing their plunder? For how long will the oppressors relentlessly inflict suffering on the people? How long will it be before the people are victorious? Will those who fight this injustice have the last laugh? When shall I ever see home again? So many unending questions shoot through the mind. One is truly hit by the injustice and the irony of the fact that those who fight for the dignity of their people and countries should have to leave while the plunderers remain behind.

Anger and frustration are followed by a sense of loss, the agony of being torn away from home and all that it symbolizes: the space in life where one's roots sink deep; the earth that has nurtured one's growth physically, spiritually, culturally, and imaginatively; an environment with which one has habitually and intimately interacted. One suddenly and deeply misses all the familiar natural scenery that had been taken for granted since childhood. The rhythms of speech and conversation to which one had been attuned since childhood painfully echo through the mind. Forced breakage from the intimate human contact of the family, extended family, friends, and fellow citizens "out there," whom one may never have personally met but whose presence one has always vicariously and communally experienced, takes away from one's humanity; rupture from the many struggles that one has always willingly embraced, well knowing the cost—all these become a tearing away from self. Obliteration of the perimeters that define and embrace one's creativity takes a great toll on one's creative energies, accelerating the process of destabilization. Thus stripped of the form and content of the creative essence, the writer has a new form of oppression to deal with: the struggle to release the imagination and to continue to create in a barren environment. Some succeed in doing so, others do not.

The other nerve-racking experience accompanying the immediate trauma of entering exile is a knifing, screaming conscience. Haunting memories of the people and colleagues whom one has left behind in the thick of battle recur with a vengeance. Unending questions engender doubts about the decision to go into exile. The question marks persistently tease—no, taunt—the mind day and night. Should I have really left? Was it not selfish to flee to safety, leaving comrades behind to struggle on without me? Will those who do not know me think that I have abandoned the struggle to go abroad and live in safety? How can I assure them that I am still traveling the same road with them and will never be derailed? What is happening to those I left behind under arrest, in detention, in jail? Do they trust that I am fighting for their freedom? The questions are truly unending. The creative imagination is drained as the mind takes such a beating. It becomes a struggle to simply remain sane and keep clear of chronic depression.

At this juncture, I cannot help punctuating these generalized observations with illustrative personal anecdotes from 1982, when I landed in the United States of America to embark on my exile, accompanied by my daughters, Mumbi and Njeri, then aged seven years and eight months and six years respectively. The first few months were simply torturous. I suffered from acute insomnia, terrorized by recurring nightmares in which I "saw" former colleagues and comrades (a number of whom I had left in detention) being subjected to the most dehumanizing punishment and torture by the police. I would literally go through my sleeping hours wrestling with unbroken nightmares in which the most horrific things would be taking place. Often I would wake up sweating profusely or screaming in terror.

One of my recurring nightmares was about being raped by a sadistic criminal who held my mouth shut so that when I tried to scream, no sound would come out. The nightmare was, of course, rooted in a reality I had encountered when I was arrested and held by the police for interrogation in 1977. Hysterically laughing and saying what fun it would be to "do it to a doctor," a raving criminal, detained for interrogation on charges of robbery with violence, had grabbed me in the dark room where I and others were being held along with him. When my captors first threw me into the room, one of them had sneeringly told me that he was putting me where people end up once they "play" with the government, even when they happen to be "doctors." This mischievous, casual comment was, of course, meant to do just what it had succeeded in doing: inciting a person like the robber and setting him against me. The experience was traumatizing. I was saved from my would-be abuser by an elderly man, also locked up, who appealed to the criminal's sense of shame and who stood between my assailant and me, sheltering me. I will never forget this humane act of love on the part of that dignified old man who did not even know me.

It is said that deep psychological scars never quite disappear. My experience in Kenya's police interrogation "chambers" (irony of ironies!) had clearly plowed so deep into my psyche that the scarring was still raw years afterwards. The nightmare drama would not go. Soaking with sweat, I would find myself sleepwalking and screaming as I tried to escape from the "interrogation chambers"—my bedroom. I frightened my daughters out of their wits as I screamed and fought with my assailants; I would call out the names of incarcerated comrades as I struggled to free myself: Alamin Mazrui, Maina wa Kenyatti, Kamoji Wachira, Edward Oyugi, Koigi wa Wamwere, Raila Oginga, Titus Andungosi, and others. I remember how panic-stricken I would become as it grew dark, as nightfall became inevitable. I would do everything possible to procrastinate and defer the act of getting ready for bed, giving in only when I could no longer stop my eyes from closing with sleep. I was terrified of going into my bedroom. Eventually, I suffered an attack of acute gastritis which threatened to give way to ulcers. It took me two years to slowly recover from the ailment, but it will take me forever to forget those sadistic, terrorizing nightmares and the burning, draining pain of the acute gastritis. The agony evacuated every ounce of energy in my system. I could virtually feel the drainage happening.

In connection with the attempted-rape nightmare, an important point needs to be made. It is my position that the story of the woman who has survived police harassment, whether as a captive or as the partner who remains behind when the spouse is arrested, still remains to be told. The stories of Winnie Mandela (1985), Caesarina Kona Makhoere (1988), Ellen Kuzwayo (1980), Angela Davis (1988), Assata Shakur (1987), and others have not really received sufficient articulation in settings where state oppression reigns. This is certainly the case for female survivors of police harassment in Kenya. The intimidation, insecurity, and general state of terror forced on the woman (who normally remains behind to hold the home together) are unimaginable. In a sense it is true that she is the true heroine of the drama of police brutality. The cumulative weight of the burdens she carries—supporting her partner, organizing legal representation, keeping the home together, confronting the agents of terror, taking care of herself, and so on—is unimaginable as it cuts across every angle of her precarious existence.

As a direct captive, she is subjected to both the brutality leveled at her male counterpart and to sexist abuse. My own captors seemed to be more angry with me for being a *female* political activist than for anything else. In fact, when I complained about being locked up with men, a vicious officer told me that I had no right to complain since I had chosen to "play with politics" *like a man.* During interrogation I was asked repeatedly whether I was not ashamed of my disgraceful conduct as a woman: women—particularly mothers—should behave with greater self-respect and not go around "politicking," I was told. One of my interrogators actually wondered whether I really was a "proper" woman and threatened to have me stripped so that he could check me out. He felt sorry for the "poor" children who called me "mother" and pronounced me a curse: not anyone's mother. His deepest commiserations were reserved for my husband who, according to my tormentor, must have suffered untold embarrassment from having me as a wife. Sexist insults are used as tools of torture against female victims of state repression, as is the violation of aspects of their biological uniqueness such as menstruation, motherhood, sexuality, and so on. These violations must have touched a very raw nerve in me because the interrogation scenes in which my femaleness was belittled played themselves out over and over again in my nightmares, evoking the original humiliation with unbearable pain.

The other narrative that exile literature has yet to tell is the story of the children who are forced into exile because they are their parents' children. The suffering that my daughters endured, especially during the initial period of our exile, is heartrending. The negative consequences of traumatic experiences for children are especially harsh, particularly when these threaten their sense of security and their dreams for the future. For my children, the sight of their mother crumbling under the weight of psychological terror must have been truly frightening. Traumatic experiences of this nature can end up causing serious health problems, including eating and weight disorders, insecurity, loss of hair, confused identity, and so on. I feared terribly for my daughters. Indeed, under these circumstances enormous guilt can overcome a parent who is finding it hard not to take the blame for what is happening to the children. It takes a lot of dialogue to help the young ones understand that humiliating and painful conditions must be endured without surrendering one's dignity and conscience.

Thus, already facing the formidable task of building a new home in a strange environment, the exiled parent also has the impossible duty of ensuring that the children accept this temporary(?) home, which they hate or resent because they are not there by choice. When this new home happens to be in the context of Western capitalism, which is crippled by racism and the denigration of human dignity that accompanies it, the task becomes another source of stress and pain. The tensions and their subtexts make the compounded text under composition nervous reading. Hearing young children in moments of desperation pleading or demanding, "Mummy/Daddy, I want to go home!" can be devastating. Here, another personal anecdote is in place.

I will never forget one late afternoon, during the third or so month in exile, when I returned home from a long day of lecturing only to find that my second daughter, then about six years old, had called a taxi to our residence. The taxi was just pulling into our driveway as I was approaching the compound. The driver explained that someone who sounded "kind of young" had ordered a taxi to the residence. On entering the apartment and while trying to sort out the mystery, I saw the young would-be traveler break into sobbing. Apparently she had wanted to be taken to the Greyhound Bus depot, where she would catch a bus to Syracuse (a three-hour journey from Canton, upstate New York, our home in exile at the time) and then board a plane back to Kenya. She had taken more than her fill of racist taunting and bullying from some of her schoolmates. She wanted to go home. When I explained to the young would-be traveler that she needed money, a ticket, and a passport to undertake such a journey, she sobered a little and proceeded to demand a "family meeting!" In exile, family meetings had become a tradition for me and my daughters: they were a means of sharing and reflecting upon our experiences in search of collective solutions; they formed the foundation of what has become a friendship between us, resting on democratic discourse, dialogue, and exchange and ensuring our individual and collective growth.

The scene was frightening and unbearably painful, especially amid the many negative silences permeating the very air one breathes in Western cultures. At such moments one realizes the indispensability of the warmth of the extended family. As intimated earlier, young children are very negatively affected by the sudden crumbling of a parent they have always known to be strong and in control. Their insecurity manifests itself in very frightening ways. For instance, one of my daughters went completely bald. Over several months, she, her sister, and I traveled to five American states seeking medical help, but nothing that was prescribed seemed to work. We ended up at Howard Medical School, where one doctor finally linked my daughter's hair loss to internalized stress. What I will always remember is how he took time to talk to the children and me, insisting on reliving our exile experiences with us. This elderly African American medical specialist stood there talking to us, in no apparent hurry, as if we were members of his family, explaining how a lot of children in the Black community were beginning to lose hair from stress. That was a turning point in what I knew was going to be a long journey in exile. I decided I would move back to the African continent and look for a home somewhere. Reconstructing an extended family would be a lot easier there.

Thus, the heart and conscience of the exiled writer who is also a parent remain under constant trial. When family pressures arise, the pain is devastating. By what right does the writer, even as a parent or guardian, impose a personal political decision on young children? One watches in anguish as the supremacy of the mother tongue(s), formerly spoken by the children with fluency and ease, gradually erodes; one struggles to enforce their usage at home, but the responses come back in the language utilized throughout the day in school and in the playing yard. Before one knows it, the foreign tongue has assumed dominance. Indeed and ironically, this becomes the language that the young exiles use more readily to express their innermost hopes and fears. At this point one clings to another more important thing: the nurturing of the young ones with the kind of ideological consciousness that will, in the final analysis, determine whether the language one speaks is truly human or merely a preoccupation with words. You see, even fascists have been known to be experts in their mother tongues, but this has not made them human.

The exiled parent whose children have lost expertise in their mother tongue(s) then faces many painful and insensitive questions, like "How could you let this happen?" The question is asked with much self-righteousness—sometimes by the very same people who should know that, while jetting from one destination to the next to lobby for their freedom from incarceration, there was no time for (the now-exiled parent) to perfect the children's imperfectly spoken mother tongues; unfortunately, the babysitters used while (the exiled parent was) attempting to internationalize the struggle were not African linguists. In this regard, my daughters and I will never forget the team of African women at St. Lawrence University in Canton—Njeri Marekia, Njanja wa Rwenji, Jeannine Anderson, Mumbi Kiereini, Julie Odaka, Samia Awori, and many others—who not only became our extended family in exile but also babysitters and language teachers during my many absences from home on campaigns to release political prisoners. My daughters' functional Gikuyu and Kiswahili are to be partly credited to the efforts of these beautiful young ladies.

Also frustrating for the exiled writer is the problem of communicating with a foreign audience. At home, dialogue with one's audience begins from a putative common point of understanding or departure, and where this is not the case, the two sides recognize their differences right from the start. In other words, one knows one's audience. In the new surroundings, the exiled writer has to open with prologues, introductions, preambles, forewords—formats that rob the debate of steam even before it gets going. Where this is not the case, the "script" is burdened with asides, stage directions, footnotes, and endnotes that interrupt the flow of the argument to such an extent that they become hiccups, irritatingly jerking the flow of the narrative voice. Needless to say, this checked exchange sabotages the screaming urgency of themes which are matters of life and death on the home scene, but mean little if anything at all to the audience in the land of exile. One feels too tired to begin to explain the teasing urgency that presses so heavy on one's own heart. In this sense, the exile experience reveals to a writer that the home audience is a very vital component of creative production; with this audience, the writer simply plunges into the debate. In exile, the writer's situation is that of one obliged to make conversation with a stranger. The process of communication can register many awkward pauses on both sides. At times the task becomes even more awkward when one has to introduce not only oneself but also what one has written. What do you say when a host asks what you would like to have said about you?

This search for an accountable audience is accompanied by a more critical task, one I've already touched upon: the search for a welcoming and embracing new home. The task of building a new home in a strange and sometimes estranging, if not hostile, environment can be formidable. In the country of refuge, the exiled writer can be relegated to the unflattering status of an irrelevant detail: being there without being of much significance. To go from being the nerve center or the throbbing artery at the heart of the self-expression of one's indigenous community, from being an initiator and executor of vital processes in the struggle for self-definition, to being a mere observer in the new situation can be a very trying experience. Here, again, another personal anecdote is called for: the story of how my mother admonished me to learn to build new homes and new circles of audiences.

My father died during my first year in exile. Apart from having lost both of my in-laws a few years earlier, this was the first time that I had to deal with a death in my immediate family. The news affected me more adversely than I could have imagined. There were so many pauses and unfinished conversations between my late father and me: political, historical, domestic, familial, and personal. The year I left Kenya, he had broached the subject of dictating "his book" to me to write. At long last the ice between us was going to crack. Then—exile. Death. The shocking news. There I was, with my two young children: the three of us commiserating with one another, or rather, they comforting me, for they never really knew their grandfather. They always referred to him as "cucu's husband" (grandmother's husband). We couldn't seriously "recall" him together or collectively relive any moments of his life; consequently, being cut off from home was heavy. I could not go to Kenya for the burial. Miles away, I constructed my own funeral in the cold of the American north country. In my aloneness, I truly missed other members of the family, colleagues, and friends who normally provided a sure and solid network of solidarity in this kind of situation. I went into a depression.

As usual, especially during this type of crisis, my mother came up with words of profound wisdom. She said something to this effect: "Those who have chosen the path you have taken cannot afford to cry for home. Instead, they should learn to build new homes wherever they may be, whether this be in the trees, in the deserts, or on water." She pointed out that a number of my colleagues who were "home" were wasting away in prison and detention. Others were "on the road" without jobs, without security. A lot of people in the country were going to bed hungry. "You, of all people, cannot afford to cry for home," she firmly concluded. The story of this dialogue has since been captured in a poem I've entitled "My Mother's Poem."

Without a doubt, many exiled African writers will largely agree with these words of advice, but they will also hasten to point out that building these new homes is not an easy task. It can be quite a precarious experience. Illustration: after my initial two years in exile, which I spent at St. Lawrence University (thanks to an institution that gave me a warm home at no notice) intensively engaged in internationalizing the Kenyan struggle for democracy, I packed my bags to return to Africa. Among the several offers that I had received from universities on the mother continent, I accepted a post as professor of English and literature as well as departmental chairperson at the University of Zambia in Lusaka. On my way to Zambia, I stopped over in London where a production of *The Trial of Dedan Kimathi* (Ngugi wa Thiong'o and Micere Githae Mugo, 1976) was in process. Just as I was getting ready to leave for Lusaka, I was informed that I was an unwanted person in Zambia: a protest from Kenya at state level had resulted in the cancellation of my work permit. I was stranded in London, jobless and homeless, with two children. My family sent for the children at great cost and risk. Unforgettable friends by the names of Pat Haward and Irene Staunton made sure that I did not end up in the streets. Fortunately, the long nightmare ended with an offer for a home in Zimbabwe from President Mugabe and his late wife, Amai Sally Mugabe. It was a great honor. I had been a part of the Zimbabwean independence struggle from my graduate student days in Canada during the late sixties and early seventies, right up to the end of the liberation war and victory for the people of Zimbabwe. However, at no time had I imagined that the land of Munhumutapa and Mbuya Nehanda would end up being my future second home.

It has been argued that unless adopted at birth, the child who comes to a new home never quite assumes the status of a son or daughter in the adopting family. There is a lot of truth in this statement. For the exiled writer, the adopting or adopted home often remains borrowed space. One remains a polite guest, an understood outsider who listens rather than spearheads debate; one who sits at the periphery rather than at the center; a provider of solidarity rather than a bona fide citizen who acts decisively to help change things. When serious internal rifts surface and one assumes sides, there are rude reminders that "foreigners" should keep out of domestic affairs. Such an ambiguous position of imposed and even self-imposed semivisibility can become another act of unintended censorship: a state of limitedness that can cause frustration and lead to unproductivity. The challenges that go with accountability, participation, and decisive, creative involvement or action, within or outside the struggle, are altogether missing. The twilight position becomes a handicap, not a stimulant to creativity.

However, there are many ways in which the exiled writer makes it a vocation to build my mother's advocated new home. For instance, setting up solidarity groups to address the abuse of human rights on the homefront brings one face-to-face with similar problems in the adopted home. In upstate New York I became actively involved in voluntary work at a huge maximum-security prison where I met the most intelligent men of African origin, mostly African Americans, that I have ever associated with. The incarceration of the young was especially painful. The viciousness and racism of some of the prison warders were frightening. The line between "econo-political" prisoners—the victims of American capitalism—and genuine outlaws became extremely thin after one got to know these men.

The experience at Ogdensburg maximum-security "facility" (oh, the ironies of language!) was an education in how, under capitalism, the denial of basic human rights (through economic deprivation and oppression) has condemned some of the most promising members of the working class by criminalizing them for being poor. This networking not only helped me to extend my definition of political prisoners but also led me to seriously interrogate the meaning of democracy. More than this, the work opened up a lot of genuine conversations between myself and the community around me. Free conversation with metaphorically and psychologically exiled people, even as they occupy physical space in their own home countries, definitely helps to construct a new home space for the writer in exile; and the realization that there are struggles wherever human beings are, even though these may assume different accents, is liberating. One learns that the linkage of struggles globally is the secret to meaningful victory. This understanding inspired me to activate my mother's advice, and it has proved to be so empowering that the construction of new temporary homes has become more of a reality.

In the foregoing discourse I have attempted to demonstrate how the exile experience can negatively affect the process of creativity. However, the handicaps that lead to writer's block for some artists do not register with equal impact upon other writers. Indeed, some writers have been extremely productive and prolific during exile, just as certain individuals are known to perform best under pressure. Such people find ways to shatter the barriers that stand in their way and continue to create. They cultivate techniques of wooing a cold and hostile environment, teasing the barren terrain until it yields poems, stories, songs, novels, autobiographies, and other creative fruits of all kinds. In their imaginative obstinacy, such writers even learn to fertilize toilet paper, giving birth to prison literature that defies the suffocating space of a jail cell, exploding the loneliness of solitary confinement and breaking through the gray walls of houses of incarceration to reach the outside world. This breed of writers has my highest admiration. As for me, it took the security of my second home in Mbuya Nehanda's ancestral home to take up creative writing again. In the meantime, travel along other roads that demanded just as much creativity left me wiser and more resilient for the trials of exile. The journeys also confirmed my belief that were I to be taken back in history and offered a chance to travel a different route—meaning the anti-people road—so as to escape being exiled, I would respond with a resounding NO. The struggle for human rights and dignity is a human vocation that I will live and die for, whatever the cost. And it *is* as deeply costly as it is precious.

If all this sounds like an apologia, try being a woman, a mother, a single parent and head of household, a professional worker, an academician, a researcher, a political activist, and writer—all in exile! Just try.

Poems for Liberation of the Land

Micere Githae Mugo

MY MOTHER'S POEM

For my beloved mother and in celebration
of progressive African Orature, with all
its sustaining wisdom and aesthetic appeal.

The day after
                    my father
                    was buried
tormenting images
                              of uncaptured time
                              between him and me
piled up
            on my breaking neck
breathing
            heaviness and sorrow
dragging
            my cracking memory
across gaps
                    of lost moments
                    of escaped contact.

The day after
                    my father
                    was buried
my space
            in life
was saturated
            with mourning
Unspoken
            torturous thoughts

jettisoned pain
        across
        the warring zone
        of antagonistic
        lost contact.

The day after
        my father
        was buried
the distance
        between home
        and exile
suddenly doubled
and through windows
                of helplessness
I hurled out
        courage
turning it
        into a heap
        of despair.

The day after
        my father
        was buried
I drowned
        the telephone line
        with rivers of tears
I soaked
        my mother's ears
        with my weeping
I choked
        with lumps
        of words
        trapped in my throat
        as I reached out
                for dialogue
                and home.

The day after
                my father
                was buried
My heart could
                no longer
                find a home
                in exile
So it reached out
                through the telephone line
                across the Atlantic
                to try and touch
my mother

Then came
                the healing words
words embalmed
        with motherly love
words weighted
        with orature wisdom
words spoken
        the day after
        my father
        was buried.

Daughter, do not
romanticize home
Do not, daughter
for many who are home
                have jail
                for home
Thousands who are home
                have streets
                for home
Millions who are home
                are crying
                for home

The whole land
                is crying

                              for home
The whole land
                    is crying:
                    "The waters are bitter
                    what shall we drink?"

Daughter, do not
romanticize home
Do not, daughter
You who have
                    chosen the path
                    of people's struggles
                    must find the courage
                    to build new homes
                    to start new lives
wherever
                    you are
be it
          in the air
be it
          on the seas
be it
          in the trees
be it
          in the desert.

Create new life
Create human beings
                    out of these
And build
new homes
On whatever
                    patch of ground
                    your feet tread
walk well
step solidly
                    leaving behind you
                    firm footprints
walk well

along the path
　　　　　　　you have chosen
　　　　　　　to take.

The sun shone through
　　　　　　　the telephone line
its warmth
and brightness
　　　　　　　lifted the mist
　　　　　　　that bogged down
　　　　　　　my vision.

The sun shone through
　　　　　　　the telephone line

wiping my tears
warming my heart.

The sun shone through
　　　　　　　the telephone line
releasing
　　　　a flood
　　　　of unchecked
　　　　powerfulness
that lifted me
above the cliff
　　　　　　　on which I stood
　　　　　　　overlooking a sea
　　　　　　　of drowning despair.

The sun shone through
　　　　　　　the telephone line
　　　　　　　as I looked beyond
the day after
my father
was buried.

A QUESTION TO OPPOSITION LEADERS

Refrain: How could you?

How could you
            crumble an agenda so long
                an agenda
                so painfully drawn
                an agenda
                written with the people's
                sweat, blood and tears?
How could you?

How could you
            shrivel an agenda so alive
                an agenda
                so collectively assembled
                shrinking it into a single
                egoistic, trashable item:
                state-house occupancy?
How could you?

How could you
                license hunting finger cutters
                to chop people's votes
                while you musical chaired
                your state-house ambitions
                sitting on the laps of our struggles
                sinking the platform of our demands?
How could you?

How could you
                abort our democratic manifesto
                miscarrying an entrusted mandate
                while camel-loaded with oppression
                the masses roast like ants
                on the burning charcoals
                of hunger, poverty and dispossession?
How could you?

How could you?
How *could* you?
How could you?
How?

We planted you firmly
          on the people's
          raised platform
We cemented the base
          with our unbreakable
          collective will
We invited you
          to come and launch
          the jump forward
          into the future
          of our collective
          realization
But you missed
the springboard
          flinging yourselves
          and all of us
          onto the concrete
          of verbal civil war
          and bruising duels
You missed
the obvious target
          dragging back
          onto our breaking backs
          the crushing boulder
          of ruthless repression
          even as we dislodged it.
How could you?
How could you?
How *could* you?
How could *you?*
How?

In the collective name
          of our struggling millions,

mightier than your ego,
reroute your derailed
democracy-bound train.
Passengers are still aboard
ready for the protracted journey
preparing to assume the driver's seat
on the lifelong pilgrimage
along the path of self-determination.

In the collective name
of our struggling millions:

Will you?

WE WILL RISE AND BUILD A NATION

In defiance of neocolonial dictators,
reminding them that even the darkest
of nights breaks into daylight and
that their days are truly numbered!

At independence
      we garlanded our leaders
      with embracing hearts
          hearts
              whose unbending
              veins.
              had survived
              the burning heat
              of colonialism
              and the blazing hell
              of dehumanization.

At independence
      we celebrated our leaders
      with earnest minds

minds
whose flaming
imagination
had withstood
scalding years
of psychological
warfare
emerging whole
but with telling scars.

At independence
we embraced our leaders
with trusting hearts
hearts
they soon shredded
flinging the tatters
to the winds of
betrayal
auctioneering our faith
in the cutthroat
markets
of transnational
business.

At independence
we craftily wove together
the frayed hanging threads
of our fringe existence
making a monumental cloth
out of which we designed
our national liberation flag.

At independence
colonial collaborators snatched
our national liberation flag
highjacking our independence
with cunning serpentine imposture
twisting it into a rope

with which they strangulated our hopes
leaving us under neocolonial barrenness.

Under neocolonialism
           antinationalists have mutilated
           our national identity
           massacred our national symbols
           and buried them
           under the primitive arithmetic
           of ethnic subtraction and division.

Under neocolonialism
           our bodies are consumed
           with keeping perpetual wakes
           through nights of econo-political
           funerals
           Our nerves are wrenched
           by persisting rending screams
           from abused human rights victims.

Under neocolonialism
           our dignity is scattered like chaff
           across the nothingness of peripheral
           survival
           our minds are terrorized with living
           horrors
           even as *Mworoto, Wagalla* and *Burnt
           forest*
           shoot poisoned ethnic cleansing
           arrows
           through the shields of justice and
           liberty.

But we refuse
        to leave our anger
        scattered
        on the wasteland
        of our enemy's plunder

We swirl
>   with the sweeping fury
>   of a dust storm

We exhume
>   the graveyards
>   of our collective
>   conscience
>   leveling the tombs
>   of our destroyed nationhood
>   our assaulted peoplehood

We swirl
>   with the sweeping fury
>   of a dust storm
>   turning the graves
>   inside out
>   molding from the remains

new women
new men
new youth.

Tomorrow
We will rise
>   with the sweeping fury
>   of a dust storm
creating a new nation
ready to extinguish
the hellfire
of dictatorship.

We will blast
>   the iron bars
>   behind which
>   our children lie captive
We will convert
>   Kamiti Prison
>   into a people's park

                    into our children's
                    playing field
We will fly home
                    exiled matriots
                    banished patriots
                    landing them home
                    on a newly built
                    Me Katilili Airport
We will plow
                    the barren fields
                    of our ravished
                    national economy
                    producing a surplus
                    of our full growth
                    and human potential

We will rise
                    and build a nation
                    molding from the pieces
                    of an oppressive history
                    an unassailable monument
                    grafted with justice for all
                    enshrined with limitless hope.

The Locus and Logos of Exile

Aliko Songolo

I

The central theme of the twentieth annual conference of the African Literature Association (in Accra, Ghana, March 24–31, 1994) was "Beyond Survival: African Literature and the Search for New Life." Implicitly, this theme raised some of the issues with which this workshop is concerned: strategies of resistance and survival for the artist as an artist under conditions of constraint or displacement. The panel on which I participated at that conference was entitled "Scorched Earth: Literature, Ecology, and Dictatorship." Its intent was to discuss the ecology of African literatures, that is to say, the environment in which those literatures live, thrive, survive, or die; how they represent that environment; how they relate to and interact with other institutions within it. The panel was to focus on the so-called postcolonial period, or more specifically, on the post–Cold War years, particularly in those countries with regimes that have perfected scorched-earth policies in the face of internal and external pressures for change: not only such notorious places as arap Moi's Kenya, apartheid South Africa, the Generals' Nigeria, Eyadema's Togo, or Mobutu's Zaire, but also less noticed yet equally oppressive regimes such as Biya's Cameroon, the late Houphouët-Boigny's Côte d'Ivoire, or Bongo's Gabon.

Some of the questions raised by both the theme of the conference and the panel make it possible for me to link the issue of survival to that of exile in African literature and art. The writer or artist may be said to "survive" either by prudently refraining from speaking the unspeakable or by suffering a more or less forced eviction from home. In either case, it seems that the act of survival and that of speech become equally compromised, although in different ways. The question that may still be posed in the latter case is whether it matters if such eviction keeps the victim within national/cultural boundaries and, going one step further, whether it matters if the eviction is coupled with physical incarceration.

These considerations suggest that exile is not always located where we might think, and that the condition of exile is not as simple as it might first appear. This is why I propose to discuss several central issues pertaining to the question of exile: 1) What is the *locus* of exile, that is to say, what spaces and conditions can be identified as spaces and conditions of exile? 2) What is the *logos* of exile, that is to say, to what extent does a discourse produced in such a space and under such conditions bear a distinctive mark or identity? 3) How does the experience of exile shape the expressive and discursive formations of the artist? 4) What is the relationship between the artist and the internal and external forces that dictate the discourses produced in exile? In the context of these questions, I propose to examine literature and art from Zaire in general, the novel *L'écart* by V. Y. Mudimbe in particular, and an art exhibition held at the University of Wisconsin—Madison's Elvehjem Museum of Art (October 1992–January 1993) under the theme "African Reflections: Art from Northeastern Zaire."

II

While the notion of exile can be, and indeed has been, theorized almost beyond recognition of the reality it represents, it is important to examine some of its current definitions and ramifications. Edward Said, one of the most insightful critics of Western culture and a celebrated exile within it, has characterized exile as "the unhealable rift forced between a human being and a native place, between the self and its true home."[1] This seemingly straightforward definition of exile needs elaboration in order to make more explicit the complications that this concept entails as an ontological experience. Said's formulation suggests that once the rupture has occurred, there can be no repairing it; any attempt to do so can only be futile and illusory, and even if such an attempt were to succeed in terms of a physical return home, the "home" would already be something other than what the exile left behind, and at the same time, the exile would also be other than the person who left. In other words, "You can't go home again."

However, even if the exile can't go home again, the break with home is hardly ever a totally clean one: what has been left behind continues to haunt the consciousness of the exile. As Said explains in a more recent essay:

> For most exiles, the difficulty consists not simply in being forced to live away from home, but rather, given today's world, in living with the many reminders . . . that your home in fact is not so far away. . . . The exile therefore exists in a median state, neither completely at one with the new setting nor fully disencumbered of the old, beset with half-involvements and half-detachments, nostalgic and sentimental on one level, an adept mimic or a secret outcast on another.[2]

This explains why the exile expends much energy, time, and other resources attempting to heal the rift, as it were, and this project may manifest itself in various ways, including nationalistic political activity, and intellectual, scientific, or artistic productivity, all aimed at recreating at least the psychological comforts of home. Thus, exile is often the force that drives its victims to great creative impulses. Said observes, for instance, that "the canon of modern Western culture is in large part the work of exiles, émigrés, and refugees."[3] He cites the names of Samuel Beckett, Vladimir Nabokov, Ezra Pound, and, in other fields of achievement, Herbert Marcuse and Albert Einstein, among others.

There is, then, an essential tension at the core of the experience of exile: on the one hand, this unalterable displacement from home and hearth, and on the other, this permanently unfulfilled yearning to recapture the customs, the language, the culture—in short, a yearning to reconstruct some form of a lost wholeness. There is also an essential ambiguity. If the physical aspect of exile is clear enough, its metaphysical counterpart, though somewhat muted in Said's formulation, is equally important, for the rift occurs also between "the self and its true home." The true home of the self may or may not be synonymous with the geographical space; it may represent an entirely inner space. Exile, then, is also—perhaps above all—a state of mind, and as such it is a condition that has at least as much to do with personal identity as with nationality, ethnicity, or the physical boundaries of "home."

There is need to make a distinction between different types of exile. In a cogent critique of the work of Edward Said on this question, Abdul JanMohamed generalizes and in a sense naturalizes the concept of exile by naming it "border-crossing." He identifies four different modes of such "border-crossings" within which he couches the experience of being away from home: "the exile, the immigrant, the colonialist, and the scholar, the last typified by the anthropologist studying other cultures (one might add the tourist and the traveler as subcategories of the scholar/anthropologist)." [4] JanMohamed argues that between the exile and the immigrant, the difference lies in their respective stances toward their new social environment: while the latter is generally positive about his or her new situation, the former generally evinces a critical attitude. Like the immigrant, the colonialist is in the new environment more or less voluntarily, but he or she makes the new culture an object of military, economic, and administrative mastery. If there is any resistance here, it is against the dangers of "going native," which motivates the negative stance of the colonialist toward the new environment. Finally, while the anthropologist's stance is positive, the home culture exerts discursive control, and the knowledge that may be garnered from this experience benefits the home culture most.

In their book on Franz Kafka and the concept of minority literature, Gilles Deleuze and Félix Guattari use the term "deterritorialization" to describe the displacement not only of persons but also of identities and of discourses and their meanings.[5] As Caren Kaplan explains, deterritorialization "describes the effects of radical distanciation between signifier and signified. Meaning and utterances become estranged." [6] Examples of this kind of estrangement include Deleuze and Guattari's definition of a minority literature, that is, a literature that is written by a minority person or group in the language of the majority and, more significantly, the revolutionary conditions created by such a literature inside the literature of the mainstream. A second instance is that of artifacts or works of art collected by the anthropologist/scholar which may have a particular set of meanings in the culture in which they were produced, but which take on other meanings in the culture where they are exhibited, or for that matter, from one point in time to another within the same culture, particularly if other disruptions have occurred in the intervening period. Yet another kind of estrangement is that of the artist who, almost by definition, occupies the peculiar position of being the voice of conscience for the society. As such, he or she may do more than merely depict social life; instead, his or her work may become a caricature of the society and its institutions, designed to prod it back to whatever values sustained it. However, this role seldom endears the artist to the mainstream of society. The artist is perceived as eccentric (in the literal sense of being off-center), becomes marginalized, and therefore enters a state of exile. Even while physically within the boundaries of the society, in a very real sense he or she is already on the outside looking in.

A full elaboration or critique of these various views of the concept of exile will not be possible here. One thing that can be said, however, is that some of these definitions may mask the scourge that exile represents by appearing to romanticize the fate of those few—the intellectuals, the artists, the well-to-do—who are capable of crossing borders and finding at least material well-being, if nothing else, or even occupying positions of preeminence on the other side of the border; those, in short, who lead a life of privilege despite, and sometimes because of, their displacement. On the other hand, we have the voiceless refugees, or as Said puts it, "the uncountable masses for whom UN agencies have been created . . . with only ration cards and agency numbers."[7] Within the last few years, the world has seen tremendous increases in numbers of such uncountable masses as a result of civil wars, wars of liberation, totalitarian rule, the Cold War and its aftermath, and so on. For several decades now, the continent of Africa has been leading the world in this regard, and in any given number of African countries, displacement bears myriad faces. About a decade ago, the number of African refugees within the continent exceeded five million, but that was before Rwanda, Burundi, Liberia, Somalia, the Angola and Sudan of recent months, and the latest forms of "ethnic cleansing" in some regions of today's Zaire. When we speak of the African diaspora, we might as well start referring to the continent itself instead of limiting that term to the New World.

Such mass exiles, including what we euphemistically call "the diaspora," are the subject of part of Edouard Glissant's monumental book, *Caribbean Discourse.*[8] Transplantation (*transbord: transship*) of masses of peoples (call it diaspora, slavery, or refugee status) disrupts nationalities, ethnicities, identities, cultures, and then reassembles them helter-skelter at the other end of the journey as so many artifacts, deprived of their original meanings and struggling to create new ones. It is the struggle involved in creating and re-creating identities, cultures, and polities that Glissant calls *"Retour"* and *"Détour"* or, in J. Michael Dash's translation, "Reversion" and "Diversion." Reversion is the obsession of a transplanted population with a unitary origin, and a single-minded, nostalgic quest for an original wholeness.

In Glissant's view, however, there is a difference between a population that is displaced through exile or dispersion but continues to survive elsewhere as a people (as in the case of the Jewish people), and a population that has been transplanted through the slave trade and changes wholesale to something other than the original. While both populations will undoubtedly be obsessed by a single-minded, nostalgic quest for unitary origin and original wholeness, the task for the descendants of slaves is made all the more arduous by the systematic erasure of all collective memory. By its very nature, slavery forces the population to desecrate and to view with derision the rituals and myths of origin (e.g., "Africa is savage"); domination by the Other (the Master, the Colonizer, etc.) favors such desecration and derision and replaces the myths and rituals of origin with the illusion of assimilation into the dominant culture. In this way, the structures of domination short-circuit all attempts at resistance, and the transplanted population is irrevocably cut off from its original culture and is simultaneously deprived of the necessary tools with which to conquer the new land. Nonetheless, some values, skills, and techniques that are necessary for survival endure in the form of traces, scattered across the culture, that can be organized in the manner of Lévi-Strauss's *bricolage* into significant forms of resistance, notably through artistic and literary creativity.

III

For their part, colonial conquest and occupation created many similar as well as different kinds of exiles *within* African societies. For instance, those chosen few who were called *assimilés* or *évolués* in the French and Belgian systems (with special identity cards to prove it) were set apart from other members of the society to serve as junior civil servants or, eventually, political *interlocuteurs valables*. They adopted Western mores, culture, and language. However, since this did not suffice to integrate them into French or Belgian society, they found themselves on the margins of both European and African cultures. The film *Lumumba: la mort du Prophète,* directed by Raoul Peck, tells of a different kind of exile that was inflicted on other selected Congolese. Since the Belgians did not allow the Congolese to leave the country until the late 1950s, the few who were "chosen" to serve as human specimens to be exhibited at the Colonial Fair in Belgium two decades earlier were kept there to die in exile, undoubtedly for fear that the revelation of their experiences upon their return would undermine the colonial enterprise and Belgian authority in the Congo. Exile in this case entailed suppression of discourse even before it occurred.

Though not well known outside Zaire, literary discourse in French is of significant vitality and quantity despite the atrocious political and economic conditions that have prevailed there for over three decades. Indeed, a survey conducted in 1989 showed that in that year alone, close to 194 titles were published in Zaire, while the combined publications of Senegal, Ivory Coast, Cameroon, and Congo—four of the most productive countries in Francophone Africa—totaled about half that figure.[9] This high rate of production was brought to my attention publicly and brutally when I gave a lecture before the Union of Zairean Writers at the American Cultural Center in Kinshasa on the subject of recent developments in the African novel written in French. At the end of my presentation, the president of the union stood up and chided me for not knowing my country's literature, even though I had featured two of the most prominent of current Zairean novelists and had stated that I considered them to be among the trendsetters in African literature today. He asserted that those writers who left the country were no longer relevant to the Zaire experience. In the name of his union and for my enlightenment, he gave me a box full of books written by its members, all recently published in Zaire, which I accepted gratefully, though not without a sense of embarrassment. Having now read most of their short stories and novelettes, I have wondered, if relevance is to be a relevant criterion, whether these writers—engaged as they are in a process of conscious or unconscious self-censorship for fear of official censorship in various forms, including termination of state subsidies for publication, and death—were not living a much more insidious form of exile than the group that left the country.

In recent years, then, Zairean literary production seems to have developed in two distinct directions: a diasporic tradition, or a literature of exile, and a literature of rootedness, each with its peculiar significance. It would not be uninteresting to look at the literature written by two or three writers from each group for the purpose of comparing the relative constraints under which literature as a social discourse is produced, and quite incidentally, the relevance of the two sets of discourses, although I consider the question of relevance a very slippery one indeed. While this approach would recognize that the question of exile cannot be as straightforward as one might think, it would still stop far short of accounting for its complexity.

In a 1992 article in which she surveys recent narrative literature from "postcolonial" Zaire, Janice Spleth notes that an unusually high number of works feature "intellectuals—educators, priests, students, and professionals—as major characters who are in some way alienated from society." [10] After analyzing the theme of political alienation in the novels of Georges Ngal, V. Y. Mudimbe, Bolya Baenga, and Pius Ngandu Nkashama, Spleth ends her article, almost as an afterthought and a surprise, with the following sentence: "It is worth noting . . . that not one of the writers in this study is currently living in Zaire."

If much current fiction from Zaire is written by authors who live in external exile and depicts characters who struggle in internal exile, it is even more fascinating to observe that the first narrative in French that claimed Congolese authorship was a hoax. In 1932, the French Academy gave a literary prize to a certain Badibanga for a collection of fables entitled *The Elephant Who Walks on Eggs,* published in Belgium the year before. However, Badibanga was never identified, and it is pretty much an accepted fact today that the fables in the Ciluba language were translated by a Belgian writer in rudimentary French to deceive the academy which, like many people then and now, prized exoticism. But the deception also aimed to show that Belgium was performing its "civilizing mission" well. In 1948, the Belgian authorities themselves set out to showcase Congolese talent even more abundantly by organizing a literary competition as part of the annual Colonial Fair. The myth of *Ngando,* written by Paul Lomami-Tshibamba, which won the prize, was the last piece of serious literature written by a Congolese until after independence in 1960. The roots of Zairean literature are thus firmly planted in exile, regardless of its place of actual production: exile due to language, but above all exile due to the fact that what this literature had to say was dictated and manipulated by the colonial power. The Zairean writer's own discourse was under others' control: it was a discourse in the expression of which the writer played a subsidiary role.

V. Y. Mudimbe is one of the major writers to emerge from Zaire since independence in 1960. Known in the United States mostly through his philosophical and theoretical work, especially *The Invention of Africa* (1988), Mudimbe is also a poet and a novelist. Although only one of his four novels was probably completed during his physical exile, they all share what I would call "metaphors of exile" in their form as well as in their content, particularly the last two, *L'écart* and *Shaba Deux.* Both narratives depict diaries left by their dead writers who lost their lives under mysterious circumstances but evidently because of their words, deeds, or thoughts of resistance.

In *L'écart,* translated as *The Rift,*[11] Mudimbe tells the posthumous story of a young scholar, Ahmed Nara, who has recently returned from long years of study in Europe and who proposes to write his doctoral thesis on the history of the Kuba people.[12] After ten years of research both in Europe and now in his country, the young historian dies before writing a single line of his thesis. However, he leaves behind a diary consisting of seven notebooks, all written during the last week of his life. The diary gives the reader a glimpse into Nara's apparently disturbed mind and the possible reasons for this state. In it, for seven sleepless nights, Nara writes down his own life story, his most private thoughts about his friends, and about the revolution he deems necessary in research to reorder knowledge and to render it relevant to his African society.

Nara argues (most of the time in interior monologue) against European anthropologists and historians who project images of their own *ratio* on the surface of Africa as he himself seeks to be more directly engaged in the specificity of local knowledge and to be sensitive to it. Archives must not be limited to "the particular expressions actualized by the brief history of Europe." The new historian, he argues, must also examine the oral traditions, reformulate the symbols found in local cultures, and avoid easy conclusions about rituals. Defining history from the perspective of oral tradition, Nara compares it to memory: a thought understanding itself at the root of its own consciousness. "Science was, in my mind, a memory. I could dig it up, read it in my own way; if need be, find it in error and discard it." [13] For him, the anthropologists have either dismissed the norms of African tradition as primitive or aestheticized them beyond their sociocultural limits. He therefore calls for a critical practice that reveals the meaning of a people's life to itself instead of using it as metadiscourse about the West.

He writes in his diary about the problems of being an African scholar in a field that is crowded with European historians and anthropologists who not only lack understanding of African history, but also are not interested in acquiring it because their judgment is clouded with the inevitable ideological underpinnings of their own societies; in other words, their discourse on African societies is not intended to particularly enhance African understanding of itself. Furthermore, they exercise power over his ultimate success or failure. Thus, when Ahmed Nara informs his thesis supervisor that he intends to write the history of the Kuba people, the latter responds that there is no need to undertake such a project because the Kuba have already been studied in depth and are by now well known. When Nara asks if they have been studied by an African scholar, the supervisor responds, "Do you think that would make a difference?" Nara dares not answer, but he reflects: "When the Germans are satisfied with descriptions of their history written by the French, and the French with English studies of theirs . . . Only then will I give in." [14]

Nara's research project leads him to read all the anthropological studies already done on the Kuba and to carefully go over all the sources used for these studies, sometimes forcing himself to learn an esoteric foreign language such as Flemish in the process. He finds that he will have to begin from scratch, to reconstruct entirely anew the environment in which the Kuba lived, to decolonize the knowledge which has been accumulated on them up to that point, to bring genealogies up to date, and finally to advance a new interpretation that would be more attentive to their milieu and their "real history." However, despite his determination and a great deal of thoughtfulness, Nara remains paralyzed in terms of actually producing a thesis. Although he speaks much about his research, the reader does not see him engaged in any written analysis of what he is supposedly discovering. The questions he asks can be classified into two categories: those of a purely technical nature, such as what to do with the new information he is finding; and those intended to bring African epistemology out of exile: how to reevaluate, revalorize, and reorder knowledge so as to attain a certain authenticity that would lead to a decolonized science of anthropology.

What Nara is doing at the *Bibliothèque nationale,* then, is to appropriate the archives and construct his own methodology by which to study history differently. And even though his questions remain unanswered, and his death appears to be something of a sacrifice to the ideological and epistemological battle that rages within him, what is important here is that he has asked the questions which might have led him (and, implicitly, *will* lead future scholars) to new answers instead of merely following in the footsteps of his teachers.

IV

"African Reflections: Art from Northeastern Zaire" was an exhibition held at the University of Wisconsin—Madison's Elvehjem Museum of Art (October 1992–January 1993). It displayed a magnificent set of art pieces collected in the Belgian Congo, today's Zaire. Although it occupied several large rooms of the museum, it exhibited only a fraction of some four thousand objects collected between 1909 and 1915 by the American Museum of Natural History's Congo Expedition, led by Herbert Lang and James Chapin, a mammalogist and ornithologist respectively.

Upon entering the exhibition, I encounter a site of at least double exile. First, clearly, I am in the presence of fragments of several cultures, the cultures of the Mangbetu, the Azande, and other peoples of a place named "Northeastern Zaire" in anthropological literature. Moreover, these "deterritorialized" cultural fragments are being displayed in a cultural, spatial, and temporal context altogether alien from their origin. I attempt to question the various displays. As is the case with literature, these art pieces constitute above all a system of signs, a discourse: they say something. But what are they saying? To whom? Who controls this discourse? To what ends? And since they have endured—as we are told all good art should—what do they reveal about the condition of their society, then and now?

From a purely historical perspective, the exhibition promised to reveal much about the place and the time from which these objects originated. After all, 1909 was only one year after the owner of the Congo Free State, King Leopold II of Belgium, ceded his territory to his government as a colony. What was the stance of the American Museum of Natural History (which must have had to negotiate the terms of the expedition) toward the atrocities that Leopold's administration of the territory perpetrated? By 1915, the end date of the expedition, the world was engulfed in the First World War, in which the Belgian colony played a role. What was the nature of this role? Finally, the year of the exhibition, 1992, was the twenty-seventh year of Mobutu's dictatorship—a rule every bit as brutal as Leopold's reign of terror or the Belgian colonialism that preceded it and served as its model. On these and similar questions, the exhibition is silent.

The second instance of exile stems from my own estrangement as a viewer from Zaire (although not from "Northeastern Zaire") and my futile search for a complicitous voice: I am unable to grasp the significance of the exhibition either from the perspective of Zairean artists, with whom I putatively share a bond of cultural kinship, or from the perspective of my fellow American viewers, with whom I presumably share a sense of aesthetic discernment. Instead, I begin to establish links between the Zaire literature of exile discussed earlier and this collection of objects that are arranged for other eyes than mine: I am an intruder. I begin to think of the artists who produced these works of art not in terms of the collective Mangbetu or Azande but as individual artists, in the same way I think of writers by name. But since for the most part they remain unidentified, I begin to think of them in the same terms as I think of Badibanga, the invented writer. Other questions come to mind: Who created the art, or rather, who commissioned the art? For what purpose? Who made the art available to the American Museum of Natural History? In exchange for what?

What was the relationship between the museum and the nascent colonial administration in 1909? What about with the king of Belgium, Leopold II? Why is the exhibit totally silent on the atrocious conditions of today's Zaire?

When I visited the museum a second time under the guidance of a docent, I was immediately made aware of who controls the discourse of this collection: the members of the expedition (whose names identify the pieces in lieu of the artists' signatures) and the Mangbetu Kings Mbunza and later Okondo. With its title, "African Reflections," the exhibit presumably invites its spectator at a minimum to express admiration at the beauty of the objects or, as some surely have, to express disapproval about exhibiting certain objects. At any rate, the exhibit forces some kind of dialogue between itself and the viewer who, once engaged in this dialogue, is no longer a mere spectator but a participant in an act of discourse. The word "reflection" in the title of the exhibit acquires for me several undecidable connotations. It means thought, meditation, careful consideration of a subject. But whose thoughts? It also means the casting back of an image, as when one looks into a mirror. But what does the viewer see in the reflected image of the exhibit? Finally, related to specularity is the idea of representation — representation of an absence: in the absence of the African cultures of the Azande, Mangbetu, and others, the viewer gazes at their stand-ins.

The knowledge and the beauty that the viewer derives from the arrangement of the stand-ins have less to do with the Azande, Mangbetu, and others and more to do with the meaning of "reflections" which my docent revealed to me: the interaction between Herbert Lang, the expedition leader, and King Mbunza. Such complicity, reeking of mendacity and abuse of power — a prefiguration of Mobutu's cold-war alliances — could only elicit in me the same feeling of malaise about this art of exile as Badibanga's literature of exile did.

Conditions in the Third World
A Playwright's Soliloquy on His Experiences

Ola Rotimi

First, I need to clarify my choice of some key words in the title of this paper. The words are: *conditions, soliloquy, playwright, experience,* and, of course, *the Third World*.

The *conditions* described here relate directly to Nigeria, my country. The word *soliloquy* has been chosen for the following reason, which should also clarify my use of the words *experience* and *playwright: soliloquy* implies a verbal outpouring of an essentially personal stream of consciousness. This presupposes that the conditions highlighted in this paper pertain to *my personal experiences*. Hence the focus on the *playwright* as case study, since this happens to be my occupational identity. Now, how important is the geographic reference point of this discourse? More specifically, and patriotic verve aside, how important is Nigeria to deserve this focus?

A handy measure of Nigeria's significance is, first, the size of its human mass. Estimated at eighty-eight million, it is vaunted to be the most domineering congregation of Black peoples on planet Earth. (For convenience, let's forget that the chronically fickle temper of Nigeria's census figures tends to render such statistics arguable!) Second, Nigeria happens to be a major producer of crude oil—some of the finest in the market. This endowment, reinforced by its richness in tin ore, coal, cocoa, kola nuts, timber, and rubber, places Nigeria among the most beatified sites in the world.

In spite of these bounties in human and material resources, Nigeria paradoxically belongs in the *Third World*. By this nomenclature we refer to those nations also known as the "underdeveloped countries," the "developing world," "the South," or whatever euphemism appeals to your diplomatic sensibilities when describing the politico-economic state of a country that is inclined to perpetuate harsh, retrogressive human conditions.

The fact that the sociopolitical experience of a playwright in Nigeria is not too different from that of any playwright (any writer, for that matter) anywhere in the Third World accentuates the demoralizing similarities among the nations that constitute that World: Guyana, Gambia, Somalia, Panama, Kenya, Haiti, Nicaragua, Sierra Leone, the Philippines, Costa Rica, Rwanda, and so on. In a lecture a few years ago, I diagnosed the symptoms manifested by these Third World nations as:

—worsening high blood pressure in illiteracy;
—acute diarrhea in population explosion;
—psychotic tendencies in human rights violations;
—technological epilepsy;
—scientific paralysis;
—industrial anemia;
—a recurrent state of political delirium;
—malignant tumors of ethnocentrism;
—sickle-cell religiosity;
—a ruptured hernia of corruption; and
—the "mother" of all maladies: Acquired Immune Deficiency in Economic Growth.

It needs no ghost come from the grave to tell us that under these conditions the creative artist of any description is manifestly operating in a chronic state of ill health.

Put together, these conditions tend to forestall the release—as much as to distract the vitality—of literary creativity, with unnerving consequences to the writer. An enduring state of anomie engenders malaise and disenchantment. This state is so unsettling in virtually every respect that it disorients and even frustrates the will to create or to produce.

It is my personal experience with this anomie in Nigeria's polity that my soliloquy here is meant to intimate. I belong to a peculiar generation—specifically, that crop of young men and women whose cultivation for national service matured at the point of the nation's break from colonial rule. For further identification, I add that these were young men and women who had been conditioned by Euro-Western upbringing and who were not only animated by the ardor of nationalism but also intensely inflamed by passions of hope. It was a hope nursed by the optimism that Nigeria—indeed, all of Africa, which had long been pillaged, deprived, dehumanized, and laid waste by exterior forces in grim collusion with misguided forebears in the land—would be rehabilitated and launched on all fronts to new altitudes of unity, progress, and self-affirmation.

Such was the rosy optimism impelling people of that generation—including this soliloquist—in those dying hours of colonialism. In hindsight I recognize that, blissfully starry-eyed as those young men and women were, their optimism impelled them headlong into the challenges of national service without stint. Those of them undergoing training overseas wound up precipitately rushing home, rejecting the allure of well-moneyed employment, ignoring the comforts of enhanced amenities, forsaking the pampering provisions in a relatively much improved social order. Such were the dreams—such, the visions. Such were the hopes—such the aspirations, the convictions.

They came forward—men and women then in their twenties and thirties—well addressed in education, motivated by impulses to prove themselves. They came out; they came together; they came forward, offering their bodies, their minds, and, of course, the heartbeats of their enthusiasm. They converged upon the land, determined to join, to contribute, to be involved in the building of a new Africa! Then came the reality, like some bad dream dominated by a headless madman in an unending chase after the dreamer, like some suffocating stench from the putrescent bowels of a collapsed public cesspit. The reality in the land subdued that generation—bleary-eyed eagerness and all—just subdued it into a state of shocked disillusionment. It came directly from the least expected source: the leadership in the land. And like some insatiable curse, the disillusionment has persisted to this day, even getting worse in places like Nigeria.

It started as an aberration. A majority of the rulers of the newly independent country—leaders trusted to stimulate the eager generation into advancing the state of the nation—began to falter or simply to abnegate the principle of nationalist struggle outright. These events seemed atavistic in the main: our own leaders colluding with external forces to plunder the land and its peoples; unwholesome vestiges of colonial interests allying with local leaders to subvert nationalist directions. Confusion pervaded the land as former "brothers in the struggle" against colonialism turned into conjurers of old hatreds to propel their own ambitions for power. National development fossilized and was heartily supplanted by a syndrome of rabid self-enrichment commingled with the jingoism of tribal interests. With some groups it has been a doggedness to hold on to power in perpetuity, daring the intervention of counteractions that are bound to culminate in a holocaust—as was the case in Liberia, Sudan, Somalia, and, more lately, Rwanda. The result is a classic example of Absurd Drama—a drama that reflects a world, a nation, a society that offers no sense, expects no logic, despises reason, and begrudges hope.

When, for instance, an interloping military dictatorship brazenly cancels the people's choice of civilian leadership—a choice expressed by the citizenry at a democratically conditioned election adjudged to be the fairest and freest ever recorded in the nation's history of electioneering—in order to keep its hold on power by armed duress—where lies the logic, sense, or sanity in such a situation? It happened in Nigeria in 1993. The political and economic climate resulting from the whimsical cancellation, by the military junta, of the popular choice of civilian leadership has remained chaotic to this day. It is even getting worse, as ancient ghosts of ethnic hate are increasingly invoked to becloud issues of principle and to undermine national harmony among the three hundred ethnic identities in the land. Who stands to gain from this chaos? Ultimately, the proportionately few scions of the military order, in league with self-seeking political hustlers—self-styled guardians of the interest of the ordinary people! But not all the people are fooled. Despite the promises of an improved quality of life from the military rulership, the ruled still see through the facade of hypocrisy. As an old African proverb says: "Who does not know the magic of tossing a morsel of meat into the mouth and making it disappear?"

The atavistic game is being replayed everywhere at the expense of the masses. But only a self-deceiver would claim ignorance of the multimillionaires, even billionaires, in the land today who hardly have a single industry to show as evidence of labor in that country of unceasing suffering and degeneration. The latest scenario in the unending saga of economic and political reprobacy by those claiming to be custodians of the well-being of the people of Nigeria was revealed a few months ago: a substantial amount, totaling some $12.2 billion, earned by Nigeria from a bumper sale of crude oil during the Gulf War in 1991 mysteriously vanished into thin air. The military government, which has kept the nation in a stranglehold for over twelve years, has maintained fetish silence over the evanescence of that enormous windfall—a windfall that should have helped repay no less than one-third of Nigeria's external debts, and thereby brought relief and some measure of social sanity to the land and its impoverished peoples. As far as the rulership is concerned, it is sufficient for the world to know that those billions in hard currency have sprouted wings and taken flight at a velocity that even the magical wizardry of a Houdini couldn't match!

A situation of anomie becomes unbearably unsettling when the same morally dubious rulership churns out decrees to silence its critics—decrees that transform the people's last sanctuary, the judiciary, into a mere puppet serving the vindictive whims of government; decrees that prescribe detention without trial by a government that endorses assassination, zealously implemented by mindless security agents, as a handy policy tool.

Whether in Nigeria, the Philippines, or in Kenya, the story has tended to remain the same: armed coercion serves as an instrument for the perpetuation of misrule centered on self-interest. All this occurs to the detriment of the collective well-being and progress of the nation. As a result, the ordinary man becomes captive in a nation where nothing seems to work, from the basic water supply to health facilities.

In broad terms, these are the conditions confronting the playwright in the underdeveloped world since independence—conditions which have tended to disconcert his being, trouble his conscience and, ineluctably, determine the content of his creative concerns.

How does the playwright come to grips with these conditions? For one, he devises ways of venting his angst through plays that employ the riddle of metaphors. This way he increases his chances of staying alive and out of detention so that he can continue to "talk" with his people about the anguish of their common predicament. He shares his feelings with the ordinary people by couching his distaste for misrule in satire. Examples such as Wole Soyinka's *Kongi's Harvest, Opera Wonyosi, A Play of Giants;* Kole Omotosho's *The Curse;* Femi Osofisan's *Once upon Four Robbers;* and Dele Fatunde's *Oga Na Tiefman* come readily to mind. But the playwright soon learns that the targets of such satire are either too testy (as in Kenya) or too obtuse (as in Nigeria) to decipher the crucial message for change advocated through the plays. Thus, no palpable change occurs; instead, an insidious condition of cachexia continues.

Another option adopted by the playwright for venting his feelings is to write plays that offer some hope to the masses, hope for a future where the "beautiful ones" may one day be "born to redress the ravages of the nation." This kind of drama (which I noted in another essay as illustrative of a new theme of the "utopian model" in contemporary African literature) highlights five basic attributes that define an ideal ruler of the people. This ideal mandates a protagonist that is shorn of tribal bigotry; result oriented; principled; foresighted; and, above all, unyieldingly committed to the well-being of the people under his charge. Examples of plays that fit into this category are Ngugi wa Thiong'o and Micere Mugo's *The Trial of Dedan Kimathi* (mirrored in the eponymous hero); Ebrahim Hussein's *Kinjeketile* (also portrayed in the eponymous hero); and my *Hopes of the Living Dead* (embodied in the character of the leper, Harcourt Whyte).

Still seeking a medium for (perhaps) more mordant attacks on a perverse rulership, I am currently experimenting with form and content borrowed from folk traditions. In this regard, I have been attracted to animal characters in African folktales for grotesque depictions of the human targets of my satirical plays. No doubt this is similar to the faunal characters that populate George Orwell's *Animal Farm.* These bizarre depictions are to be in playlets. One such playlet of mine is pointedly entitled *How Not to Rule the Third World.*

All told, the playwright in Nigeria (or the Third World) cannot but be affected by the spasms of his nation's sociopolitical tendons. In this context, expression of his anxieties cannot be confined to writing for the stage alone. He realizes he must also use other channels to articulate his response to the anguish in which his being and that of a majority of his people are circumstanced. The nation's press media fulfill this goal—if the local press itself hasn't been forcibly silenced already by some intimidating decree or closed down outright, as is again the fate of Nigeria's more progressive media houses.

A fourth option—perhaps the ultimate—is getting involved directly in activism: picketing, demonstrations, public rallies, and so on. Without a doubt, indictment of misrule through the press and through public activism are emotion-, mind-, and energy-sapping distractions to artistic productivity. But such distractions are crucial, it would appear, to the artist's mental equilibrium. In any case, they help to drain (purge?) some of the vexing inundations of the mind that could otherwise slow down creativity and atrophy the will to live. Indeed, for the contemporary playwright in the Third World, there seems to be no hope of imminent relief from worsening social inequities, economic stagnation, and political chaos. The diurnal provocations from freewheeling political fatuities are simply so persistent as to render his creative output sporadic, his very existence unsure from moment to moment. Nonetheless, his impulse for self-expression seems to be just as unrelenting, forcing him to seek some space wherein to keep on writing within the boundaries of his nation, at best—or, at worst, in self-exile away from his motherland. What matters in those circumstances of reined expressiveness (harried in the former, culturally estranged in the latter) is the fact that the writer refuses to compromise the principles of his stance vis-à-vis the excesses of the wielders of inordinate power and coercion in his particular world. Somehow, this relationship of the writer to the rulers of his world is reminiscent of the relationship between the rock and the scorpion in African folklore: the scorpion represents the powers-that-be and the rock personifies the dissident. Now, the story:

Scorpion this day strikes out its venom full on Rock for daring to impede his reckless thrust along a footpath. Soon after the sting, Scorpion pulls back to gloat at the consequence. Stunned and discomfited by what he sees, Scorpion blurts out at Rock:

> You stubborn son of the devil!
> I stung you hard,
> Yet you wouldn't die
> Nor would your likes stop popping up
> In my path!

All considered, it is this writer's opinion that the restoration of hope and the rekindling of optimism in the peoples of Africa is still possible, as is the prospect of redirecting energies toward the rehabilitation and enrichment of the continent itself—a world too long pauperized from without and from within. However, the creation of a climate that will engender an improved quality of life in that World needs must begin with ONE action, namely . . .

First, a background:

In recent years, the Black diaspora has made vocal demands for reparations from the White World—reparations meant to offset the rapacity of the slave trade and colonialism. In this writer's opinion, this demand seems to be out of focus. The concern should not be with reparations; rather, and more defensibly, it should address the idea of repatriation. Pointedly, this is repatriation of all the billions sponged from Africa since independence by insatiable, venal rulers together with their relations and minions. The period in question here spans roughly the last three decades—a relatively manageable compass of time and a far more recent setting for judgment.

So much for background. Now to the desired action:

The White World should be exhorted to desist from plying Africa (and by extension, the Third World) with venomous placebos in the form of loans from the World Bank, the International Monetary Fund, the Paris Club, the G-7 Nations, and others of that ilk. The interest charges alone are enough to cripple the debtor nations; added to this are recurrent reschedulings of the repayment terms. Besides, these purported "aids" only serve to aggravate the socioeconomic deprivations of the ordinary people in the recipient nations. The avarice and skewed programs of misrule have always guaranteed that condition.

In place of "munificence" in loans, the White World—if it has a conscience—should work in concert with the United Nations and the International Court of Justice to ferret out the billions secreted into the money vaults of Europe and America and proceed to impound the thieveries in the name of morality, logic, justice, and humanity. The crime committed by the "owners" of such mammoth sums is proving to be as catastrophic to life as were the murders perpetrated by the villains in the Nuremberg trials. By any measure both are, infinitely, crimes against humanity. How else can one describe an act by which, for instance, a single Mobutu Sese Seko of Zaire can boast billions of dollars robustly stashed away in a personal account sequestered far out in an enclave in northern Europe called Switzerland, while a growing multitude of ordinary Zaireans die from joblessness, starvation, disease, and abject want?

Once impounded by the world bodies, the amounts should fitly be repatriated to the respective countries of their plunder. Quibbling over "right of ownership" simply has no place in this action, except where our universe chooses to be hypocritical. Common sense and logic are enough to conclude that the multimillions "owned" by a single person with hardly any personal means of production—except the opportunism of being the ruler of a people —were stolen from the people.

The benefit of such action to our universe is fundamentally twofold: first, it is bound to effectively deter kleptocracy in the governance of the Third World, where systematic checks and balances have yet to be established as the bedrock of national polity; second, in addition to discouraging the deadly syndrome of governance by thieving, an action of this kind would also curb the incidence of human misery, particularly among the proverbial poorer peoples of the Third World, since the repatriated loot would go to ameliorating their condition and restoring their human dignity.

Indeed, only in this way can mankind begin to espy some hope, to perceive some signs of enduring peace, of diversified progress, and of shared comfort—all coalescing into the suppression of repression in our universe.

How Not to Rule the Third World
A Parable Playlet

Ola Rotimi

NOTE TO THE DIRECTOR/PRODUCER

It is important to the meaning of this play that the characters who constitute the machinery of state government are masked in *animalian* representations (beasts and birds, primarily). In this context, the more *grotesque* the animal chosen, the better. However, there must be an obvious link between the *habit* for which the particular animal-metaphor is *notorious* and the *trait peculiar* to the *human* characterization. Furthermore, the masks employed must be fabricated so as not to impede speech, while the costumes *must* be a realistic reflection of the human fashion of the times. Of course, those for the LIONS must be, naturally, *leonine*.

CHARACTERS	SUGGESTED ANIMAL-METAPHORS
RULER: alias KING	Pig, complete with bloated paunch
HIS WIFE: alias QUEEN	Ditto
NOBLEMAN 1	Wart Hog
NOBLEMAN 2	Toad
NOBLEMAN 3	Vulture
NOBLEMAN 4	Rat
WIVES OF NOBLEMEN	In accordance with the depictions of their respective husbands
SECURITY CHIEF	Baboon
BODYGUARDS	Apes
SHEPHERD	
BEGGARS	
GOATHERD	
LIONS	
2 VOICES	

The palace of the ruler of a Third World country.

The KING, *his household, and* NOBLES *are engulfed in merriment: dancing, wining, munching, etc. They are all gorgeously attired. After a while, a* NOBLEMAN *raises his voice, diminishing the din of revelry. In pairs, the* NOBLES *and their spouses go up to the* KING, *curtsy, and adulate him.*

NOBLES. [*severally, with devout sycophancy*] Hail to his Majesty! Ruler for life!
Protector of the people!
May our Lord live long!
Defender of the land!
Your most revered Majesty, may your reign be without end!
KING. I thank you. . . . Noble Ones, respectable Ladies of our land. I thank you all. Indeed, for your sake, I will live long. And for your sake and that of the land, my reign shall be one of bounty and merriment.
In rushes a SHEPHERD, *clad in rags, breathless with terror.*
SHEPHERD. Oh, King! Help . . . help!
SECURITY CHIEF. [*furiously*] What d'you want, and who are —?
SHEPHERD. Help me, your Majesty — help!
KING. Well, who are you?
SHEPHERD. One of your humble subjects, your Majesty — a simple shepherd.
NOBLEMAN 2. So, what d'you want?
SECURITY CHIEF. And how dare you burst into this ceremony like this!
NOBLEMAN 1. Speak up!
SHEPHERD. A lion, dear Elders, your Majesty — a lion.
KING. A lion!
SHEPHERD. Indeed, your Majesty. I was in the field where my sheep were grazing. Suddenly, this . . . lion! Big, strong, vicious! Leapt straight out of the bushes, crashed full-bodied upon my sheep, killing two in an instant!
KING. [*nonchalantly, helping himself to some drinks*] I see. . . .

The NOBLES *take this as their cue to resume guzzling food and drinks served on trays by gaudily uniformed palace stewards.*

SHEPHERD. Pray, your Majesty, help me!

KING. In what way, may I ask?

SHEPHERD. Pray, your Majesty, call up the hunters in the land, have them search and kill the lion!

KING. [*to the gathering*] Ladies and Noblemen, our dear shepherd here wants me to . . . [*to the* SHEPHERD] what was it, again?

SHEPHERD. I'm praying his Majesty to summon the hunters in the land to attack the lion before—

The courtiers break into jeering.

NOBLEMAN I. What insolence!

WOMAN I. An ordinary peasant now tells the King what to do?

NOBLEMAN 2. The nerve!

SECURITY CHIEF. That's democracy for you!

All the courtiers burst into another toady chorus of laughter.

QUEEN. But then . . . [*to the* KING] your Majesty . . . Elder Ones . . . Ladies and Noblemen, our good friend may have a point here. Let's hear him out.

KING. All right.

QUEEN. What part of town did the lion . . . ?

NOBLEMAN I. The rules, your Majesty. Procedure. There are rules and procedure to governance, my royal Lady. Our talk at this moment is SECURITY. Security of the land and its people from danger—from threats to lives, limbs, and property.

NOBLEMEN. [*severally*] That's right!
Indeed!
Of course!
Precisely!
No more, no less!

NOBLEMAN I. Very well, then. It is the responsibility of the Chief Security Officer in the land to question this intruder. That's the rule; that is the procedure.

KING. [*to the* QUEEN] Not a free-for-all affair, my dear—this thing called governance. [*To the* SECURITY CHIEF] Do your work!

NOBLEMAN I. Interrogate the alarmist!

SECURITY CHIEF. [*pompously, to the* SHEPHERD] You—d'you know me?

SHEPHERD. The land's Security Chief.

SECURITY CHIEF. Good. Now tell me: is it the King's sheep that are being attacked?

SHEPHERD. No, my Lord.

SECURITY CHIEF. Oh, the sheep of someone else at this gathering, perhaps? [*The* SHEPHERD *shakes his head slowly, in deep embarrassment, as the crowd again guffaws at his discomfiture.*] No-o-o again?

SHEPHERD. They are *my* sheep.

SECURITY CHIEF. Then why, may we ask, should the hunters in the land be summoned?

SHEPHERD. To protect other sheep in the land from—

SECURITY CHIEF. Hn, hn, hn, hn, hn—our talk is NOW, okay? The sheep being attacked now! Not other sheep in some distant future!

WOMAN 2. That's them for you—these troublemakers in the land —always mixing things up to cause confusion everywhere.

NOBLEMAN 1. They call it democracy—

WOMAN 3. Everybody talking—rubbish!

WOMAN 1. No respect!

SECURITY CHIEF. [*threateningly, to the* SHEPHERD] Answer my question: whose sheep are we talking about?

SHEPHERD. My sheep, my Lord.

SECURITY CHIEF. I see. . . . Well, don't you have hands? Why don't you attack the lion yourself? Answer me, troublemaker! Or I'll get you locked up! Why d'you come to us?

SHEPHERD. Sorry, Sir, but the next attack by the lion could be on the sheep of anyone here! [*A wave of alarm arises at both the intrepidity of the* SHEPHERD *and the horror of the possibility of his dire prediction.*] It could even be the sheep from the very special flock of his Majesty's!

KING. I see. . . .

NOBLEMAN 1. [*to the* SHEPHERD] How dare you talk like that?

SECURITY CHIEF. [*to a* BODYGUARD] Detention! Lock the rebel up!

SHEPHERD. [*naively*] But it could be the sheep of any one of you the next time!

QUEEN. [*horrified*] The Heavens forbid!

SECURITY CHIEF. Alarmist! When that time comes, we'll know

what to do. [*joins the* BODYGUARD *in jostling the* SHEPHERD *out.*]

NOBLEMAN 1. Bloody alarmist!

NOBLEMAN 3. Indeed, your Majesty—a troublemaker, pure and simple!

WOMAN 1. Too many of them in the land anyway—I keep saying it!

WOMAN 2. It's his sheep that'll get devoured by lions!

QUEEN. They'll never give us peace! [*breaks into tears.*]

WOMAN 3. Now see how the filthy groundhog has upset our gentle Queen!

Other WOMEN *cluster round to comfort the* QUEEN.

WOMAN 1. [*furious, charging out after the* SHEPHERD] It's your sheep that'll be feast for ten lions, d'you hear me? Twenty lions . . . a million!

SECURITY CHIEF. [*reenters in time to intercept* WOMAN 1] It's all right—the law of the land will deal with the rebel. [*Soothingly, to the* QUEEN] Don't worry, your sweet Majesty. If he comes out of detention alive, let him thank his God for leaving him permanently disabled!

NOBLEMAN 1. Sorry for the rude interruption, your Majesty.

KING. I think we must now let our women retire with the Queen for their banquet. The men will remain behind. There's some important business to engage in before our banquet.

As WOMEN, *in company of the* QUEEN, *retire . . .*

NOBLEMAN 3. [*lustily*] Three hearty cheers to the King and Queen: hep, hep, hep!

NOBLEMEN & WOMEN. Hurray!

NOBLEMAN 3. Hep, hep, hep!

NOBLEMEN & WOMEN. Hurray!

NOBLEMAN 3. Hep, hep, h-e-p!

NOBLEMEN & WOMEN. Hu-r-r-a-a-y!

Only the NOBLEMEN *and the* KING *now remain. Even the* BODY-GUARDS *have been gestured out by the* SECURITY CHIEF. *The drinking still goes on, however, as the* NOBLES *hover over drinks and food located all over the scene.*

KING. Noblemen—er . . . it is crucial that we all speak in one voice. We must brace up against those eternal rebels . . . especially those subverts styling themselves "JOURNALISTS of a

FREE PRESS"—whatever that means! Who wants to bet? First thing tomorrow morning, this little ceremony will be criticized and blown out of proportion by a Press desperate to hang us before the public as self-indulgent, corrupt, extravagant rulers!

SECURITY CHIEF. We'll shut down such a Press!

NOBLEMAN 1. Meanwhile, our integrity has suffered abuse!

KING. That's why we need to speak in one voice. [*To* NOBLEMAN 2] Information Chief . . . what will be your Press release—the official statement of the purpose of this ceremony?

NOBLEMAN 2. [*reading from a sheet of paper*] On this occasion of our nation's Thirtieth Anniversary, the Head of State and his Executives are appropriately launching a war! A war against whom? Against a sister nation? No! More patriotically, it is a war against two dominant problems. Dominant problems that have long bedeviled progress and development in this potentially great nation! We address the problems of—one, corruption . . . and two, wasteful spending!

Ovation.

KING. Another reason for this celebration, of course, must also be borne in mind—no need to reflect it in the Press release . . . the people won't understand anyway. What's crucial is that we all know what to say. One voice. Now, [*clearing his throat*] the people all know that this country recently received fresh loans from the rich nations. Well, that we are here in celebration of this achievement is not wasteful spending—it's simply a matter of records. We're here to simply mark the "transfer of resources"—that's all. And in this consideration, the fact that two-thirds of the loans received have already gone into the arrangements and logistics for this celebration hardly makes us corrupt leaders. It's a matter of proportion. Celebration of a major national achievement deserves a major financial outlay. Are we all clear on that? [*Another ovation.*] One voice!

A fresh commotion develops outside.

VOICE. Help . . . h-e-l-p!

NOBLEMAN 1. Not again!

GOATHERD. [*bursting in amid resistance from the* BODYGUARDS] Where's the King?

SECURITY CHIEF. Who the devil are you?

GOATHERD. Goatherd, my Lord—a humble goatherd, going

about his business. As has been the tradition from the days of my forebears . . .

NOBLEMAN 1. Cut out the history!

GOATHERD. A lion, your Majesty . . . attacked my goats! Killed four at a go!

SECURITY CHIEF. And what has that to do with the palace?

NOBLEMAN 4. That's their idea of democracy: carry every filth to the doorstep of the Head of the land, hm?

SECURITY CHIEF. Answer my question!

GOATHERD. But you are all here!

SECURITY CHIEF. So?

GOATHERD. And this is the home of the Head of the land . . .

SECURITY CHIEF. It's your head that needs a deep crack down the middle! [*To the* BODYGUARDS] Lock up the saboteur! [BODY-GUARDS *manhandle* GOATHERD *out of sight as the* SECURITY CHIEF *blares savagely after them*] Ten years! No trial!

NOBLEMAN 1. Now we're talking!

SECURITY CHIEF. [*still addressing* BODYGUARDS *off stage*] You hear? And that's a decree!

NOBLEMAN 3. Now we're dealing with them—the bloody troublemakers!

KING. [*in a drunken drawl*] Er . . . my Nobles . . . dedicated . . . as ever. I . . . a-gree—greet—you all. Now, I think . . . perhaps we should listen to the complaints of these . . . er . . . common folk once in a while. Or what d'you think?

NOBLEMAN 1. [*also tipsy*] Not now, your Majesty. This is not the right time!

NOBLEMAN 4. There'll be time enough for that.

NOBLEMAN 2. Precisely.

KING. Security, . . . what d'you say?

SECURITY CHIEF. We're on track, my Lord, right on track!

KING. What does that mean?

SECURITY CHIEF. Our action is right, your Majesty. To show understanding to the complaints of the governed, my Lords, is to send the wrong signals for radicalism. Our democracy has no room for "government by the people." It's either we govern the people, or we don't. No power-sharing nonsense!

NOBLEMAN 4. That's right.

KING. "Government by the people"? What's that?

SECURITY CHIEF. That's how one ruler described "democracy," your Majesty.

KING. "Government by the people"?

SECURITY CHIEF. Even worse. He says it's "of the people, by the people, for the people. . . ."

KING. A ruler said that?

SECURITY CHIEF. A long time ago, though—a long, long time ago in history.

NOBLEMAN 4. A ruler in these parts?

SECURITY CHIEF. Of course not!

KING. That explains it.

NOBLEMAN 3. A dreamer . . .

SECURITY CHIEF. They're all over the world, confusing people with funny ideas.

KING. My point is that complaints by the common people never end!

NOBLEMAN 3. Never.

NOBLEMAN 4. Oh, I don't mind their complaining—if you get my meaning. My point is that they complain at the wrong time. Always do . . . if you get my point . . . [hiccups].

NOBLEMAN 1. That's it: timing. There simply have to be rules, procedure—a format to anything we . . . do in life. Timing. So complain if you have to, blast it! Complain long or complain short, but . . . timing counts. In all things. These people simply have no sense of . . . [hiccups] timing—period!

KING. What bothers me is their common statement.

SECURITY CHIEF. Common statement, your Majesty?

KING. That what they see as their problem today could darn well turn out to be the problem of any of us in this secure palace tomorrow. Now, that . . .

SECURITY CHIEF. My answer to that was clear, my Lord. When and if any of these problems crop up—what am I for? We shall not be caught unready, your Majesty.

NOBLEMAN 2. Precisely!

Rowdy ovation by all, accompanied by the clinking of glasses. The jollity is barely subsiding when there's a knocking on the door, accompanied by a pliant female voice.

SECURITY CHIEF. [*to the* BODYGUARD] Who's there?

The BODYGUARD *opens the door from outside. Two raggedly clad female* BEGGARS *totter in, diffidently.*

NOBLEMAN I. Who are these?

BODYGUARD. Beggars, my Lord.

SECURITY CHIEF. How dare they . . . [*He whips out his belt, charging at the* BEGGARS, *but freezes at the command of the* KING.]

KING. Stop!

Hushed suspense prevails. Meanwhile, the BEGGARS *have recoiled in fright, out of sight.*

KING. Noble Ones . . . you must understand this: not every time must force . . . violence . . . be our response to provocations from those we rule. Oh, no. Dialogue—it is very important. Now, watch. . . . [*To the* SECURITY CHIEF] Bring them back in—the beggars—bring them in.

The SECURITY CHIEF *gestures to the* BODYGUARD *who ushers in the* BEGGARS *again, but they remain at a respectful distance from the* KING.

KING. Tell me . . . what is it you want?

BEGGAR I. We are . . . still waiting, Father of our land.

SECURITY CHIEF. Waiting for what?

KING. Ssshh! Let me handle this, will you?

SECURITY CHIEF. Forgive me, your Majesty.

KING. [*to the* BEGGARS] Talk to me: I'm ready to listen.

BEGGAR 2. We're many, Father, many—and with children.

KING. You say you're waiting. Waiting for what?

BEGGAR I. For whatever is left of the food from this merriment, your Greatness.

KING. Merriment did you say?

BEGGAR 2. [*benignly*] Our spirits join in your merriment, Fathers of our land.

KING. Thank you, but is the merriment over yet?

BEGGARS. Not yet, our royal Father.

KING. And you want food left over from it. How is that?

BEGGARS. For ourselves and our children—hunger ails us, Fathers of our land.

KING. So we learn; and you want food left over from this merriment.

BEGGARS. It is so, our Lord.

KING. But you too have just admitted that the merriment is not over yet.

BEGGARS. True, our Lord.

KING. So how can you talk of food that is left over when the eating still goes on? It does not make sense, does it? [BEGGARS *shake their heads in agreement with this logic.* NOBLES *laugh at the disconcertment of the* BEGGARS.] Well, then, people: now that we agree in our reasoning, do what is right. Wait outside. When we're through—that is, if you'll let us have peace to be through—why, you shall have the food left over.

BEGGARS. [*hesitantly*] But the crowd outside is growing bigger, my Lord—and the children are crying!

KING. No problem. Anyone too impatient to wait is free—why, ours is a democracy—free to move on to some place else. [*He gestures to the* SECURITY CHIEF *to take over.*]

SECURITY CHIEF. You hear? Now, out! Wait outside, or keep moving! Come on . . .

The BODYGUARD *shoves the* BEGGARS *out and slams the door.*

KING. [*with the sobriety of a sage*] See what I mean? Once in a while, dialogue. Everyone feeling free to talk. That's democracy, brothers. That's . . . to act . . . er . . . civilized. [*He chuckles triumphantly.*] Which brings me back to that ruler who said government should be "of the people, by the people, for the people . . ."—well, we must forgive him. Perhaps the fellow said something like that while he was in the kind of state we're in at the moment: blessedly drunk!

Self-indulgent guffaw by all.

NOBLEMAN 4. Objection! There's a difference, your Majesty. I object! Indeed there is a difference. When, in appreciation of life, we do get drunk, the fact remains: we still talk sense— no matter how [*hiccups*] potent the drink—we still talk [*hiccups*] sense!

NOBLEMAN 2. Precisely.

KING. [*thoughtfully*] "Of the people, by the people, for the people"? Without a doubt, what the fellow really [*hiccups*] meant was: "what, when, and if," not "of, by, and for!"

NOBLEMAN 1. "What, when, and if"?

KING. You heard exactly what I said. In a democracy—and I mean true democracy . . . unmixed demo- [*hiccups*] cracy—the ruled must be free to indulge in the right to hear the kinds of things they love to hear from those who rule them. In turn, those who rule must retain the right to do what they want to do—when they want to do it. And if they feel like doing it—whatever it is they want to do—when, where, and how!

NOBLEMAN 2. Wisdom!

A cacophony of inebriated acclamation.

KING. The key word here is balance, see?

NOBLEMAN 2. Precisely.

KING. That's what's missing in that fellow's vision of democracy. No bal- [*hiccups*] ance! He piles up everything on "the people, the people, the people"! No consideration, no thought, no grain of sympathy pinched over for the [*hiccups*] ruler. The consequence? An epidemic of swollen-headedness afflicts the people. And d'you blame them? Do you? With so much . . . responsibility piled upon them, won't they become delirious, for Heaven's sake?

SECURITY CHIEF. Breeding rebels and saboteurs!

NOBLEMAN 1. Not while we live!

NOBLEMAN 2. And long live the King in his wisdom!

KING. Well, [*hiccups*] Noble Ones, I hope you've learned a sound lesson from what you've just witnessed.

Glasses clink and the revelry is about to pick up again when another commotion swells—this time, from the recesses of the palace.

VOICE 1. Hurry! H-e-l-p, everybody! Two lions have leapt into the King's backyard and are attacking his cows!

KING. What's that?

SECURITY CHIEF. [*motionless, ears cocked intently*] I'm studying the development, my Lord! [*To a* BODYGUARD] Lock the door! *The* BODYGUARD *bolts the front door.*

VOICE 2. [*from the rear quarters*] Out! Get out, everybody! The lions are right inside the Queen's chambers, attacking the women!

Horrifying wails of women issue forth from the rear rooms of the palace.

KING. [*to the* SECURITY CHIEF] Did you hear that?

SECURITY CHIEF. I'm analyzing the situation, my . . .

NOBLEMAN 1. [*in panic*] Our wives!

NOBLEMAN 2. [*tearfully*] Precisely!

VOICE 1. Now there are five! Five lions all over the p-a-l-a-c-e! *Frantically they scamper about, confounded with terror. The lamentation from the rear rooms intensifies.*

SECURITY CHIEF. Guns! Everybody draw your guns! If no guns, then bottles—whiskey bottles, champagne—anything!

KING. Hunters! Call up the hunters!

SECURITY CHIEF. Take cover, everybody! [*He scales through a window to safety.*]

NOBLEMAN 1. Let us p-r-a-y!

The rest fall on their knees. Too late. Five huge lions crash through the door into the midst of the crouching, wailing, trapped conclave.

BLACKOUT

Cartoons in Cameroon
Anger and Political Derision under Monocracy

Célestin Monga

INTRODUCTION

One paradox of authoritarianism is its ability to emphasize the need for new vectors of communication and to inspire writers, journalists, and artists in their permanent quest for new forms of opposition. Indeed, in an environment where brutality is the only accepted form of "dialogue"—which is typical of francophone sub-Saharan monocracies [1]—there is a higher propensity to invent new languages and new means of informal resistance.

However, the history of political cartoons in the world does not correlate with the quest for freedom. The founder of the modern school of political cartoons was the Englishman James Gillray.[2] Between 1803 and 1811, after the revolutionary movements in Europe, he invented political caricatures, beginning with Napoleon as a subject. Almost at the same time, similar initiatives were observed in France, Italy, and Germany. The first caricatures were lithograph sheets, passed about from hand to hand, usually issued by the artists themselves at first and subsequently by publishing houses. The use of caricature in American politics dates from the 1832 presidential campaign. As noted by Bishop, "campaign papers made their first appearance, and were devoted entirely to personal abuse of the two opposing candidates."[3]

The emergence of political caricature in Cameroon and in most African countries was quite different. The need for a graphic weapon for political purposes was justified under the colonial period by the absence of freedom of speech. But national archives have kept very few of the first caricatures. This paper focuses on the most recent trend, which began in 1990–91 with the struggle for a multiparty system. The following section presents a historical background to various perceptions of humor and briefly analyzes the new Cameroonian cartoons in a theoretical perspective. The final section highlights some of the lessons which can be drawn from this subversive popular discourse.

THE GRAMMAR OF HUMOR IN CAMEROONIAN CARTOONS

This section focuses on the origins of political cartoons in Cameroon, the analysis of the aesthetics and ideological positioning of the three main artists, and the intellectual structure and the emotional dynamics of their work.

Genesis of Political Cartoons in Cameroon

Cameroon reintroduced multiparty democracy in 1991, but President Paul Biya maintained his control over a highly centralized political and administrative apparatus. Although the former single party, the Cameroon People's Democratic Movement (CPDM), no longer holds the majority in the unicameral National Assembly, it still controls the executive branch of the political system through a coalition with parties represented in the government. Moreover, under the 1996 constitution, the president has extensive powers over the legislature and the judiciary.

The constitution provides for freedom of speech and of the press and outlaws discrimination on the grounds of political opinion. However, since the adoption of the constitution, numerous de jure and de facto restrictions and inhibitions encumber the exercise of free speech. In 1990 and 1991, independent newspapers were banned; intellectuals and journalists were regularly arrested, put on trial, and sentenced for disseminating "subversive statements" or "reports which are likely to cause alarm to the public or to disturb public peace." Radio, the medium through which most Cameroonians used to get their news and the only one with national extensive coverage, was strictly controlled by the authorities. The single state-owned television station was used only as a channel of propaganda for the ruling party. To protect its radio and television monopoly, Biya's regime refused to issue licenses for private radio stations.

For all these reasons some independent journalists based in Douala decided in 1990 to initiate political caricatures in the private press (*Le Combattant, Challenge Hebdo, Le Messager*) as a means of communication. The rationale behind this decision was simple: all private papers had to submit their drafts to administrative censorship prior to printing. However, unlike the regular articles and surveys on politics often viewed as subversive, cartoon pages were not considered to be "threats to public order." The government officers in charge of censorship did not pay much attention to political caricature, estimating that its impact was negligible.

Indeed, the influence of cartoons was highly underestimated. Since they were easy to understand and unusually funny, they attracted readers in both rural and urban areas, increasing the readership of the private press, even among illiterate groups of the population. Their success was so fast that the number of newspaper buyers in 1991 was almost four times as great as in 1990.[4]

Aesthetics and Positioning

The typical Cameroonian cartoon is confined to a few figures in one of the weekly newspapers. While there has been a steady advance in artistic merit since 1990, there has been little change in the general style of each of the four major cartoonists: Nyemb Popoli (*Le Messager*), Jean-Pierre Kenne (*Challenge Hebdo*), Tex Kana (*La Nouvelle Expression*), and Go'away (*Cameroon Tribune*). Most of the cartoons are about the size of half a page. The characters depicted are generally outlined, and they are never presented in natural attitudes. They appear almost invariably without background, and most of them are giving utterance to sentiments or thoughts which are enclosed in a loop above their heads. Faces are not precisely drawn, even though some of them are carefully designed portraits.[5]

Evidently, politicians are the favorite figures in caricatures. Paul Biya, the head of state, is generally pictured as the national godfather of an international mafia, the local chief agent of the disaster, except when pictured by *Cameroon Tribune*'s Go'away, who usually presents him as a prophet.[6]

Drawing is not taught at all in the country, and all those who are skilled in it are self-taught. None of the four Cameroonian cartoonists has a college degree—many journalists in the country

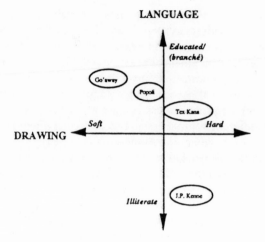

LANGUAGE

Educated/ (branché)

Go'away

Popoli

Tex Kana

Soft **DRAWING** *Hard*

Illiterate J.P. Kenne

The Positioning of Political Cartoonists in Cameroon

have the same background—but they claim to have an intuitive knowledge of national politics and national issues.

Caricature is used as a means of communication in three dimensions, each of which is exploited differently by the major cartoonists:

The drawing: It is usually strong, but the composition of the pictures can be crude. Following the French school of caricature, they make great use of the technique of disproportion—that is, exaggerating the size of the head and the length of the legs. Go'away is probably the most consistent in the quality of his drawing. Tex Kana and Popoli tend to sketch their figures roughly.

The comic effect of the whole picture: By combining several figures in the same picture and making an intelligent use of the loops, cartoonists increase the comic potential of their work. Popoli is probably the best in this domain, mastering several figures and stories like a novelist. He can be very subtle. Go'away tends to unveil his political opinions very bluntly.

The political message: The mingling of politicians and other prominent personages (religious leaders, famous artists, influential intellectuals, etc.) in situations illustrating the political developments or the news of the week provides opportunities for cartoonists to convey their political messages. Being affiliated with a governmental media, Go'away is usually full of praise for President Biya's government; he only targets the opposition leaders and always tries to depict them along the lines of the official discourse, whereas Popoli, Kenne, and Tex Kana, who do not formally belong to any political party, strongly oppose Biya's regime and devote most of their loops to criticizing his policies.[7]

These different approaches and focuses can be represented in a three-dimensional diagram. Along each of these three dimensions, there are different types of readers. Their positioning does not give many insights into the real message of Cameroonian political cartoonists. In order to understand their message, it is worthwhile to analyze the internal structure of the various forms of humor which emerge from the drawings.

Intellectual Structure and Emotional Dynamics

Before attempting to analyze the technical structure of Cameroonian cartoonists' humor, one might think of using some theoretical considerations listed by philosophers, anthropologists, and psychologists since Aristotle. Let's recall some of the available frameworks and theories of humor and laughter.[8]

In Aristotle's view, laughter was intimately related to ugliness. René Descartes held that laughter was a manifestation of joy mixed with surprise or hatred or both. Francis Bacon, like Cicero, believed that the first cause of laughter was deformity. Thomas Hobbes adopted the same point of view in one of his famous writings: "The passion of laughter is nothing else but sudden glory arising from a sudden conception of some eminence in ourselves by comparison with the infirmity of others, or with our own formerly." Along the same lines, Henri Bergson wrote that "in laughter, we always find an unavowed intention to humiliate and consequently to correct our neighbor."[9] William McDougall emphasized the therapeutic virtues of laughter, observing that it "has been evolved in the human race as an antidote to sympathy, a protective reaction shielding us from the depressive influence of the shortcomings of our fellow men."[10]

Any discussion intending to provide tools for dissecting and analyzing specimens of humor in Cameroon would be incomplete. It is impossible to draw up an exhaustive list in which jokes and witticisms would be classified according to the nature of the frames of reference whose collision creates the comic effect. Furthermore, patterns of association vary from one cartoonist to another, and the very peculiar way in which collective memory keeps and processes history here makes impossible the task of explaining the subtle equation of humor and the mechanics of laughter. Indeed, as A. Koestler put it, "to analyze humour is a task as delicate as analyzing the composition of a perfume with its multiple ingredients, some of which are never consciously perceived, while others, when sniffed in isolation, would make one wince."[11]

The theories mentioned in this sample are very different since each one has its own theoretical frame. However, on this one point nearly all of them would agree: that humor and laughter are always related to aggressiveness. As pointed out by Koestler,

> There is a bewildering variety of moods involved in different forms of humour, including mixed or contradicting feelings; but whatever the mixture, it must contain a basic ingredient that is indispensable: an impulse, however faint, of aggression or apprehension. It may appear in the guise of malice, contempt, the veiled cruelty of condescension, or merely an absence of sympathy with the victim of the joke—a momentary anesthesia of the heart, as the French philosopher Henri Bergson put it.[12]

But they would not help very much to fully capture the Cameroonian humor and wit as it emerges from political cartoons. Indeed, the Cameroonian frames of reference which emerge from today's political cartoons seem to emphasize a strong sense of collective anger.[13] When looking for the philosophical background and the psychological mechanisms that play a particularly crucial role in generating laughter in Cameroonian cartoons, one ends up concluding that there is no single frame of reference for these artists' work. Indeed, the ingredients that are used seem to be extracted from several psychological and social intellectual sources. Obviously, many cartoonists are heavily influenced by what could be roughly termed an African conception of humor. But their work generally goes beyond that "traditional" framework. Their inspiration seems to be primarily punctuated by contemporary issues. In fact, the only recurrent source of inspiration that can be invoked with a certain degree of certainty for all the major cartoonists is their reliance on new forms of everyday wit, their extensive use of new languages that people invent in their daily struggle for survival as a collective response to oppression. Very often, their cartoons are filled with popular jokes derived from the painful decay of the social fabric, jokes that one also finds in literary works by writers like the Congolese novelist Sony Labou Tansi, or popular singers like Petit Pays, Papa Wemba, or Prince Eyango.

Almost all the time, the common pattern underlying the stories (the secret formula for comic effects) lies in that common denominator: the figures presented are very angry; the artists themselves always seem to be angry; so are the readers, who expect the caricatures to translate their anger into laughter. A glance at the various types of caricatures makes one realize that even within the set of publications of the same cartoonist, there is in fact a wide spectrum of humor, from coarse to subtle forms. The cartoonists also tend to alternate different frames of reference, but according to only one basic principle: they constantly create a clash between several social codes (personal thoughts versus official discourse; common sense versus official logic; private interests versus public responsibilities, etc.).

More than others, Popoli's work displays the richness of a relatively new tradition of African laughter articulated by the first generation of Cameroonian writers and humorists—Ferdinand Oyono, Ambroise Mbia, Guillaume Oyono Mbia—and subsequently deepened by popular artists like Essindi Mindja, Narcisse Kuokam, Jimmy Biyong, and Jean-Miché Kankan. He is an expert in the use of parody—a very aggressive form of impersonation, as we all know. His drawings are generally designed to deflate what he perceives to be hollow pretense, to undermine the pathos of politicians by harping on their weaknesses and contradictions.

Tex Kana's approach focuses on the critique of the political arena: the demystifying of an apparently static scene and the disclosing of the underlying transactions whose emergence highlights and transforms this surface. By choosing to concentrate his drawings on the sociopolitical crisis, he undertakes the huge task of dismantling the prevailing structures of domination—an idea that is intrinsically optimistic, since he tends to view the present as history and to promote the notion that the future will certainly be better. His jokes and anecdotes tend to have a more linear structure. His stories are constructed in such a way that there is always a single point of culmination—usually the final moment of the scenario, the last image of the cartoon. It is almost as if he chooses to privilege the mystery of his story.

On the other hand, Jean-Pierre Kenne's style tends not to rely on a single effect, but rather on a series of minor climaxes. Each image is full of meaning, and the whole story reflects the general skepticism prevailing in the country. His cartoons feature a set of characters trapped in the contradictions of the quest for freedom. Indeed, his work is a genuine rejection of the inauthenticity of African political life. His famous characters Tobias (the husband) and Mamy Nianga (the wife) represent average citizens caught in the turbulence of everyday life. For this old couple, the intractability of a so-called democratic society, the arbitrary nature of human existence, and the failure of emerging cultural frameworks to project a realizable better future yield existential despair and justify some sort of cynicism. Ultimately, Kenne advocates the celebration of the naive state of mind that would lead people not to trust the dynamics of political changes.

Because of the huge success of cartoons in Cameroon after 1991, the authorities eventually perceived the necessity to control their diffusion: first, by launching several newspapers using work from conservative cartoonists like Go'away; then, through its traditional means of coercion: between 1991 and 1993, the government used the police force to arrest editors, dismantle printing presses, harass vendors, impound magazines. This shift in media policy reveals the great concern cartoons have caused top-level decision makers.

BEYOND THE DRAWINGS:
THE ESSENCE OF SUBVERSION

The language of cartoons usually includes words like *good, bad, just, fair,* and so forth. Many puzzling questions have to be raised: What do users and readers of these words mentally associate with these words? How is the idea of justice in politics, for instance, represented? And is such a representation wholly determined by the various cultural environments from which cartoonists emerge, or are there, perhaps, as Alvin L. Golman would suggest,[14] certain innate structures that dispose cartoonists and their readership toward some specific conceptions of justice and fairness? Are there some common patterns of moral thought that are referred to by the cartoonists? Do the artists influence the way ordinary people think about moral attributes, or is it, on the contrary, a reverse correlation?

The popular success and the importance of cartoons in the national media also raise other questions: What emerges from them? What type of message are they conveying? And what lessons can we take away from such a phenomenon? Answers to these questions are complex, since they touch on various issues and several academic disciplines. Let's simply emphasize seven lessons one might draw from cartoons in Cameroon:

1. The persistence of a subversive memory in the country: Many researchers recently argued that the democratization process is failing in sub-Saharan Africa because of the lack of a "democratic culture" in those countries.[15] According to this school of thought, democracy is a function of democratic demand and democratic attitude from people. Observing that "there are very few democrats in African countries,"[16] they conclude that the collective demand for freedom is still very weak and could not sustain major institutional changes. The success of political cartoons in Cameroon and the politics of parody that emerged through this new means of communication clearly show how aware of the issues people are, how sensitive they are to decisions affecting their future, even when they are illiterate. It also shows how prudent one must be when evaluating bizarre notions such as political culture or social awareness.[17]

2. The banalization of authority and the absence of trust: Another observation drawn from the cartoons is the very high level of contempt people have toward all representatives of public authority. People in power are highly mistrusted; none of them is respected. Moreover, people seem to have exorcised their fear of dictatorship to the extent that whoever symbolizes public authority is totally discredited. This appears very clearly in representations of Biya in all the magazines.[18] By the same token, anyone who challenges the government is quickly perceived as a Messiah—beginning with the cartoonists themselves. Yet, whatever merits protesters have in challenging authority under *monocracy,* it is important to point out

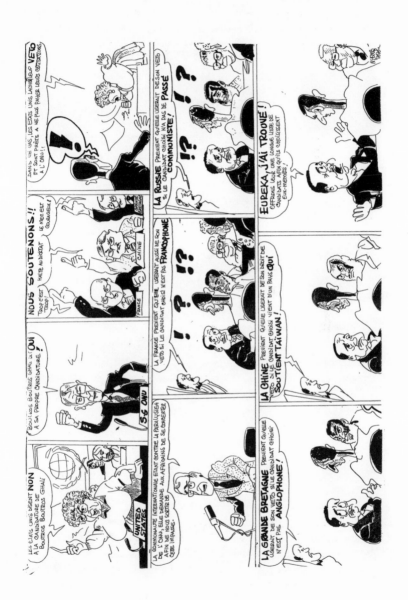

that mere opposition to a dictatorial government does not confer wisdom. As Derrick Bell has noted, "the protester is not a prophet. Confrontations with authority [only] test the legitimacy of power. They are neither right or wrong in some absolute sense. . . . The protester, while always seeking to carry the banner of truth and justice, must remember that the fires of commitment do not bestow the gift of infallibility."[19]

3. *The leadership crisis:* Even though cartoonists seem to be grateful to Fru Ndi (the main opposition leader) for his struggle for democracy and justice, they also criticize him for not taking enough initiative. In many caricatures published by papers which usually oppose the government (*Le Messager, La Nouvelle Expression*), Fru Ndi is sometimes depicted as not being fully prepared to lead the country. More generally, all the political leaders are strongly challenged in the cartoons. It is surprising, however, that cartoonists—and beyond them, most journalists and writers who analyze the political scene—never suggest (or try to explore) the reasons for that national leadership deficit. The steady deterioration of families and communities, the brutal repression of political parties for many decades, the weakness of the emerging civil society institutions (churches, unions, professional associations, women groups, etc.) where leadership qualities are usually nurtured and where traditions of resistance and organizational skills are passed on to new generations—all these possible explanations are rarely put forward.

4. *Politics as a zero-sum game:* In cartoons, politics is war. Each side (opposition/government) has its radical elements and perceives the other as the enemy. There is no rule in the game except to "kill" each other. The 1996 constitution is described as a piece of paper daily violated by the head of state; likewise the law is simply meant to serve the personal political agenda of those in power. The opposition leaders have no real recognition (formal or informal), no protection, no foreseeable future. Those Cameroonians who are suspected to have links with the main opposition party (Fru Ndi's Social Democratic Front [SDF]) are promptly sent to Coventry. Several people have lost their jobs, even within private corporations, simply because of their opinions. From the government's perspective, SDF members have no future in the country. In reaction to such treatment, the SDF staff called for civil dis-

obedience in 1992, creating a very tense political climate in the country. Thus, Cameroon's politics is characterized by permanent Manichaeism, well depicted by cartoons.

5. *The commodification of power:* After the legislative and presidential elections of 1992, many political leaders who were theoretically opposed to Biya's regime joined his government. The three opposition parties represented in the National Assembly, which then constituted the majority, chose not to work together in voting for the constitutional changes they advocated before the elections, but rather to form a coalition with the former single party; thus, the parliament became monolithic. Opposition leaders did not sign any political platform or agreement for a specific program or policy; they simply accepted being part of the same government they had challenged only a few weeks before. Because of this political recomposition, which occurred without leading to any concrete change for the population, the cartoonists developed the idea that politics was simply a race run by hungry politicians— *"la politique du ventre."* [20] Power became a sort of commodity, primarily used for raising money.

6. *The "hostage syndrome":* President Biya is usually depicted as weak, inconsistent, and lacking the necessary skills to run the country. Yet he has been in power since 1982, after six years as prime minister. The explanation from the cartoonists is simple: the president is supported by the French government (France is the former colonial power) and international financial institutions (the World Bank and the International Monetary Fund). These foreign institutions are considered to have the true power in the country. They appointed Biya as president, and since then they have been providing him with money for his Swiss bank accounts and with the financial and military support necessary for the implementation of his brutal policies. Thus, the Cameroonian people are presented as being hostages of an international mafia.

7. *Nihilism:* Finally, it also appears from cartoons that some form of nihilism is currently in ideological fashion in Cameroon. The most popular characters (Kenne's Tobias and Popoli's Tonton Doba) are generally fatalistic about everything. Even though they are surprised and disappointed with the functioning of their social life, the economic crisis, the disruptive behavior of politicians and civil servants, the brutality of police forces, and the lack of respect

they get from young people, they never think of acting differently in order to change the course of events. In spite of all the injustice and trouble they may get into, they are always willing to accommodate and to live with their diminished expectations.[21] As Cornel West observed in the African-American community, "nihilism is to be understood here not as a philosophic doctrine that there are no rational grounds for legitimate standards or authority; it is, far more, the lived experience of coping with a life of horrifying meaninglessness, hopelessness, and (most important) lovelessness. [It] is a disease of the soul."[22] Most of the Cameroonian cartoonists depict a tragic vision of modern life. Fueled by the dilemma of life in a society that has not yet reconciled Western and traditional values, the characters are victims of "the ambiguous adventure" that writers such as Cheikh Hamidou Kane and Chinua Achebe describe brilliantly in their novels.

One might say that they seem to follow James Wright's wise and humorous philosophy about life: "Well, this is the only life I have. In many ways, it's a snarled mess, but I like it."[23] However, it is unlikely that such an attitude will help the process of intellectual reconstruction so needed in Cameroon and the other African countries currently suffering from political, social, and economic crises.

CONCLUSION

These observations suggest mixed feelings and two types of impressions: first, cartoons have become a very powerful means of communication; and, second, they can help sustain the democratization process. However, given their focus on politics, their propensity to easily satisfy larger and larger shares of readership at any cost, and the relatively low level of intellectual rigor in some of the newspapers in which they appear, their final impact might be somewhat perfidious. Furthermore, in a country where freedom of speech remains a mere slogan, they also tend to amplify all the rumors, mixed signals, and "crude" information coming from the political arena. What is at stake here is not simply the construction of a new totalizing narrative in some newspapers. It is the promotion of a specific and demobilizing conception of politics, and the surreptitious elaboration of a new intellectual and sociocultural order. I suggest that the rich dialectical pictorial practice introduced by Cameroonian cartoonists is ultimately deficient, that is, not voluntarist enough to yield the intellectual rewards that one might expect from prominent social critics and producers of knowledge. Like their peers in the media business, Cameroonian cartoonists should shift their focus from the mere finger-pointing exercise that has been their main preoccupation up to now to more subtle analyses of the more profound issues facing their society. Given their impressive ability to raise social awareness, their intellectual contribution in the democratic project would be very useful in the difficult and chaotic phases ahead. It is not an easy task.

Earth and Sound
The Place of Poetry

M. Nourbese Philip

> *Cydymdreiddiad* — that subtle knot of interpenetration, which . . .
> grows in time (in people's consciousness) between a territory and
> its people and their language, creating a sense of belonging to a
> particular stretch of the earth's surface.
> —Ned Thomas, *Derek Walcott, Poet of the Islands*

> Every person belongs to his period, to his part of Time which is the
> "place" of his experience. He dwells in that part of the total fabric of
> living mankind extended through Time.
> —Maurice Nicol, *Living Time*

"You better know your place!" In the Caribbean that most often meant you had stepped out of line — as a child; less frequently, it was addressed to one's social inferiors. As a poet that caution has come to have greater significance for me — to know my "place," so that "place" becomes that *from* which, rather than *about* which, one writes.[1]

For the poet, a primary relationship is with the word. Just as important is the relationship between poet and place, and bonding with place is as essential to the poet's development as bonding between parent and infant is to the development of humans. I define "place" as that certain location in time and space where historical, social, cultural, and geographical forces coalesce and/or collide to produce the individual. Land — possession, ownership, rejection, abandonment, or merely recognition and acknowledgment of it — plays a significant part in the configuration of these forces. Without attachment to land, which encompasses more than legal ownership and entails a recognition and acceptance of belonging first to *the* land and then to *a* land, neither identification of place as I have defined it nor bonding with place is possible.

If the poet is truly bonded with place, it then forms the matrix of her work: place remains within the poet although she be in exile or never write a word about it. A rooting in place would, however, of necessity preclude the latter alternative.

True poetry — a poetry of truth — depends very much upon such a rooting in place despite the forces of displacement and alienation that prey upon most poets today. Where poets are displaced, where they lack cultural security, identification of the particular displacement or displacements is often the precursor to the identification of one's place. Displacement — from homeland, language, culture, or race; from the means of production or the product of one's labor; from one's truths or wisdoms; from a belief in one's self and one's potential; from all to which one is truly entitled — has been, and continues to be, effectively accomplished in both Third World countries and the northern metropolises. For displaced poets, the struggle and search is for that place — psychic, psychological, spiritual, economic, geographical, cultural, or historical — that is theirs by rightful belonging.

The displacements of which I speak lead often, if not always, to a disjunction in the psyche which can be, and often is, for poets and writers a source of intense creativity: displacement leads to marginality; marginality allows one a certain distance from, and lucidity of vision about, the mainstream society, which in turn allows the poet to explode the myths and lies by which such a society fuels itself. It is often also a source of tension, invaluable and essential to the creation of any work of art — a manifestation of that "paradox of literary art [which] demands a relationship of both operative distance from, and intricate inwardness with its object."[2] That operative distance is what marginality can provide. If, however, the disjunction created by displacement becomes too wide a fissure, too much creative energy may be lost and marginality then becomes a purely negative force. There is in fact a precise balance that must be maintained if marginality is to be made to work for the displaced poet.

As a displaced poet — triply displaced through race, gender, and language, and now quadruply through place — finding my place has meant an encounter with history, time, memory, and with language and its loss.

Time present and time past
Are both perhaps present in time future,
And time future contained in time past.

T. S. Eliot, *Burnt Norton*

Slavery, servitude, life as a chattel in utter displacement from
language, land, culture, religion and even family—these were the
events that defined the African's first relationship with the land in
the New World. They undoubtedly shaped that relationship after
slavery—a relationship that was to result in an extreme lack of attachment to the land. To leave the land for the city—city jobs and
homes—was often the most effective way to put as much distance
between themselves and a land that tied them to a despised past.

In the Caribbean islands, this was, oddly enough, an alienation
from the land that was shared by the white European who, despite
his ownership of the land, was in no way attached to it. His alle-
giance was to Europe—England, Spain, France, or Holland. For
the most part, he viewed the land primarily as the means by which
he gained access to a splendid life in the metropolis. If they could,
Europeans lived in London, Paris, Madrid, or Amsterdam, not in
the colonies where the overseers ruled.

Unlike the American South, no plantocracy with its discrete
culture developed; European landowners would take what they
could from the land, and heaven help them if they were forced,
through circumstance, to live in those outposts. By contrast, white
settlers of the former Dominions—Canada, Rhodesia, Australia,
South Africa—succeeded in becoming so rooted that, after displacing the aboriginal populations, they claimed to have a greater
stake in the land than the indigenous peoples themselves.

It would be the overseers, the lesser sons of lesser sons—those
who could do no better—who would settle these islands as Europeans. Their world—a tawdry imitation of life in the metropolis—
would always be and often was judged from the perspective of
the metropolis. All eyes turned toward the mother country: their
children were educated there and, if possible, settled there. It is
perhaps ironic but illustrative of this that when finally many of
these islands were being run by Black bureaucrats, these men and
women would continue to enjoy their "home" leave (to England),

initially instituted for the Englishman and his family to return "home" for extended periods of time.

It would remain for the Asian who came as an indentured worker in the second half of the nineteenth century (after the abolition of slavery) with his family, culture, and religion intact to conceive and develop a much different relationship with the land. As part of their contract of indenture, Asians were offered land at the end of their indentureship period in lieu of a return passage to India. Furthermore, the use of indentured Asians by colonial governments to reduce wages meant that Africans were essentially prevented from employment on plantations at a fair wage. Through this process of colonization, the African and Indian so learned to hate and despise each other that they became mutually displaced from each other's experience and reality. Across the chasm bounded on the one side by "nigger," on the other by "coolie," they faced each other's differences.

Bequests and Legacies

> . . . There are other places
> Which also are the world's end, some at the sea jaws,
> Or over a dark lake, in a desert or a city —
> But this is the nearest, in place and time,
> Now and in England.
>
> T. S. Eliot, *Little Gidding*

Colonizers leave many legacies, most of them unfortunate and destructive; one which they did not bequeath to the English-speaking Caribbean was that of attachment to and love of land and/or place. While the European despised the colonies — the Caribbean — his attachment to *his* land and *his* place was unstintingly nurtured and developed, so much so that we have, in the English language at least, a vast body of literature that justly merits the description "literature of place":

> There'll always be an England
> While there's a country lane,
> Wherever there's a cottage small
> Beside a field of grain.
>
> Ross Parker and Hughie Charles, *Song of Second World War*

That Blakean "green and pleasant land" of England which gives rise to that "affectionate joy in our landscape, which is one deep root of our national life and language"[3] would, in the Caribbean, produce the "poor/land/less, harbor/less, spade" of Edward Kamu Braithwaite's *The Arrivants.*

Not only was there an absence of attachment to place, but also a condemnation to wander the earth seeking a place to land. Alienation—exacerbated by the forced migration of generations of young people who grew to maturity knowing, almost simultaneously with awareness of self, that any future lay elsewhere, overseas, abroad, anywhere but "home"—was what fueled dreams, and far too many bided their time until they could leave for "big country."

Thus one grew to discount the physical environment as ever being able to offer sustenance—economic, cultural, or spiritual. One lived the promise, the hire purchase dream, the credit of elsewhere on these "stepping stone islands that skim broken waters of memories that leak into nowhere, where else and elsewhere."[4]

This environment—combined with an excellent system of education that succeeded outrageously in displacing one from an understanding of one's history, from the veracity of one's surroundings, from the importance of one's beginnings—would result in absolute and utter alienation: psychic, racial, cultural, and historical. Within such a context, attachment to land or place was impossible.

Earth and Sound

> (*Et le soleil n'est point nommé, mais son puissance est parmi nous.*)
> *Va! nous nous étonnons de toi, Soleil! Tu nous as dit de tels mensonges!*
> (And the Sun is unmentioned but his power is among us.)
> Come we are amazed at you, Sun! You have told us such lies!
>
> St. John Perse, *Anabasis*

Literature, and in particular poetry, only begins to belong to a place when the poet belongs; the poet belongs when the language belongs; the language belongs when it arises from and reflects the essence of all that combines to produce place. In this process the bond between poet and place remains indispensable. Place for the poet from the Caribbean must include language and the poet's attempts to solve the dilemma of language. At its most simple the dilemma can be resolved to an either/or dichotomy: either one writes in the demotic variant (dialect), or one writes in standard English. Within this framework, choice of one or the other is often seen as political, and much bad poetry gets written in the name of linguistic validity. The issue is, however, a more complex one. The place we occupy as poets is one that is unique—one that forces us to operate in a language that was used to brutalize Africans so that they would come to believe in their own lack of humanity. No language can accomplish this—and to a large degree English did—without itself being profoundly tainted.

The Africans in the New World, however, succeeded in transforming the leavings and detritus of a language and infusing it with their own remembered linguistic traditions. They produced what I refer to as the demotic variant of English in the Caribbean. The challenge facing the poet who is at all sensitive to language and to the issues that language generates is to use the language in such a way that the historical realities are not erased or obliterated, so that English is revealed as the tainted language it truly is. Only in so doing will English be redeemed. As a poet from the Caribbean, one can never be less than self-conscious when working in the English language.

In *Poetry of Place,* Jeremy Hooker writes that "places can be said to receive a voice, in that an actual community achieves its first public articulation through one of its members."[5] This was a reference to the poets Hardy and Clare who belong very much to the tradition of a literature of place. My concern at this point, however, is not with the literature or poetry of place, but to identify and articulate the *process* between "place and people (which) form(s) reciprocal relationships."[6] One outcome—a long term one—of this process, however, is a literature of place.

I am interested in how "our feeling flows into places, and an accumulation of feelings—historical, cultural, and personal— flows back from places into our consciousness."[7] Whether and how the poet becomes the conduit of this flow and gives voice to that "sacred knot of interpenetration which . . . grows in time (in people's consciousness) between a territory and its people and their language, creating a sense of belonging to a particular stretch of the earth's surface"[8] is bound to influence her and her work.

On the "interpenetration . . . between a territory, its people and their language," Margaret Drabble writes:

> Our language itself preserves some of the attributes of our early landscapes, and our ways of looking at them: it is no accident that Tennyson is so fond of words such as glimmer, wan, dim, ghastly, misty, dusk, chill, dreary, drooping, sodden, drenched and dewy — most of them words that have no counterparts in the brighter languages of the South — for they describe the half-tones, the melancholy, the dim wetness of a Northern world.[9]

Ten degrees north of the equator, we had, and still have, no parallel words to describe a landscape ruled, often tyrannized, by the mighty, all powerful, ever constant sun. I use these overblown adjectives deliberately because, coming from a land of almost constant sun, its qualities and attributes and one's responses to it are much more complex than one could ever garner from tourist advertisements.

One took it for granted yet avoided it; worked around it, getting as many things as possible done before midday. It was that which must not be looked at for too long; that which was not shade; that which dried the grass, bleached clothes, dried cocoa and coffee beans; that which was there when there was no rain; that which was there *with* rain and which offended when it didn't appear. Constancy, faithfulness, reliability, and relentlessness are the word associations that come to mind when I think of my primary experiences with the sun, which glowed, scorched, whitened, bleached, heated (water), and melted (pitched roads); it was that which was completely without secrets. These are words that I have appropriated in service of an experience and circumstances that have largely been defined by the pallid Northerner, unaccustomed to the sun and either seeking its tanning effects or avoiding overexposure to it. Ezra Pound put the issue another way: "Different climates and different bloods have different needs, different spontaneities, different reluctances, different ratios between different groups of impulse and unwillingness, different constructions of throat, and all these leave trace in the language, and leave it more ready and more unready for certain communications and registration."[10] Being the inheritor of many unwelcome legacies, not the least of which is a language still "unready for certain communications and registrations" that speak to my reality, I must, as a poet, make it more susceptible to that reality. Rooting the language in place (as I have defined it above) must of necessity be part of that process.

From the perspective of the African in the New World, all colonial languages are languages of destruction, not intended to engender attachment to anything except the master; all ideas of self, land, and place were, and too often still are, images from outside and abroad.

What must be done appears paradoxical: we, as poets, must so use a language whose primary purpose vis-à-vis the New World African was to destroy, exclude, deny, subjugate, or marginalize—never to affirm—so that at least we "leave a trace in the language, and leave it more ready" for our poetic legatees. If we succeed, as we must, we will have reconstructed a new language, one rooted in place. When the poet begins to see place from the perspective of one who lives within, not without, as that *from which* and not *about which* one writes, this process has begun.

Language and place must interpenetrate and allow access to each other. In this process the poet becomes the medium, the membrane through which this interpenetration occurs, so that finally a balancing of what I call the equation of language and place occurs, giving rise to that "one deep root of our national life." In "The Artist in the Caribbean," C. L. R. James wrote:

> Exceptional mastery in the medium is intimately related to the natural surroundings in which the artist has grown up, to the society in which he lives, and his national or even regional ancestry. These may or may not be directly related to the specific artistic tradition which he has inherited or encounters in his search for a mode of expression, but they most often are. . . . The universal artist is universal because he is above all national.[11]

In a more overtly political argument he continued this theme of land and place and its importance to the individual:

> An Indian living under a fig tree in India with one little piece of cloth around his waist, he can tell the British, "Get out of here, the land is

mine. It ain't much but I live here. My great-grandfather lived here.
We have lived here for a thousand years. You get out." But the West
Indian Black from Oxford, and from New York, and from Harvard—
he can't say that. You know why? Because he never owned it. He
went there as a slave. He has no sense in his head of having owned it.
So today he cannot say, "I want it back," because he never owned it.[12]

In 1983, ten years after James made that speech, and during
the aftermath of the invasion of Grenada by the United States of
America, the Antiguan writer and intellectual Tim Hector would
cite the latter statement in his analysis of the events that led inexorably to the invasion.[13] Failure to bond with land and/or place,
failure to attach one's self to it in any sense, Hector argued, was
one of the primary causes of the catastrophic outcome of the
Grenadian revolution. In the absence of such a bond, we remain
forever adrift from all lands, all places, wanderers unable to attach
ourselves truly to any one place.

A COUNTRY HERE NOT MINE

> . . . Un pays-ci n'est point le mien.
> Que m'a donné le monde que ce mouvement d'herbes?
>
> (A country here, not mine.
> What has the world given me but this swaying of grass?)
> St. John Perse, Anabasis

How does one make something, anything—a land, a language,
a history, a place in time—truly one's own and in as many senses
as possible? How does one develop a sense of belonging and identity with place as defined above? There are no easy answers, least
of all that of private ownership and control.

The poet must, often uneasily, often tentatively, find her own
unique answer to the question of place, be it through language,
through connectedness with a particular geographical locale, or
through an understanding and acceptance of a particular historical experience. There is even the possibility of possessing a land
or a place imaginatively—in the manner in which Australian Ab-
origines are said to possess their land. As poets we often create
and dwell each within our own spirit country.[14]

"Nous sommes les fils du volcan," says the Martinican poet Aimé Césaire—"children of the volcano" poised on the edge of catastrophe. The volcano, in this instance Mount Pélée, becomes the symbol, not only of those people who live in its shadow on the island of Martinique, but also of the volcanic eruption of history that brought the African to the New World:

> Et puis, j'ai un peu l'habitude de dire que si je voulais me situer psychologiquement, et peut-être situer le peuple martiniquais, je dirais que c'est un peuple *péléen*. Je sens que ma poésie est péléenne parce que précisément ma poésie n'est pas du tout une poésie effusive, autrement dit qui se dégage . . . se dégage perpétuellement: je crois que la parole est une parole *rare*. Cela signifie qu'elle s'accumule. Elle s'accumule pendant longtemps, elle s'accumule patiemment, elle fait son cheminement, on peut la croire éteinte et brusquement, la grade déchirure. C'est ce qui donne son caractère dramatique: l'éruption. Ainsi ma poésie est une poésie péléenne. En tout cas, me pensant, *c'est toujours en termes de terre, ou de mer, ou de végétal que je dessine*.[15]

Not only has Césaire rooted his work in place but he has assigned a vital role to the land, animals, and plants that belong to it.

> In fact Césaire recognizes a direct relationship between the animals and plants that make up the wildlife of Martinique and the lot of its human population. As a general rule it is the people who are called upon to heed these supposed lower beings and learn from them. . . . It is the role of Césaire, the educator of his people, to lead the people back to their true personality in order for them to see in the gesture of these plants and animals the rebellion that they should be leading against their oppressor.[16]

Attachment to and rooting in place and/or land is an issue that the Australian poet Les Murray confronts in his work, both poetry and prose. He writes:

> Australians do have strong feelings about land; I say Australians without qualification by color because this, surely, is one of the prime areas in which the attitudes of black and white Australians converge. Black activists, more than any other political group in the nation, recognize that at least some country people have a depth of love for their region, their holding, or district, which approaches that of a tribal Aboriginal for his spirit country. Having just such an attachment

for my own region, I tend to think of anyone who lacks any sense
of such a bond as an immigrant, however long his people may have
been here.[17]

By such a definition, most Caribbean people remain immigrants
in lands where they and their ancestors have lived for at least three
centuries, albeit most of it in servitude. If, as D. M. Thomas writes,
"love of country is a primary theme of any developed national culture," we displaced peoples have yet to develop our national cultures.[18]

NEW WORLDS

> We shall not cease from exploration
> And the end of all our exploring
> Will be to arrive where we started
> And know the place for the first time.
>
> T. S. Eliot, *Little Gidding*

That physical land mass of the Americas and the Caribbean, "discovered" by Christopher Columbus, is what we have come to
think of as the New World, in opposition to the Old World. For
me, however, the New World has come to encompass those new
worlds that come into being with the liberation and empowerment
of groups long alien to power—women, Blacks, native peoples,
peoples of color. The Old World has continued to exist within the
New World (traditional meaning) in the form of oppression, pre-
dilection for war, racism, and sexism. According to my definition
of New World, however, we can now truly have "new worlds"
existing within the belly of the Old World. The New World is no
longer defined by geography and history, but by certain values,
ideals, and struggles.

The New World poet is therefore in search of place which implies a context, rootedness, and wholeness which more secure
peoples and cultures take for granted. Confrontation with time,
history, self, and the obduracy of a language that at times refuses
to yield its essence; recognition of phenomena never seen before;
sightings of unidentified but recognizable objects: herein for me
as a poet lies the significance of such a quest.

What the result must eventually be—not necessarily in our generation, for we are all at work building foundations for future generations of poets—is a fundamental shift of emphasis, so that in opposition to the center, the periphery begins to be balanced. Validity of vision, poetic or otherwise, will not solely depend upon the location—be it London, New York, or Paris—of the poet, but upon the authenticity of vision, inspired and determined by relative and particular truths that are in essence universal. The result will be a poetry rooted and nurtured in place.

"You better know your place!" To know my place I have chosen to follow an often fragile thread through a labyrinth of miseducation, disinformation, and amnesia, collective and personal. I have chosen to "mine" a language—both in the sense of making it mine, as well as plumbing its depths and, if necessary, exploding it; I have chosen to excavate painstakingly the layered deposits of memory; to stalk a history busy with larger events; to lay waste the citadels of lies to find that place.

OH CANADA!

> For me there was nothing to follow but everything to discover.
>
> Magdalena Abakanowicz

The Québecois writer Max Dorsinville, in his work *Le Pays Natal*, identifies the theme of return to the *pays natal* as the distinguishing theme of all Third World literature:

> L'impératif culturel consiste en une recherche d'authenticité artistique faite de symbiose entre l'écrivain, le pays et le peuple. . . . A la lumière de ces impératifs prédiqués sur la "matière" du Tiers-Monde, une thématique nous paraît centrale dans sa littérature: celle du retour au pays natal.[19]

This return, he argues, may be real or symbolic, "animé par une double vision faite de contrastes entre des expériences vécues à 'l'étranger' et celles issues de la réalité du milieu natal." Return, even the symbolic, implies an acceptance of the *pays natal*, the land of birth, the earth, and the body. "Le retour au pays natal équivant à une acceptation de soi, mais le soi collectif s'inscrit dans la durée biologique et ontologique du pays-nature."[20]

The collection of poems *She Tries Her Tongue; Her Silence Softly Breaks* represented for me just such a symbolic return to the *pays natal*. The *pays natal* of land and of body, for, in all its aspects and with a preternatural force, the body erupted into this work. The effect of this eruption was to force upon me as a poet the awareness that the "place" of poetry was not only the Caribbean or the New World, but also, and in the most profound way, the body.

> when the smallest cell
>
> > remembers
>
> how do you
> how can you
> when the smallest cell
>
> > remembers
>
> lose a language?
>
> > Universal Grammar [21]

For many reasons, some of which are outlined above, the exported peoples of the English-speaking Caribbean have traditionally drifted toward three major areas—England, the United States, and Canada. In England, with its long and respected traditions of Commonwealth literature, the African writer of the New World is able to fit herself into an already existing tradition. In the United States, with its long tradition of African American writing, this is also possible. Writers like Paule Marshall, whose background is Caribbean, offer examples of how the African American tradition has been able to absorb the African writer from elsewhere.

What makes the Canadian situation unique is the fact that there has been no tradition of writing that is in any way receptive to the African writer. The African Canadian literary tradition—if we may call it that—is presently being formed, or rather wrested out, of the harsh and unfriendly literary culture of Canada. Furthermore, Canada's own national identity is constantly seeking to reassure itself that it exists, a condition that in turn affects the literary climate. The dominant literary and artistic culture meets the description coined by the Australian poet Les Murray in describing his own Australian culture as a "mandarin tradition": it is a tradition—CanLit—that has developed from above in the boardrooms of officialdom. For the Black writer, there has been, until very recently, nothing to follow, join, or even resist.[22] One is, therefore, constantly forced to uncover, discover, and recover one's own rootedness in "place" which oftentimes does not embrace Canada. "Nothing to follow, but everything to discover": this is how Magdalena Abakanowicz, the Polish sculptor, describes her development from tapestry to sculpting with fabric. Those words best sum up my experience as a writer of African Caribbean background and heritage in Canada.

The results of this experience are, however, not necessarily entirely negative. It is, I believe, only in exploration and discovery that something new is possible, and traditions can at times be too overwhelming. What Canada has offered is an opportunity to begin with a blank page. Terry Eagleton writes, "Great art is produced not from the simple availability of an alternative, but from the subtle and involuted tensions between the remembered and the real, the potential and the actual, integration and dispossession, exile and involvement."[23] Discovery of and rooting in place creates for me the needed counterweight to an alien culture and the tension so indispensable, whatever the outcome, to creation.

Whose Idea Was It Anyway?

M. Nourbese Philip

From fireplace to desk—up and down—round and round—first the desk, next the room, and back to the fireplace again he paces. The room is large, well appointed with furnishings that underscore and emphasize the owner's stability and comfort—even his wealth. Velvets; brocades; the gleam of polished wood; silver, even some gold—all in abundance. Before the fireplace is the rug, in all likelihood Persian, but certainly of the Orient; the intensity and depth of its colors—red, sepia, burnt sienna, beige, and black—are held in perfect balance by its intricate patterning. It muffles his footsteps, provides further evidence, if any is needed, of wealth.

The paneled walls are hung with paintings that further bespeak their owner's station in life. The fire's energy is caught and reflected in the occasional glint of gold leaf that frames the novelty and luster of the still-new medium, oil. Portraiture: a group of plump women in diaphanous clothing; still life: a bottle of wine—the darkest of green—luminescent, a glass, some fruit with the sheen of freshness still upon it, pastries . . . all eternally ready to be consumed; landscape: a hayfield and in it a hayrick silhouetted against a red setting sun; classicism: Actaeon fleeing his hounds and the beautiful Artemis; biblical: a woman—Mary Magdalene—in deep meditation, her hand upon a skull. Every genre is represented. There are, as yet, no Raphaels, Titians, or da Vincis; no Pisanellos or Caravaggios; they will undoubtably come later. For the present these are the lesser works of lesser masters, and their illusion is better served by the firelight. Their purpose is to reflect back to him who paces, as nothing else does, his solidity, his wealth, his burgeoning power—his being.

The desk, fashioned from a dark wood—mahogany perhaps—and richly colored, faces the fireplace; its polished surfaces gleam in the fire and lamp light. As befits the man who paces, it is a large desk; on it rests a globe—a Martin Behaim globe—a hymn book, a psalter, a book of arithmetic, and Ptolemy's *Geographia*.

Every so often the man interrupts his pacing to stand before the globe, and with the tip of his right index finger he sets it spinning—almost gently at first—only to increase its speed until its outlines are a mere blur. He laughs. Abruptly he uses the flat of his palm to stop the revolutions. The globe shudders and trembles under the impact of the sudden arrest.

Can we put an exact date to the man's pacing? A time? The fire and the light through the window suggest a dying day. Did he, that morning, leap out of bed with an exclamation, a shout as of surprise or discovery—of excitement? He might have echoed Archimedes: "Eureka! I have found it!" An idea that would equal Newton's discovery of the principle of universal gravitation, Galileo's discovery of the Milky Way, Copernicus's centering the motionless sun at the heart of our galaxy, the *cogito ergo sum* of Descartes. Such an idea, such a thought, such a plan that would . . . but as yet he had no idea of its enormous potential.

Who was he? A man, of course. Neither peasant nor serf—a nobleman perhaps—possibly a lord. Would a nobleman have sullied his thoughts with an idea so crass yet so utterly brilliant? Spanish, Portuguese, English, French—was he any of these things? Does it matter? He was European, undoubtably manifesting the European mind long before the word "European" would come into vogue. Some no doubt called him blessed, a genius; but generations of mothers' sons and daughters would curse him, unknown though he was, into eternity. Too many and too few would die; too many and too few would live out the diabolical plan that would change the world to come, forever. Philosophy, medicine, jurisprudence, economics—no discipline would be left untouched; anthropology and craniology—new branches of knowledge would develop to manage the unmanageable.

Was it an idea that was solely his, or were there several like him, within his own nation and without, who would serendipitously conceive and nurture the same idea at the same time? An outburst—a veritable epidemic—of synchrony; a natural effervescence within national psyches that collectively manifested itself in these isolated instances of Promethean thought?

Were they all men who had risen with the morning sun from their beds of linen sheets, laundered by the many hands of their many servants; men who had then washed themselves perhaps, dressed or were dressed—noblemen or good solid burghers, or merchants with an eye for profit? Did they then shake their wives awake and, with a quietly controlled excitement, say in unison: "Listen, my dear; *Écoute, ma femme; Oiga, mi esposa;* Listen, listen, I have an idea," or perhaps, "I had a dream . . . last night . . . a dream, *un cauchemar,* in which I saw one hundred thousand ships . . . at anchor . . . under sail. . . ."

They—these women—would have listened, as they had always listened to everything their husbands had to say, eyes widening under the import of what was told them, the brilliant simplicity of it all—seeing in their mind's eye larger houses, mansions perhaps, more servants, gold, jewels. Such an idea! And did he, did they— wives and husbands all—then embrace their children, flaxen or dark-haired, downy skin still damp and soft with sleep? Did he caress their youth, their innocence, their years not yet burdened with age, with doubt, with ideas? The infinity in their gaze turned toward history—he not saying much, but transferring to them his excitement—his sin, perhaps? Or was it merely business?

Did he not circle? No, that would come later; but did he not note the date, record it in his diary as he would have any event on his freehold estate or at his business? On such and such a day, in the year of our Lord, I conceived—no, the idea came upon me— no, I saw clearly how . . . "On the sixth day of January, A.D. fifteen hundred and thirty-five," he might have written; or if he wished to reveal his learning: *anno Domini;* or *le huitième jour d'août;* or the fourteenth day of March, fifteen hundred and two, in the year of our Lord—he could just as easily have written fifteen hundred and three, fifteen hundred and twelve, or fifteen hundred and sixteen. "I sat at my desk," he would have continued, or "I walked in my garden admiring the roses of an evening"; "I sat drinking port after dinner on the evening of . . ."; "Just before I rose from my bed . . ."; "While at prayers in the chapel . . . as the Reverend Father . . . during the *Te Deum Laudamos* (or was it the Nicene Creed?) . . . a blinding flash of light, a sound as of rushing wings or water, a low murmur, . . . almost a sussuration of voices, a clap of thunder . . . and there it was: the idea." A brilliant insight it might have been called four centuries later, like Einstein's: "mine eyes have seen . . . the fusion of past, present, and future—change."

An idea such as this could not have been nurtured amid smoke, grime, and filth—though even amid the picking and killing of fleas, ticks, and other vermin, its brilliance and luminescence would have lit up the hovel that wombed it. No, it demanded light; it demanded space; it demanded leisure.

Wheresoever it happened to have been conceived, it deserved to have been reported, recorded, annotated, copyrighted, data-banked, chiseled in stone: on the ___ day of ___, fifteen hundred and whatever, or maybe it was fourteen hundred, but certainly no later than fifteen hundred and eighteen—we know the Spanish crown sanctioned the idea in that year—and most certainly in the year of our Lord.

In today's world, an idea of such magnitude would call for boardrooms, flow charts, bottom lines, and an advertising campaign to rival those of Coke and Pepsi; its purveyors pin-striped, tailored—male and female both—blond, blue-eyed, and Christian, for that was the lynch pin of the idea: the full and dark flowering of the messianic, crusading spirit of Christianity.

> The Bishop strongly recommends that when cargoes of Negro slaves arrive in the harbour, priests should immediately be assigned to instruct them in the Christian faith and to teach them the doctrine of the Church in order to baptize them, and also to see to it that the Negroes hear Mass and go to confessions and communion.[1]

Surely the progenitor and architect of this idea—if we could identify him—should take his place alongside those who, like the Portuguese navigators, Cristóbal Colón, or Adolf Hitler, have stood in the way of history and altered it.

> It was a truly wonderful sight to see them all standing there, for some were fairly white and well-formed, some were as yellow as mulattoes, and some were as black as Ethiopians. . . . But who would have been so hard of heart as not to feel pity for them in their distress? Some lowered their tear-splashed faces, others bewailed themselves loudly and turned their eyes towards the heavens, and still others struck themselves in the face and threw themselves to the ground. There were those who sang lamentations, and although we did not understand the words, the melodies told of their great sorrow.[2]

Maybe the idea was happenstance, developed by small accretions of practice—a few here, a few there—as gradual as a meandering river gracefully yet inexorably eroding a shoreline. An idea that was merely the result of the accumulation of capital needing to expand, to create new markets:

> It is no less than four months since traders took five hundred from Cape Verde to New Spain in one boat, and one hundred and twenty died in one night because they packed them like pigs or even worse, all below decks, where their very breath and excrement (which are sufficient to pollute any atmosphere and destroy them all) killed them. It was indeed a just punishment from God that these brutal men who were responsible for carrying them also died. The sad affair did not end there, for before they reached New Mexico almost three hundred died.[3]

A phenomenon of such gargantuan proportions and scale must have been deliberately conceived—by someone, somewhere, sometime: the man stands before the globe; his arms are folded, his head lowered as if in thought. Suddenly he throws his head back, exposing a smooth and cleanly shaved white throat, and laughs again and again. When he stops he sets the globe spinning again with his finger . . . waits for the speed of its revolutions to lessen, and with a gentle motion—a caress almost—he brings the globe to a halt. Lightly, at first haltingly, he traces his right index finger down along the newly opened Indian Ocean, around—the finger moves surely now—Bartholomeu Dias's discoveries at the Cape of Good Hope, up, along the West coast, and across—now his finger is fully confident—the varnished ocean, painted blue . . . to a new world not yet discovered, but which he would help to birth.

The fire is dying now; its light reddens the outline of his robe all along his right side, bleeds onto his right cheek, painting his skin with a sanguinary glow as it embraces his head with its fiery corona. It is hard to tell in the dim light, but his eyes are blue, like the painted ocean, his hair is blond, his skin fair, and he laughs again and again.

Preface to *Testimonies of Exile*
On Territories, Tied Tongues, and Translations

Abena P. A. Busia

All my friends are exiles,

born in one place, we live in another
and with true sophistication,
rendezvous
in most surprising places—
where you would never expect to find us.

Between us we people the world.

With aplomb and a command of languages,
we stride across continents
with the self-assurance of those who know
with absolute certainty
where they come from.

With the globe at our command,
we have everywhere to go,
but home.

When I wrote that poem, I had two images at heart: the vast, limitless horizon described, and the small caged fortress place against which the horizon figures. As a world traveler my kingdom is large, but the existence of that small barricaded fortress called home reverses the size of the regions of travel; affective affiliations alter the size of the realm. The boundless world becomes a caged horizon, and the small place called home, a vast Eden closed against you. Home becomes that partially known place you belong to fiercely, but are always away from. This is the condition of exile. In reflecting on exile, despite the fact that we might be at times quite ambivalent about the terms, I keep returning to the dilemma that it is used in contexts which assume that we know where and what home is; that we know who "we" and "they" are; that we have a sure sense of place and being, centers and peripheries, to help us articulate the manifold implications of the movements of our personal and collective histories. Yet a lot of the time, when I have to think about it, I feel fragmented, bewildered by life's geographies. And those times when I don't have to think about it, I do not, in the daily routines of life, walk around torn by any sense of in-between-ness; I simply live my life.

The condition of exile both invites and precludes nostalgia. The homeland, which increasingly in the mind of a child becomes an imagined homeland, is a place not to which one will not return, but one to which one cannot return. It invokes nostalgia as an ordinary, fixed place of perpetual longing and belonging. However, the realities of having left, the reasons for leaving—political threat or persecution, economic deprivation, or war—preclude sentimental fixations.

And then there is always the other threat, the threat of that other betrayal: that your place of sojourn might actually become home . . . might actually become more familiar and easy to walk through than the place you have invested so much in claiming, in aggressively belonging to. For exiles are always in exile from somewhere, and sometimes what we become troubled by is the idea of ever relaxing that tension and acknowledging that we may have actually arrived somewhere else, and a somewhere else that has, on the whole, been kind to us.

> And we have asked for courage Not
> to belong, Not
> to identify, Not
> to regret.
> Not to confine the spaces of our souls
>   to the places of our first heartbeat
> Not to let withering umbilical cords
>   keep us parched
> making more barren
> the strangeness of our foreign homes.

No such petitions succeed, and that is a ceaseless anxiety.

Perhaps *Testimonies of Exile*[1] is an attempt to control that anxiety. I did not set out to write a collection of poems on the condition of various exiles; the poems grew individually, out of the experience of being a wandering child, a displaced young woman, a migrant academic. Only later did I recognize their relatedness. As poems they are an integral part of a more than twenty-five-year journey, signposts along the roads I have traveled since I started writing as a child. I grew up at home and in exile in five different countries spread across the globe, and thought this a common experience. I did not fully comprehend that we were in "exile" until the day of the coup that overthrew Nkrumah in 1966. It was only my parents' elation at the possibility of a return home that taught me that our sojourn had not been voluntary; by then I was thirteen years old, and had been away from home for seven years.

To my parents I owe a great debt for this gift of a sense of security in the face of all odds. Having grown up with this sense of surety in movement, it was years before I realized this was not the usual condition of life for university professors and their families, and that we were an unusual family. Still later I appreciated that we were an extraordinary family among many such families, for wherever we went, there was a community of people just like us, from all around the world, because they also could not go home. Whether in Ghana, Holland, Mexico, or England, it seemed the people we met were all people in transit who had come temporarily to rest in the place they encountered us for the short time before either we, or they, moved on.

This experience, at once exciting and potentially alienating, served as constant background to my early life. Yet my parents and my brothers and sisters and I remained together throughout all the changes. It is this unity, not merely spatial but spiritual, which became for me the dominant constant: everywhere I went, there they were; every strange experience they shared with me. And out of this otherwise ordinary drama of the shared experiences of everyday life I wrote poems to work out the uncertainties of political and spiritual exile.

> and I am a woman ravished and naked
> chanting the words of a little girl lost
> treading the edge of the waves
>
> trying to recapture . . .
>
> the dream of a virgin robed in moonlight
> reaching gestures across the waters
> singing a song of home

> I am a black man's child, still
> stranded on the shores of Saxon seas.

Seven years apart, the first time by a student, the second time by a colleague, I have been asked the same question: why do I inscribe myself in my exile poems as "a black man's child"? Why do I speak of Ghana as my *father*land so specifically? And it brings home to me always that Ghana, the Ghana of my exile condition, is my *father* land. It was because I was my father's daughter, not my mother's, that I grew up away from home. She, too, was a part of the home he carried with him from place to place, and when he passed, home is where we took him. And also, in a very real sense, the politics that led to our exiles (and we have had two) were marked by my father's role as a "founding father." To this day, the civilian traditions that oppose themselves to the increasing militarization of our country, in whatever guises, are called the Nkrumah and the Danquah-Busia traditions. So when I think of myself as an exile, I recall that it is a condition inherited from my father.

Yet even away from home, Ghana has shaped me, has shaped all of us, the brothers and sisters of those "wilderness years" to whom I dedicate this collection. We laugh among ourselves in our home that the houses in which we grew up could have been anywhere; the ways in which we were brought up, our mores and manners, the things we were taught to hold sacred, remained constant, and Ghanaian. As frequently happens, these were the values of the society upheld in the household, the values shared by our father but inculcated on a daily basis by mother. These were all Ghanaian. In terms of the social conventions and rituals of daily living under which we were raised, we might as well have been in Wenchi or Jamestown, Accra—with one singular exception: though the familiarity of history and custom may have helped inure us, in our early years, from a sense of placelessness, exile to me has become more particularly an exile from language.

Growing up, we did not speak any Ghanaian languages consistently in the household. We heard Twi, our father's language, spoken consistently between our parents. If today we are able to reclaim that tongue with any facility, it is because of that and only that. For we had no Ghanaian community, especially in those politically strained early years in Holland and Mexico. In Holland what marked us was that we were not from Suriname, and in Mexico what marked us was that we were not from the United States. But we were also not part of a Ghanaian community. In those years between 1959 and 1966, Ghanaians avoided us.

This meant for us as children that our linguistic community was anything but Twi speaking. My sister, who learned to speak in Holland, constructed sentences in three different languages at once, and suffered the frustration of noncommunication when there were not the right people around to act as interpreters for the different fragments of her sentences. But only now do I realize that her sentence structure was English. In fact our linguistic community was overridingly English, wherever it was we happened to be living. Thus, though English was spoken by only one of my four grandparents, and was not the first or even second language of either of my parents, it is the only language I am fluent in. It is the only language I have been speaking consistently all my life, and that my thoughts have immediate access to. It is the language of my dreams. That frightens me, and I pray for the day I wake up and realize I have been dreaming in Twi.

Those writers who have a mother tongue can choose which language they write in. I have not that choice. Speaking as I do now from a partial return (I have returned to Ghana on sabbatical, and am staying home for more than three months for the first time since I was a child), it is this loss that haunts me most. I am having to relearn, or claim the confidence of speaking, languages which are my own. This specific sense of loss controlled the opening and closing poems of the first two sections of my collection. My sister's illustration for "Caliban," a small figure dwarfed by a heavy tongue protruding out of its mouth and wrapping itself around the throat in a choke hold before falling to the ground, is how I feel. I cannot unburden myself as yet from the anxiety of language as legitimacy. What after all is it that makes us "from" somewhere if we have not lived there and do not speak its languages?

> This tongue that I have mastered
> has mastered me;
>
> has taught me curses
> in the language of the master
>
> has taught me bondage
> in the language of the master

I speak this dispossession
in the language of the master

Thus I felt it especially keenly when one major review accused me of not being a legitimate African poet because the only poem in a Ghanaian language in my collection is merely a "translation." It did not seem to matter to the reviewer that I had created the poem out of the circumstances of my own life. I had gone to some length to detail, in an explanation he clearly did not think it worth the trouble to read, that without the peculiar parentage I have, the poem would not be possible. It is a poem written in Twi, my father's language, which is a play on words on the name of the goddess as life-giving mother in my mother's language. And that, far from translating some preexisting incantation, what I was doing was translating myself. "Mawu/Mawo" is my attempt at rebirth and liberation.

Mawu/Mawo	Mawu/Mawo
mmmmmmmmmmm	mmmmmmmmmmm
mmm mmm mmm	mmm mmm mmm
mm mm mmmmm	mm mm mmmmm
mmm mmm a	mmm mmm a
mma mma aa	mma mma aa
maaa	maaa
mmmmmmaaaaa	mmmmmmaaaaa
maaa	maaa
maaaa	maaaa
mama mama	mama mother
ma ma	I, I've
wo	given birth
ma ma wo	I, I've given birth
mama ma wo	ma, I've given birth
mama ma wo	mama, I've given birth
ma wo	given birth
mawu	mawu
mawu!	mawu!
mawu ae! ma wo	oh mawu! I've given birth
ma wo	I've given birth
ma wo	I've given birth
mmaa wo	women give birth
mmaa wo	women give birth
mmaa wo	women give birth

mama mawu	mama mawu
mama mawu	mother mawu
mama mawu	mother mawu
a wo	has given birth
a wo	given birth
mawu a wo	mawu has given birth
mawu a wo	mawu has given birth
mawu a wo wo	Mawu has borne you [*sing.*]
mawu a wo wo	mawu has borne you [*sing.*]
mawu a wo mama	mawu has borne mama
mawu a wo mama	mawu has borne mama
mawu a wo mu	mawu has borne you [*pl.*]
mawu a wo mu	mawu has borne you [*pl.*]
mawu a wo mu ma	mawu has borne masses of you
mawu a wo mu ma	mawu has borne masses of you
mawu a wo mmaa	mawu has borne women
mawu a wo mmaa	mawu has borne women
mawu wo mmaa	mawu bears women
mawu wo mmaa	mawu bears women
mawu wo mmaa	mawu bears women
mawu wo mmaen	mawu bears nations
mmmmmmmmmmmm	mmmmmmmmmmmm
A!	A!

Nevertheless, my explorations of "the paradox of exile" have been done, with that one exception, in English. All of us here, whatever the circumstances of our imprisonments and exiles, share a common language. This can be a vibrant condition.

> We have lived that moment of the scattering of the people—
>   Immigrant, Migrant, Emigrant, Exile,
>   Where do the birds gather?
> That in other nations, other lives, other places has become:
>
> The gathering of last warriors on lost frontiers,
> The gathering of lost refugees on lasting border-camps,
> The gathering of the indentured on sidewalks of strange
>   cities,
> The gathering of émigrés on the margins of foreign cultures.
>
>   Immigrate, Migrate, Emigrate, Exile,
>   Where do the birds fly?

In the half-life, half-light of alien tongues,
In the uncanny fluency of the other's language,
We relive the past in rituals of revival,
unraveling memories in slow time; gathering the present.

Immigrant, Migrant, Emigrant, Exile,
Where do the birds fly, After the last sky?

The last line of "Migrations" is, like us as a community, a migrating line. I love it because it represents, for me, both our dilemma and the ties that bind us. This line is a misquotation of Mahmud Darwish's "where should the birds fly after the last sky," from his poem "The Earth Is Closing in on Us." I first heard it quoted correctly by Homi Bhabha in the opening paragraph of his article "DissemiNation," but his source had not been the poem itself but its use in the title of a book by Edward Said. Thus a line from a poem by a Paris-based exiled Palestinian poet gives rise, in New York, to the title of a fellow exile's book. This work then has resonance for an Indian migrant living in London, whose quotation of that same line is heard by myself, a Ghanaian migrant exile who used to live in England but, though officially resident in New Jersey, was at the time sojourning in Los Angeles. For me those words touched a chord which inspired yet another poem. Such is the condition of our lives. We learn to translate dividing borders into a diaspora community, to transform a lack of language into diaspora literacy. Such literacy requires shared knowledge, a knowledge of histories, continuities, and discontinuities which only our storytellers in their many guises can give us:

ACHIMOTA: FROM THE STORY MY
MOTHER TAUGHT ME

There is a place between Accra and Legon hills
where they built the famous school.
Everyone thinks of that
today
when the name Achimota
is heard.
Yet the new school takes the name
of the place
but does not reveal what that name means.
The name is A-chee-mo-ta.

It is a forest still, beside the school,
the roads, the railways, and the streetside markets.
But the forest came first,
and has always been there.
The trees still stand,
but they do not speak the history they have seen,
A-chee-mo-ta, no, not at all.
And only the name remains the reminder
of who we are, what we have been,
and what we have been through.

Sometimes it seems we are forgetting,
but so long as there are people alive who remember,
we will remember the meaning:
Here we came, fleeing
to a place of shelter,
escaping the chains and lash
we would not submit to,
and these trees hid us.
So, when traveling through
here, searching,
you do not call
by name
in this place.
A-chee-mo-ta,
you do not call,
by name,
out loud,
no, not here.

The "underground railroad" had its precursor,
long, long before, on this side of the world.
No one will tell you that today.
We too have been taught forgetting.
We are schooled in another language now
and names lose their meanings except
as labels.
We are being taught forgetting.
But some remember still
Achimota and its history
a forest, and its meaning—
the place, and its silence.

I have my mother to thank for this story and many others, for finally claiming her courage and becoming a great teller of life and life-giving stories. My sense of what it means to have a history and customs, located in specific places of grand meaning, is as much hers as father's. And their commitment taught me that we who have survived to have homes and lives anywhere must live in constant remembrance of those of our communities, through time and around the world, who did not so survive: the freedom fighters and activists, the refugees and other exiles, the disappeared and the dead.

But what is it that makes us write, what is it that makes writing a mechanism for and a celebration of survival and triumph? I don't know. I don't know if any artists can ever rationalize the wellsprings of their gift. Writing poems is the one thing I know I have been doing consistently all my life for as long as I have been able to write. I have most of the poems I have written since I was nine years old. I do know that I owe three people in particular thanks for the confidence to write. From a virtually unknown Englishman, and one of the most extraordinary teachers I had in a life full of wonderful teachers, I learned that we all have permission to try. Mr. G. W. Snelling, for twenty-five years headmaster of Standlake Primary School, taught me that poets are ordinary people too, and that all of us, even ten-year-old Ghanaian girls far away from home, have poems in us, about every subject under the sun.

And I thank my late father, my first teacher, for sharing with me his love for poetry by reading to me, from as early as I can remember, the poems, psalms, and Methodist hymns which sustained him. How great this influence was, again, I did not realize until very late. About a decade ago I was asked to speak about what in my life influenced me to write. I thought, in my head, that though my father had taught me my love of hymns and poetry, through the "dead white men" we all study I had not inherited a love for his favorite, Alfred Lord Tennyson. (My tastes growing up inclined more to T. S. Eliot, Gerard Manley Hopkins, and Dylan Thomas, and Keats's ode "To Autumn.") Then I faced the significance of this first collection, *Testimonies of Exile;* the two poems father used to read to me aloud, over and over again, were Tennyson's "Ulysses" and "The Lotus Eaters," his two poems on exile and loss of home. I had heard more than I knew.

Yet, always, living remains an everyday, ordinary condition. We continue the rituals of habit, in the execution of the dailiness of living. We don't, for the most part, give up on life—and we do build communities, somehow, wherever we are. I wanted my collection to reflect that also; so finally, a brief word on the remaining cycles. My second cycle, "Incantation for Mawu's daughters," is my testimony to the people, women mostly, who have been my companions through the years and to the late woman-warrior Audre Lorde. In addition to my family, friends have been my security, and I am blessed with many. For example, other than my sister, I have a school friend who every day for nearly thirty years, despite the boundaries of oceans and continents and several migrations, has always known on an almost daily basis exactly where— on which spot of earth—I am. That sure sense of sharing—sharing stories about places, events, loved ones—is what helps keep us whole and laughing.

LIBERATION

We are all mothers,
and we have that fire in us,
of powerful women
whose spirits are so angry
we can laugh beauty into life
and still make you taste
the salt tears of our knowledge.
For we are not tortured
anymore;
we have seen beyond your lies and disguises,
and *we* have mastered the language of words,
we have mastered speech.
And yes
we have also seen ourselves.
We have stripped ourselves raw
and naked piece by piece, until our flesh lies flayed
with blood on our *own* hands.
What terrible thing can you do to us
which we have not done to ourselves?
What can you tell us
which we didn't deceive ourselves with
a long time ago?
You cannot know how long we cried
until we laughed

over the broken pieces of our dreams.
Ignorance
shattered us into such fragments
we had to unearth ourselves piece by piece,
to recover with our own hands such unexpected relics
even we wondered
how we could hold such treasure.
Yes, we have conceived
to force our mutilated hopes
into the substance of visions
beyond your imaginings
to declare through pain our deliverance:
So do not even ask,
do not ask what it is we are laboring with *this* time;
Dreamers remember their dreams
when they are disturbed—
And you shall not escape
what we *will* make
of the broken pieces of our lives.

And, finally, the last book is a testament of faith. It is difficult, and certainly unfashionable, to talk about faith if you are not a professional faith talker—a minister or priest, a rabbi, an ayatollah, monk, or theologian. Yet faith and intellect, faith and family, faith and politics are not mutually exclusive, though we may enter the pretense that we believe them to be because it is easier, at least among many in the West, to separate ourselves from "fundamentalists" and hide among the disbelieving, or to demur with the half-believing than to take a stand among the faithful, of whatever calling. Yet for me, my defense of a nuclear-free world, my commitment to liberation struggles, my stand as a feminist, my practice as a teacher, my actions as a friend are all fueled and informed by my faith as a Christian. To walk as a Christian is a constant challenge, on a daily basis, at home or away, in love or in trouble, at peace or facing war, in the classroom or the kitchen.

I remember once as a teenager, in those awful limbo years when, having finally realized what it meant to be in "exile," I wanted so very terribly to be "home," hearing a particular sermon. The burden of it was that there was nothing we had to undergo which the Lord had not done first. And just as my little rebellious, wanting-to-be-a-homeless-martyr heart resisted this lesson, the minister gave his example: the very first thing that happened to Christ, at "two years old and under," was exile to Egypt.

For me, learning to transcend exile has been a faith walk. No aspect of this journey is simple or has facile solutions, and I thank those people and congregations who have through the years walked with me. My stand at the altar is in response to all these calls, and though it is no easy walk, I know I need not take it unaccompanied.

SERMONS FROM RIVERSIDE

i. Choices

At the moment of hesitation before the knife fall,
we are both Abraham and Isaac
trapped:

This razor's edge of human choice
is all we ever had.

"The promise of life's magnificence" is perplexing:
There never was an original innocence,
only this original contradiction;

This world is our embattled Eden
of eternal seconds of human decision
on the tips of our outstretched hands.

And every movement becomes a choice,
and each choice a bewildering journey
with no clear sign-post, save one;

To face Mount Sinai all footsteps stumble, through
the wilderness of Sin.

And the sound of the serpent's hiss,
or the bleating of the ram in the thicket,
has never penetrated the silence of Gethsemane.
With no preordained sign we make the resolution
to stretch out the fingers, to pull back the hand,
to pull back the fingers, to lower the hand.

Through Faith
before the Promise dies, the Lamb cries
and astonished children climb off the altar.

On Oppression, Prison, and Exile—Poems

Kofi Anyidoho

SANTROFI

for Jack Mapanje

I.
Santrofi   Santrofi   Santrofi

against persistent rumors
of your midnight
death by stabbing squad
I must compose this suicide note
in stupid solidarity with a foolish friend.

Like you   my mind is burdened
with ancestral indiscretion.
The slightest lie
gives us indigestion
so we must go gathering dangerous rumors
letting our minds loose on laxative
soiling popular images of decent people.

They say it's sad for a full-grown
Man with children who call him
Papa   to stagger home in tears.

But Santrofi   I couldnt help maself.

When I heard they say they say
they picked you up at deaf of night

I could not hold on to my pride.

I broke up in fears   I crumbled
home sobbing through my tears.

II.
But then the children started wailing.

So I laughed.   I laughed I told them
I was rehearsing my part in a difficult play.

So they laughed. The children laughed.
But then they asked to see my script
so they could cheer and prompt me on.

Santrofi   I had to explain
there was no script to our play.

We act it out
by daily dress rehearsals
of the various things we shouldnt do.
The drama unfolds backward
with every step we take forward.
The plot quickens and complicates
with unexpected & twisted
reenactments of scenes from future dreams.
We are hurled into false resolutions
leaving us still entangled in strange
subplots
forever groping for redirection
back into our main
conflict with its knotted
quest for a breath of air free of all toxic substances.
We grow breathless yearning
for escape from suffocating assemblies
of shameless men with their poisonous speech
persuading us all to die once more
and die all over again.

But Santrofi   against
their kind offer

of death by stabbing squads
we must insist on our dream
of life   our dream
of life   our dream
of life among the burning grass
   life among the riding storms
         among the desert sands
of life among the thunderbolts.

III.

Santrofi   Santrofi   Santrofi

you remember how
often I came for you at dawn
our shotguns all loaded and ready
for the ancestral partridge hunt?

We were such great badshots
our bullets run away from our game.

But we always came back home.
We always came back home.
Back home to our meal of modest
corn and fish and life.
We always came back home.

So when your Maimouna
in a voice grown eerie with sudden pain
told of how
some nervous men with tangled beards
came for you & walked you
into the deepness of their night
fiercely clutching stolen rifles

I have been wondering
what BigGame hunters club
you may have joined on secret oath.

I have listened every night and every dawn
for the lonely echo of the hunter's call

But all I hear is this silence
deeper than the liar's yawn.

IV.
Santrofi   Santrofi   Santrofi

so now   I am guilty.   Guilty
of harboring doubts and fears

doubts for their smiles
fears for your mind
fears for your life
fears fears fears for those joys
we dared to dream for our land.

I suppose they'll come with pincers
probing our tongue for unspoken curses.

And we wish we could hold our breath forever.

But once too often we've held
our doubts and found unspeakable
terror in silence and patience
when marvelous blockheads
took up megaphones and broke
eardrums with philosophical obscenities
and baboons in mufti & native sandals
made menacing speeches from platforms

borne on shoulders of those who chose

patience and silence in spite of doubts
silence and patience in spite of doubts

in spite of bleeding fear
in spite of leaking hurt

silence and patience in spite of doubts
patience and silence in spite of doubts.

Santrofi   Santrofi   Santrofi.

V.

Santrofi   Santrofi   Santrofi

you remember
how once upon our doubts
they planted letters in the press

and in the names of mythical voices
they painted our names with dung and slime?

Santrofi   Santrofi   Santrofi

VI.

Santrofi   Santrofi   Santrofi

Today   the fierce young ones
who broke the dawn with smoking guns
are now become Youthful Elders of State.

How come
        they see so much guilt
        in every elder's eyes?
        and hear so much betrayal
        in every intellectual's sneeze?

        They bypassed warnings
        and took huge loans
        only to import
        halfwits from
        harvard & princeton
        halfwits & gifted inventors
        of designer deaths in manmade seasons of drought.

Santrofi   Santrofi   Santrofi

        you must lay ambush at hellgate
        and watch them trespass into limbo

and lead them stranded and lost
among the ghosts of false prophets.

and do us a favor   will you?
Throw a little red pepper in their eyes.
And do not wipe away their tears.

Angels may come and offer you QueenDoms
But whatever you do
Do not wipe away their tears. *Eh! Santrofi!!*

BAYONETS

BEFORE the season of the Bayonet
there was the season of the Hoe
a season of the soul's harvest:
We grew wonder-eyed standing
humbled before the miracle
of the giant Oak locked deep
down within the tiniest mystery seed.

In those seasons of our Soul's Harvest
there were such fires in our eyes.
Our spirits flowered and petaled
into hues of faintest rainbows
offering new and newer images __
of dreams we could with ten fingers
mold into things and thoughts and hopes.

THEN   they came with BullDozers.
And then   the ArmoredCars   dressed in camouflage.

NOW   we plant grenades in backyard farms
Harvesting Coffins
in showers of Bullets and FirePower.

They pick our flesh on Bayonets.

Across cold muzzles of Guns
They break our sleep in two
Give one half to CannonBlast
Toss one half into silence deeper
Than Volcano's bleeding core.

There will be showers at SunRise
And storms at SunDrown.
Bones shall sprout tendrils more verdant
Than loveliest GreenMamba.

Rivulets of venom shall water our fields
Restoring this soil to ancestral Fertile Time.

GUILT

i.
And they opened up his wound.
Polished its tender surface
With alligator pepper
And onion paste.

But his soul was large
Enough to hold his hurt.

Grasping tight
To sharp painpoint of breath
He threw them back that final
Look
Whose depths they feared to explore.

A Look suspended
somewhere

Between surprise and wonder
Carefully balanced
Between desire to
Hope
And the need to
Believe
That fear   sometimes
Is a noble retreat from
Doom.

ii.

He swore he would be Human   *If*
Only they would let him   *Be.*

But they hanged him all the same.

Except that   even in death
They could not look him in the face.

There were such questions
On lips of this corpse
Whose memory survives life survives death.

The LawMakers don themselves
in weeds thick enough
To parry the thorniest Question Mark.

The HangMen gather
Their courage around their fear
Assuring themselves in whispers
Even they themselves cant hear:

> *It really was a duty by The Law.*
But they hanged him all the same.
And they couldn't look him in the face.
But they hanged him all the same.

NOSTALGIA

Above all   I shall forever
lament the wisdom
of those many many

Friends who disinherited their Souls
And chose the misery of alien Joys.

trapped in circles among SnowFields
their spirits freeze   and thaw   and Frost
with constant fickleness of NorthernWinds.

Once too often
they converge in smoky PartyRooms
drinking hard   to prove
a point only they   can see   can feel
arguing endless justifications
for a choice sadly made.

Between their dreams of Fame
Their hopes of instant Wealth
the nostalgic self moans its way
through MidNight Storms
into DawnNightmares

reaching into   distances   silences . . . .

*Memories alone are not enough SoulGuide
Into Futures filled with many Absences.*

Through the Bars
The Prison Experience in Poetry

Dennis Brutus

It is a special occasion for me to come back to Northwestern. I used to be on the faculty here, and it is really a very pleasant experience to come back. We did all kinds of things while I was here. Some of you may remember that we twice hosted the annual conference of the major organization in the field of African literature in this country, the African Literature Association, which was formed in Texas in 1975. I notice that in my absence things have been happening: we now have the Institute for Advanced Study and Research in the African Humanities, and I am delighted to be associated with it. So it is in many ways a kind of return for me, and a return that gives me a good deal of satisfaction, particularly in realizing that things have not stood still, that there has been constant forward movement since that time.

In the interest of honesty, I should say that I was not always very popular at Northwestern. I had a bad habit of saying controversial things, and I'm glad you don't mind that. I am alerting you now that I propose to say a few more controversial things. Our focus is on poetry, it is on exile, and it is on prison. And so I spent some time trying to think of things that might be new and insightful which would contribute to a better understanding, a better perception of what we mean when we talk about exile and prison, and the way these metaphors function both in terms of one's literary life and then in the realm of one's psyche. So I'm going to do a couple of things: one is very rapidly to stress the importance of the image of prison—and prison bars—in work in general but also in my own work, and touch on maybe one or two highlights, the essence of prison as I experienced it; another is to go from that to correct one of the misconceptions arising from it. Given the opportunity to address my own work, it seemed to me a good occasion to touch on one or two misreadings or misconceptions in the hope that it will be helpful to you. Then I will move on to look at the contemporary South African situation as someone who has experienced exile and imprisonment there. And finally I will try to draw it all together and put the South African situation into the larger global context.

I was pleased to see that your material for the conference quotes me as saying something which has always seemed to me important and perhaps more important today than ever before: "I have no problem with the statement that the artist should not merely depict the world but should transform it." I speak to you in the aftermath of your electoral debacle and on the eve of the meeting in Washington where the United States Congress will decide whether to move forward into a far more significant involvement in the global economy. So to talk about transforming the world seems to me a very significant comment to make at this time. I should remind you that the experiences of banishment, of exile, of political imprisonment—none of these is new, of course. Some of them are centuries old. The Roman empire had a special legal structure by which you could be banned; you were banned from bed and board and you were banished to the farthest reaches of the empire. And if you remember your Shakespeare, you know poor Romeo was banished—indeed that's what that whole tragedy was about: the fact that he was banished after that unfortunate killing. And you think of Spanish literature and that marvelous hero El Cid—he was banished from bed and board and no one was permitted to give him water or warmth; he was not allowed to sit beside any fire.

So these institutions are old, but they have achieved a new relevance in our own time. I think it was Aliko Songolo who pointed out that in South Africa we had a process called banning. In Zaire and in other parts of Africa you could also be banned, which meant that you were silenced; or you could be banished, as Winnie Mandela was to a remote part of the Orange Free State (one of those little ironies of South Africa: Orange *Free* State). And of course people like myself were banned and therefore silenced. It was illegal for me to write not only poetry, but also anything that might be published—such was the extent of my banning order.

Let me address one of those little points of contention straight away. In South Africa it was debated whether I was exiled or not exiled, and in fact even now you can make up your own mind about it. Let me give you the circumstances and then you can decide if it was exile, which is what *I* think it was, or something else, which the government insisted it was. When I came out of prison in 1965, my home became my prison: I was placed under house arrest for five years. I had been a journalist briefly, but I was then given an order which made it a crime for me to write, which meant that even sitting at home and trying to earn a living by writing became impossible. It was of course illegal for me to have visitors, and that meant also that my family members were unable to have visitors since any visitor *they* had could accidentally say "hi" to me and that would be a criminal act. So, being unable to earn a living of any kind, I was reduced for a while to living on charity. But this, I'm sure you know, is a very humiliating situation to be in. And to ensure that I did not get any visitors (this was one of those little ironies), there was a Volkswagen van parked permanently outside the house so that anybody who entered or left could be observed. They changed watches at eight-hour intervals so they had twenty-four-hour surveillance. All that was very annoying. One last touch: though it was illegal for any banned person to communicate with me (of course this is one of the banning orders), periodically someone who was an ex-prisoner would be sent to me with a request for help or with a message from Mandela or whatever it might be. We had a whole series of pretexts for me to meet with people, and any one of them could have led to my being reimprisoned. We need to be aware of this complex of circumstances. I was forced into total dependence on charity. It was impossible to go on living in South Africa with the constant possibility of being imprisoned; for any one to meet with me was a criminal act. This is one way in which people can be exiled, if you like, by circumstance rather than by direct order of exile. Of course, at the airport in Johannesburg I signed an agreement that if I returned to South Africa I would go to prison without trial. Surely I am justified in using the term "exile."

The other thing I wanted to stress initially was how permanent the image of bars is in the South African prison. One is constantly aware of the bars and how they separate you from the rest of the world. So that it's not enough to think of prison bars as mere metaphor. Even now when I see one of those old western movies, and I see the prison doors open and the bars clank, the image is instantly the same one I had on Robben Island. And so I'll read a little from one of the poems I wrote on Robben Island:

it was a barred existence;
one did not need to look at doors or windows
to know that they were sundered by bars.

One was constantly aware of this image, and I make the point because I'm pleased that in this workshop there has been awareness that the bars are metaphorical but also, in a very real sense, physical.

I want to pass on to some things that seem to have been misunderstood or misread in my work—and one that I am particularly embarrassed about; so this is a kind of public confession. If you know "Letters to Martha" and some of my other poetry, you will know that some of it focuses on homosexuality and on gays. I am aware that there are people who are gay who resent my work because they find in it an absence of sympathy for people whose sexual orientation is different from mine. So, with your permission, I would like to make a couple of points about that. One, I came out of a Catholic environment, educated at a little mission school, and I'm quite sure you know what that means in terms of a fairly rigid morality. Looking back now, I have some uncomfortable recollections. Fortunately, I was so innocent that I didn't know what was happening around me, but I have to say there were priests and people in the choir of whom *now* I would be extremely suspicious. But at that time I was too simple-minded to know what was going on around me. But I admit there is a hostility toward people who are gay or lesbian that is reflected in my poetry. But I want to add two other considerations which I hope will mitigate it. One, I'm talking about sexual relationships in prison, which are really an exercise of power. They are about dominance: they are about a man cultivating several young prisoners who then become his harem and are used as an image of how macho he is; this is what makes him tough in prison. And, most seriously, the systematic use of sexual assault as a technique of domination—not only of domination but of demoralization. This was a strategy used against political prisoners, a method of forcing them into submission. What I am speaking about is sex as a technique of power.

In "A Simple Lust" or "Letters to Martha," sixth in the series of postscripts, I write of a young man in the cell adjoining my cell. We are both in the section of the Island which is a maximum security section, and we're both in what is called "isolation" as opposed to "solitary": in solitary you're put in a totally dark cell and you see no one; in isolation you're merely separated from the other prisoners. And I hear this young man being beaten every night. I hear him crying out. I also know that he is not being given any food, that when they deliver the food along the corridor in the cells—they will bring me my coffee and my dry bread, my potatoes, my mealies—they will skip his cell. And so he's being starved into submission, and he's being beaten into submission. You have a composite of these pressures being applied on him. I'll read the poem rather than attempt to develop it any further:

> A studious high-school boy he looked
> As in fact I later found he was.
> Bespectacled, with soft curved face
> And with drawn protected air
> And I marveled at him, envied him
> So untouched he seemed to be
> In that brutal, hammering atmosphere
> But his safety had a different base
> And his safely private world was fantasy
> From the battering importunities of fists
> And the genitals of sodomites he fled.
> In a maniac world he was safe.

And I didn't really understand what was going on until the day I saw him in a straitjacket being carried out on a stretcher, and I understood that he'd gone mad . . . that his way of escaping the reality of the prison was to escape into a fantasy world where he didn't even know what was happening to him. So I'm talking about a very particular form of homosexual relationship which in fact becomes a political instrument—an instrument of domination.

We can turn from that, I assume, to something else. When I was in Johannesburg earlier, chairing an arts festival at the Civics Center, I met with some very peculiar questions from some of my audience. Most of them had never heard of me because of course for a long time I was nonexistent in South Africa—I'd been banned out of existence. It was a crime to quote me or to print my photograph in the paper. In any case, the questions I got were very odd;

but looking back, from several different portions of the audience, I got the same question. And only afterward did I understand what they were driving at.

There's a rather peculiar notion in South Africa today, promoted by former diplomats, especially in the old apartheid government, that the change in South Africa was the result of a miracle, that the change in South Africa was the result of a miraculous change of heart; that it really had something to do with divine intervention—a little like Saul, no doubt, on the way to Damascus: suddenly being knocked off his horse and seeing light. So people in the audience would ask me, "Don't you feel it was a miracle?" and I would hesitate; and then someone else would say "What was your experience in prison? How strong was religion for you in prison?" and so on; and they were all really driving at the same point—which I was supposed to confirm—about this miraculous change. I had to tell them, "Look, I was at the universities of the United States, organizing sit-ins and protests and getting the American universities to divest and take their money out of South Africa. I don't believe in that supernatural explanation." But they would keep at me, and it is true that I went through a period of profoundly religious experience in prison. But looking back on it, it seems to me that, if anything, religion did me more harm than good in prison. I was visited in November that year, and those of you who are good Christians will know that November is also the month of the Holy Souls, those who are suffering in purgatory. One of the things you can do on earth is suffer on their behalf, okay? So here I am in prison feeling I ought to do *something*—Heaven knows I was doing enough, but here I was thinking I ought to do more. Now, I'm allowed one visit every six months, and I'm due to get a visit from my sister-in-law Martha who's married to my brother (Martha of course is the one in "Letters to Martha"). So poor Martha gets on the ferry and comes all the way to Robben Island to see me, and I refuse to meet her because I feel I'm making a sacrifice—you know, for the sake of the Holy Souls, getting them out of purgatory, and so on. Martha, of course, is hopping mad about this, having come all the way to the Island . . .

But while I was there, I was put into isolation and I had a guard assigned to me to make sure I talked to no one. He would be outside the window whistling. And he always whistled the same tune, out of key of course, but it was from a movie called *Never on Sunday*, which is about a Greek prostitute who entertained her customers every day of the week but never on Sundays. So here I am listening to this tune night and day, it is getting into my head, and I'm beginning to get hallucinations in this cell—to the point where the paint on the wall begins to assume the shape of faces. I look at the floor, the concrete floor, and there are faces staring at me out of the floor, and eventually even my food—the crushed corn in my plate—I'm afraid to eat it. I'm going through a genuine hallucinatory process. Eventually I sense that the devil has entered me, lodged in my gut, and is driving me crazy.

Imagine all of this happening when you're alone in your cell: you can't even relate it to someone else who would help you to recover a sense of reality. So I go through this experience. I don't want to go into it, but they forced me to talk about it in Johannesburg with this whole religious business. I ended up attempting suicide: twice I slashed my wrists with the stones that I'd been breaking in the stone-breaking section with Mandela and Sissulu and the other people there. Anyway, I came out of this and I wrote a poem about it. Apart from the religious question, after I came out of prison, by great irony, I was invited to Greece to organize a global campaign for the cultural boycott of apartheid. And the woman who chaired the conference was a very famous actress who was now the minister of culture in Greece—the same woman who had been the star of this movie *Never on Sunday*. So there's another connection. Here's the poem:

> When we shook hands in the Athenian dusk
> it closed a ring that had opened twenty-four years before
> when a wisp of off-key melody had snaked into my gray cell,
> whistled by a bored guard in the sunlit afternoon outside:
> it circled the gray walls like a jeweled adder,
> bright and full of menace and grew
> to a giant python that encircled me, filling the cell
> then shrank and entered me where it lay
> coiled like my gut, hissing sibilantly
> of possession;
> twice I breathed death's hot fetid breath
> twice I leaned over the chasm, surrendering
> till some tiny fiber at the base of my brain

protested in the name of sanity and dragged me
from the precipice of suicide that allured
with its own urgent logic

Our hands meeting, uncordially, your gaze
quizzical, perhaps affronted
sealed a circle in the gathering dusk,
like the ring of dark waves advancing
on the island's jagged shore
and the dark enclosure of wire
whose barbs are buried in my brain.

That's part of a longer sequence, but you can see I'm trying to confront this question of religious experience. And I want now to move on quite rapidly, perhaps unwisely, but I want to talk about what happened in Johannesburg because it brings us up to the present and into the future. I shared in a panel in which we discussed the creator-act with people like Mbulelo Mzamane, and they talked about something that I found very interesting. They said they were encountering an "orthodoxy of reconciliation." I said, "What on earth is this?" And they said, "Look, we're being told to forget the past. We mustn't even write poetry about our experiences, or short stories. We must look forward into this new, unblemished future of hope. And we shouldn't be reminded. We don't want to be reminded." They were being told this by people who saw themselves as some kind of cultural connoisseurs who were telling the writers what they ought to be writing about. And Mbulelo said it's not only this orthodoxy of reconciliation; he complained that he found a conspiracy of silence about the past, that people no longer wanted to talk about the past. I'm glad to say that there were people who said bluntly they did not intend to be told what they could and could not write; they were not going to accept this orthodoxy now being preached that you shouldn't get out of line.

Now two things happened in the audience on the various evenings. One evening I had a great time with people like Linton Kwesi Johnson, who had been brought in from London, and other rap poets. I was chairing the session. I was told, "Well, you don't have to read poetry. It's alright, we'll let the other people read poetry." But I decided I had to get my oar in as well. And the audience was complaining that there's very little literature dealing with women and the contribution of women to the struggle, which had been a very significant contribution. I said, "Well, it just so happens that I have a poem about the women. Since nobody else has anything else about the women, maybe I should read this one." I dedicated it to women like Dulcie September, who was the representative of the African National Congress (ANC) in Paris, and Ruth First, who was the editor of the journal that I wrote for. She was banned but she continued editing, and I was banned but I continued writing. Dulcie September was killed one morning as she was opening the door of her ANC office in Paris. She turned around and someone with a gun put five bullets in her face. She died instantly. And Ruth First, in Maputo, Mozambique, received a parcel in the mail at her office where she was lecturing at the university; it looked like a book—it was a bomb instead—blew her head off and she died right there in her office. These are some of the people whom I refer to in the poem:

ABAFAZI

Where the shining Tyumie River
winds down through the
Amatola Mountains, blue—
shadowed in their distances
along the banks stand miles
of waving corn, the blade-shaped
leaves flashing as the wind rustles
through them and they throw back like spears
the shafts of light that fall on them:
the trees stand tall, aloof and dreaming in
the haze of the warm midday heat
except for the young blue spruces—
they seem alive and restless with magic
and a blue shade, as if moonlight
lingers there, is gathered around them.

All this grows from dark, rich, fertile soil;
through these valleys and mountain slopes
warriors once poured down to defend
their land and fought and gave their lives:

they poured their rich blood with fierce
unrelenting anger into this dark fertile soil:
and the men and women fight on,
and give their lives.
The struggle continues.

And as I say, this is part of my tribute to the women whose role in the struggle is now being downplayed. It seems to me important that one should stress their role rather than minimize it.

Well, then we had another evening of poetry where we talked about the African poetic tradition, the oral tradition, and we linked it with rap and reggae and what people are doing in the Caribbean as well as in Africa. And again I took the opportunity to read a poem, one I wrote some years ago. I'll now read a small bit of it about the high-school children who were killed, as I'm sure most of you will remember, in 1976 in the Soweto uprising. This is curiously distant now, and yet it is something that seems to me we ought *not* to forget. And so what I did was talk about the old ballad tradition in Europe, the notion of choral participation in the verse, and the call-and-response structure, which of course is not unlike the African tradition which came to America and other parts of the diaspora. And this is a poem where you have a kind of lead line and then a response line. In Johannesburg, I got my audience to assert that they would not forget, that they would make that commitment, that they would *not* forget. And the poem goes like this:

CATENA

commemorating the victims of Soweto
Pray you, remember them.

The alleys reeking with the acrid stench
of gunfire, teargas and arrogant hate

Pray you, remember them

We remember them

The pungent odor of anger,
of death and dying, and decay

I pray you, do remember them

We remember them

Anger drifting through smoke-filled lanes
and sudden erratic gusts

Pray and remember

We remember them

Torn bodies half-glimpsed
Through standing roiling smoke

Pray, remember them

The ghettos reeking
Fathers grieving
Mothers weeping
Bodies of children torn and bleeding

Pray, remember them:

We remember them

I hope I've given you just a slight glimpse of the South Africa of today. Certainly, it is not one that the American media will communicate to you. And it is one that you may not be aware of if you were in South Africa. So let me give you four rather crude facts.

One: as you probably know, the minister of economic affairs in the new South Africa is the same minister of economic affairs who was the minister in the old South Africa. He has since resigned, but he's been replaced by a man who is very much his clone.

Two: the general who commanded the South African army in the old apartheid days is the general who commands the South African army in the present post-apartheid South Africa.

Three (and in my mind the most troubling, perhaps): the man who headed the secret police in the old South African regime heads the secret police in the present South African regime.

Those seem to me extremely important. The fourth: we do not have a democratic government in South Africa. Instead we have something called the GNU, the Government of National Unity, which is a fusion of the democratic forces and the antidemocratic forces together. President Mandela, sure. Vice-President Thabo Mbeki, sure. But also Vice-President Mr. De Klerk, *and* the minister of ethnic affairs—would you believe, and this is really very scary—Buthelezi: the man who was the principal promoter of ethnic divisions is now the minister of ethnic affairs.

Those are some of the issues that trouble me, and there's one more. And this one must cause people to shudder all over Africa, not just South Africa. The South African government is now in the process of negotiating with the World Bank and the International Monetary Fund (IMF) about a series of what I call "conditionalities." If you've been to Ghana, if you've been to Nigeria, if you've been to Uganda or Zambia, and especially—I think, where the most naked processes are taking place—Zimbabwe, then you've seen what the IMF and the World Bank are about ultimately: not aid, but bankruptcy and the virtual recolonialization of the continent of Africa. This is what we must recognize. This is the process that confronts South Africa and all of the continent of Africa. We've entered a new world, a totally new world, and I'm not thinking of this week's disaster; I'm thinking of the fact that—post–Berlin Wall, post–Cold War—we've now entered a totally new unipolar world. The old bipolar conflict—between East and West, democracy versus socialism, and capitalism versus communism—is past. We are talking of a new unipolar world in our time in which we see an attempt to impose global oppression, global capitalism, the freedom of capital to move anywhere, transcending all boundaries and all barriers, to go wherever labor is cheapest. Third World countries are reduced to competing with each other and saying: "You come to us—our labor is even cheaper than it is in Taiwan or in South Korea or in the Philippines. And, what is more, we promise you that if you come to us, we will not allow our workers to form trade unions. We will not allow them to go on strike; we will not allow collective bargaining for minimum living wages. We will allow you to destroy our environment, to pollute and destroy it, and there will be no legislation to interfere. *And,* we promise you, you will have complete freedom to repatriate your capital, your profits, so that whatever wealth generated will not be for the benefit of the people in that country." This is what GATT is about and this is what the WTO—this new monster which will confront us all, the World Trade Organization—is about. Into that morass South Africa is being drawn as other African countries have already been drawn.

I'm going to read a couple of poems, but I will try to limit them to the topic of exile since that is what we are about tonight. I'm going to start by reading one you may have heard before. I should mention the context: when I was in China as a guest of the Chinese Olympic Committee, they took me to what is probably the most beautiful part of China, the area around West Lake. Marco Polo visited this area hundreds of years ago and, having been around the world, declared that this was the fairest place he had ever seen. And it is an absolutely wonderful place. At night you hear the nightingales singing. Weeping willows trail into the water, little delicate bridges that look like ivory filigree, and at night you hear the nightingales singing. That is about as good as it can get except—and that is what my poem is about—that even then one would rather be in one's own country; even that, wonderful as it is, does not satisfy the need to be in your own homeland. And so here's the poem:

EXILE

West Lake, China

Nightingales
in branches
on the hillsides
reflected in the smooth
black mirror of West Lake:
a much-traveled traveler said:
"fairest place in all the world,"
my obdurate heart
resisted stubbornly that beauty,
railing soundlessly
against exile.

My next poem, from new work, is based on a very unusual experience. I was in Johannesburg this year, invited to chair a festival of the arts to prove that the arts had stayed alive under the years of oppression. I was delighted to be a part of it because, in a sense,

I think I have helped to keep those arts alive through my poetry, which continued to circulate illegally after I was banned. Anyway, while I was there the organizers asked me what I would like to do as a special treat. I had mentioned that I had been to Johannesburg before—in fact I knew Johannesburg well: I had spent time in prison in Johannesburg. A whole military base had been converted into a prison called The Fort, where Mahatma Gandhi had spent time as well. So I said, "Well, it would be nice if I could see The Fort." And they said, "Unfortunately, it's been changed; it is now the headquarters of a regiment. They have their banquets and their receptions there, and they also have a military museum with all their military trophies there." So I said, "Well, I'd still like to see it." And they said, "Well, unfortunately, they are having a banquet and it's full of flowers and candles and decorations and all that, so . . . too bad." I said, "Well, see what we can do." And they said, "Alright, the caretaker will let you in for a short while and you can kind of walk around the place, although it won't be satisfactory; but at least if you want to go, you can go." By coincidence, one part of it had not yet been changed, and this they showed me: it was where the Blacks used to have a little area to bathe or shower. And it turned out that this was where *I* had been kept—I had been shot, and I was brought in and laid out on the floor in this particular area, and then I was allowed afterward to go and wash there.

To go back to this place was a very unusual experience; it was a place I had since written a poem about. Sunlight had come through a wire mesh over the window. And as it penetrated through the window, somehow the wire mesh split the light so that it had a prismatic effect, the kind of thing you sometimes see on the edge of a mirror—all those multicolors of light. At that time I was feeling particularly depressed. I had been shot in the back, and the bullet had gone right through me and come out of my chest. They had had to cut me open and take out the bullet. They stitched up the six separate holes where the bullet had entered and exited three times; the stitches had not yet been removed. Lying on the floor there, one of the few things that redeemed existence for me was seeing this prismatic effect of light split up like a rainbow on the wall. There was something cheerful about it, and it made me feel good. And so the poem is about that:

THE FORT PRISON

For NCADP and John Spenkelink, May 26, 1989

They called the single cell
over the doorway
simply *"the condemned."*
Here, prisoners were kept
who could be hanged
(but Gandhi, they said
was also isolated there).
Light was prismed through a fine mesh
so it broke, iridescent,
on the gray wall—
patches of rainbow light delighted me
but I saw how a life could shatter,
be lost into eternity.

"Stubborn Hope" is one of the few poems I wrote about exile, and roughly it makes one point: it says "exile is not amputation"; it is not as if you had a limb chopped off and you feel the pain of the nerves at the end of that amputated limb. For me, exile was something that I partly succeeded in shutting my mind to: I did not accept the fact that I was in exile; I continued to function as if I were still in South Africa, still in contact there, still participating in the struggle. And, of course, we understood that this was a struggle to liberate our country. We didn't fool around. Whether what we have now is really a liberated country seems to me an open question, one that may still have to be answered in the future. But writing about it, writing about the new South Africa, I find our situation not unlike that of the people of Haiti. There today the killings are still going on. If you listened to the radio this morning, they talked of men whose wounds were being dressed where they had been slashed with machetes. It's still happening, but now it's happening in the presence of the United States Army. And the United States Army is preparing to hand over power, when it leaves, to that military. We may end up with the replacement of one military regime by another military regime, *but* with the appearance of change because you have Aristide there (the poor man is virtually powerless)—but you have the *appearance* of a democracy.

So for me, in South Africa (and I know this is unpopular—I

think a time will come when many other people will also see what I see now) what we have achieved is this fraud of a government of national unity. This is happening now in Mozambique, where Frelimo and Renamo are under pressure to form one government; the Angolan people are being told that the MPLA and Savimbi must form one government.[1] Governments of national unity are suddenly fashionable. The West used to say to Africa, "How dare you have one-party governments! We will condemn every one-party government!" Now we're ending up with one-party governments of a new breed. So I wrote a poem about the fact that we have a long way to go toward freedom in South Africa:

STILL THE SIRENS

Still the sirens
stitch the night air with terror—
pierce hearing's membranes
with shrieks of pain and fear:

still they weave the mesh
that traps the heart in anguish,
flash bright bars of power
that cage memory in mourning and loss.

Still the sirens haunt the night air.

Someday there will be peace
someday the sirens will be still
someday we will be free.

Let me finish on a comparatively optimistic note. I'm looking at South Africa and I know how difficult the struggle is to achieve true freedom, *and I know*. I believe we're on the way toward true freedom. And so this next poem was my tribute to Mandela when he came out of prison. The day he was released, I began a poem which took me about fourteen months to finish. I had been with Mandela on Robben Island; we had broken stones together in the same section, each one; with a rock file and a hammer, we broke stones together. We walked the white beach sands together and we watched the warders beating up prisoners on the beach there. And all of these get into my poem in various ways.

FEBRUARY, 1990

Yes, Mandela—
Some of us admit embarrassedly
we wept to see you step free
so erectly, so elegantly
shrug off the prisoned years
a blanket cobwebbed of pain and grime:

behind: the island's seasand,
harsh, white and treacherous
ahead: jagged rocks and krantzes
bladed crevices of racism and deceit.

In the salt island air
you swung your hammer, grimly stoic
facing the dim path of interminable years.
Now, vision blurred with tears
we see you step out to our salutes
bearing our burden of hopes and fears
and impress your radiance
on the gray morning air.

On Prison and Exile—Poems

Dennis Brutus

PRISON

The "Abyss" is their word for time,
time in prison—any kind of prison
they can see time as a devouring maw,
a vortex that sucks away their lives;
but in that vision they assert themselves
seeing the abyss and themselves as separate:
so they take on, once more, human dignity.

ENDURANCE

> . . . *is the ultimate virtue—more,*
> *the essential thread*
> *on which existence is strung*
> *when one is stripped to nothing else*
> *and not to endure is to end in despair.*

I.

Cold floors
bleak walls
another anteroom:
another milestone behind
fresh challenges ahead:
in this hiatus
with numb resolution
I coil my energies
and wait.

II.

Stripped to the waist
in ragged pantaloons
long ago I sweated over bales,
my stringy frame—strained—
grew weary but sprang back
stubbornly
from exhaustion:
the lashes now,
and the labors are different
but still demand,
wound and stretch to breaking point:
and I still snap back, stubbornly.

III.

All day a stoic
at dawn I wake, eyelids wet
with tears shed in dreams.

IV.

My father, that distant man,
gray hair streaked with silver,
spoke of St. Francis of Assisi
with a special timbre in his voice:
loved him not, I think, for the birds
circling his head, nor the grace
of that threadbare fusty gown
but for his stigmata: the blood
that gleamed in the fresh wounds
on his palms and insteps:
in my isolation cell in prison,
the bullet wound in my side still raw,
those images afflicted me.

V.

When we shook hands in the Athenian dusk
it closed a ring that had opened twenty-four years before
when a wisp of off-key melody had snaked into my gray cell

whistled by a bored guard in the sunlit afternoon outside:
it circled the gray walls like a jeweled adder
bright and full of menace and grew
to a giant python that encircled me, filling the cell
then shrank and entered me where it lay
coiled like my gut, hissing sibilantly
of possession;
twice I breathed death's hot fetid breath
twice I leaned over the chasm, surrendering
till some tiny fiber at the base of my brain
protested in the name of sanity and dragged me
from the precipice of suicide that allured
with its own urgent logic

Our hands meeting, uncordially, your gaze
quizzical, perhaps affronted
sealed a circle in the gathering dusk,
like the ring of dark waves advancing
on the island's jagged shore
and the dark enclosure of wire
whose barbs are buried in my brain.

FOR WCJB

My brother, who died in exile

For him the battle never ended
he wore doggedly day after day
the armor of isolation and loneliness
the mask of indifference and impassivity
but a slow fury smoldered in his head
and a bitter green fire burnt in his guts like bile

he heard, his anger flaring, each distant outrage
and on the neighbor allies of oppression
his contempt ran in a steady stream like spittle:
even at the end, when his eyes clouded,
the last pinpoint gleam held steady,
and his ragged fragmented lungs rasped, "*Freedom.*"

A Song of Home, A Song of Exile

Keorapetse Kgositsile

RED SONG

Need I remind
                    Anyone again that
Armed struggle
                    Is an act of love

I might break into song
Like the bluesman or troubador
And from long distance
In no blues club
I might say
        Baby baby baby
There is no point in crying
Just because just because I'm not at home

When I try to run away from song
Walking softly in the night
A persistent voice
More powerful than the enemy bombs
Grabs me by the elbow of my heart
Demanding the song
That bathes our lives
In the rain of our blood
Stretched taut in the streets
As Moloise gasps the last breath
Of one solitary life

Should I now stop singing of love
Now that "my memory is surrounded by blood"
Sister why oh why

Do we at times mistake
A pimple for a cancer
And you brother
Who knows our tough tale

Who has been through the tunnel
On this long road
Who has seen the night
Winking and whispering
Who possesses worldwide hands
Of the worker
Who has created
This house these clothes this bed
This street I walk in the night
This light to shatter the darkness of this despair
Tell me why
I must not sing a song of love

Horror and terror are not strangers
When Duma no older than six years
Looks at shoeprints in the yard
And says: Papa who has been here
Rrangwane Uncle Thami Uncle Tim Uncle George
And you do not have shoes like this
Mama why did you leave the window open
The child knows and tells something
About the life we live

So who are they who say
No more love poems

I want to sing a song of love
For the woman who blasted the boers
Out of that yard across the border
And lived long enough to tell it
I want to sing a song of love
For that woman
Who jumped fences pregnant
And gave birth to a healthy child

I want to sing a song of love
For the old woman who in fearful nights

Still gave refuge to comrades
I want to sing a song of love
For the peasant who shared
His meagre supper with comrades
Without returns "for services rendered"

So now with my hands
Clasping guns grenades bombs
Embracing the warmth of my woman's breast
Moving to the rhythm of a mother's love
And the sad sad eye of a father
Embraced in the fixed demands
Of a troubled and expectant people
From the stench of history
And the fragrance of desire and purpose
Softly I walk into the embrace
Of this fire
That will ignite
My song of love
My song of life

JUNE 16 YEAR OF THE SPEAR

They call me freedomchild
I am liberationbound
My name is June 16
But this is not 1976

Freedomchild homewardbound
With an AK47 resting easy in my arms
The rivers I cross are no longer treacherous boundaries
Throwing me into the frustrating arms of exile
The rivers I cross are love strings

Around my homeland and me
Around the son and the new day

Who does not see me
Will hear freedomsound
Roaming the rhythms of my dream
Roosting warmly palpable as breast of every mother
Splitting every day and night
Spreading freedomseed all over this land of mine
My mothers fathers of my father kinsmen
Because I am June 16
And this is not Soweto 1976
I emerge in the asphalt streets of our want
And because 'my memory is surrounded by blood'
My blood has been hammered to liberationsong
And like Rebelo's bullets
And Neto's sacred hope
I am flowering
Over the graves of these goldfanged fascist ghouls

I am June 16
As Arab Ahmed says
My body is the fortress
Let the siege come!
I am the fireline
And I will besiege them
For my breast is the shelter
Of my people

I am June 16
I am Solomon Mahlangu
I am the new chapter
I am the way forward from Soweto 1976
I am poetry flowering with an AK47
All over this land of mine

NOTES

Kofi Anyidoho, "Prison as Exile/Exile as Prison: Circumstance, Metaphor, and a Paradox of Modern African Literatures"

1. Okinba Launko, *Dream-Seeker on Divining Chain* (Ibadan and Lagos: Kraft Books Ltd., 1993), 66.
2. See Appendix for a fuller statement on the Institute in general and the 1994–95 program in particular.
3. The main participants in the workshop were: Sandra L. Richards (African American Studies and Theater, Northwestern University); Abena Busia (English, Rutgers University); Ola Rotimi (Drama, Obafemi Awolowo University); Kofi Anyidoho (English and School of Performing Arts, University of Ghana, Legon); Aliko Songolo (English, University of Wisconsin–Madison); Dennis Brutus (Black Community Education, Research, and Development, University of Pittsburgh); Micere Mugo (Afro-American Studies, Syracuse University); M. Nourbese Philip (Toronto-based writer); Célestin Monga (Sloan School of Management, Massachusetts Institute of Technology); Jack Mapanje (English, University of Leeds); Oga S. Abah (Drama, Ahmadu Bello University); Akbar M. Virmani (Program of African Studies, Northwestern University); Leonard Houantchekon (Economics, Northwestern University); and Keorapetse Kgositsile (South African poet).
4. Wole Soyinka, *The Man Died: Prison Notes* (London: Rex Collins, 1972), 13.
5. Abdul R. JanMohamed, "Dennis Brutus," in Bernth Lindfors and Reinhard Sander, eds., *Dictionary of Literary Biography, Vol. 117: Twentieth-Century Caribbean and Black African Writers, First Series* (Detroit: Gale Research Inc., 1992), 98.
6. Jack Mapanje, "Censoring the African Poem: Personal Reflections," in Kirsten Holst Peterson, ed., *Criticism and Ideology* (Uppsala: The Scandinavian Institute of African Studies, 1988), 104–11; reprinted in *Index on Censorship* 9 (1989): 7–11. For a fuller account of Mapanje's life and work, see James Gibbs, "Jack Mapanje," in Bernth Lindfors and Reinhard Sander, eds. *Dictionary of Literary Biography, Vol. 157: Twentieth-Century Caribbean and Black African Writers, Third Series* (Detroit: Gale Research Inc., 1995), 170–80.

7. Chinua Achebe, *Anthills of the Savannah* (London: Heinemann, 1987), 123–24.

8. Kwadwo Opoku-Agyemang, "Introit," in *Cape Coast Castle* (Accra: Afram Publications, 1997), 9.

9. Tanure Ojaide, "I Want to Be an Oracle: My Poetry and My Generation." *World Literature Today* 68, no. 1 (Winter 1994): 21.

10. Andrew Gurr, *Writers in Exile: The Identity of Home in Modern Literature* (Sussex, Brighton: Harvester Press; Atlantic Highlands, N.J.: Humanities Press, 1981), 13–14.

11. Ibid.

12. Rowland Smith, ed., *Exile and Tradition: Studies in African and Caribbean Literature* (London: Longman and Dalhousie University Press, 1976), ix.

13. Ibid., 25.

14. Mary Lynn Broe and Angela Ingram, eds., *Women's Writing in Exile* (Chapel Hill: University of North Carolina Press, 1989).

15. Joseph Brodsky, "The Condition We Call Exile," in Broe and Ingram, *Women's Writing in Exile*, 1.

16. Max Dorsinville, "Senghor, or the Song of Exile," in Smith, *Exile and Tradition*, 67.

17. Ibid.

18. Léopold Sedar Senghor, *Nocturnes,* trans. John Reed and Clive Wake (London: Heinemann, 1969), 19.

19. Onyekachi Wambu, "African Europeans," *Africa Forum* 1, no. 3 (1991): 17–22.

20. "Africans Abroad," *West Africa* (March 4–10, 1991): 294.

21. Ama Ata Aidoo, *Our Sister Killjoy: Reflections from a Black-Eyed Squint* (London: Longman, 1966), 126–29.

22. Ngugi wa Thiong'o, *Detained: A Writer's Prison Diary* (London: Heinemann, 1981), 97.

23. Mineke Schipper, "Censorship on Africa," *ALA Bulletin* 20, no. 2 (Spring 1994): 61–68.

24. Ngugi, *Detained,* 97.

25. Don Mattera, *Memory Is the Weapon* (Johannesburg: Ravan Press, 1987).

26. Ngugi wa Thiong'o, *Matigari,* trans. Wangui wa Goro (Oxford: Heinemann International, 1989), viii; original Gikuyu edition published as *Matigari ma njiruungi* (Nairobi: Heinemann Kenya, 1986).

27. Wambu, "African Europeans," 17.

28. Ibid., 22.

29. A Presidential Welcome Address, delivered at the 20th Annual Meeting of the African Literature Association, Accra, March 1994. In Kofi Anyidoho, Abena Busia, and Anne V. Adams, eds., *Beyond Survival:*

African Literature and the Search for New Life (Lawrenceville, N.J.: Africa World Press, forthcoming).

30. Abena P. A. Busia, *Testimonies of Exile* (Trenton, N.J.: Africa World Press, 1990; Accra: Woeli Publishing Services, 1990).

31. M. Nourbese Philip, *She Tries Her Tongue; Her Silence Softly Breaks* (Havana: Casa de las Americas, 1988; Charlottetown, Canada: Ragweed Press, 1989); *Looking for Livingstone: An Odyssey of Silence* (Stratford, Canada: Mercury Press, 1991).

32. Elaine Savory, "Marlene Nourbese Philip," in Bernth Lindfors and Reinhard Sander, eds., *Dictionary of Literary Biography, Vol. 157: Twentieth-Century Caribbean and Black African Writers, Third Series* (Detroit: Gale Research Inc., 1995), 303.

33. Ken Saro-Wiwa, "Lord Take My Soul but the Struggle Continues: Ken Saro-Wiwa's Last Words," *ALA Bulletin* 21, no. 4 (Fall 1995): 3-4.

JACK MAPANJE, "OF ORALITY AND MEMORY IN PRISON AND EXILE"

1. Bakare Gbadamosi and Ulli Beier, eds., *Not Even God Is Ripe Enough* (London: Heinemann, 1968).

2. Latin for "I have sinned most grievously."

JACK MAPANJE, "CONTAINING COCKROACHES"

1. Mandrax, *chamba,* and cannabis are narcotics; *chamba* is a local term for marijuana. RENAMO originally referred to the guerrilla movement that fought for the liberation of Mozambique from Portuguese colonial rule, but here it has been adopted as a nickname.

MICERE GITHAE MUGO, "EXILE AND CREATIVITY: A PROLONGED WRITER'S BLOCK"

An abridged version of this paper was presented at Northwestern; the full first draft was delivered at the conference on Writers and Human Rights, September 26-28, 1989, at the Centre Africain d'Animation Culturel, Dakar, Senegal.

MICERE GITHAE MUGO, "POEMS FOR LIBERATION OF THE LAND"

Selected from Micere Githae Mugo, *My Mother's Poem and Other Songs* (Nairobi: East African Educational Publishers, 1994).

Aliko Songolo, "The Locus and Logos of Exile"

1. Edward W. Said, "The Mind of Winter: Reflections on Life in Exile," *Harper's* 269 (September 1984): 49.

2. Edward W. Said, *Representations of the Intellectual* (New York: Pantheon, 1994), 48–49.

3. Said, "The Mind of Winter," 49.

4. Abdul J. JanMohamed, "Worldliness-without-World, Homelessness-as-Home: Toward a Definition of the Specular Border Intellectual," in Michael Sprinker, ed., *Edward Said: A Critical Reader* (Oxford: Blackwell, 1992), 101.

5. Gilles Deleuze and Félix Guattari, *Kafka: Pour une littérature mineure* (Paris: Editions de minuit, 1975); see esp. chap. 3, "Qu'est-ce qu'une littérature mineure?"

6. Caren Kaplan, "Deterritorializations: The Rewriting of Home and Exile in Western Feminist Discourse," *Cultural Critique* 6 (Spring 1987): 188.

7. Said, "The Mind of Winter," 55.

8. Edouard Glissant, *Le Discours antillais* (Paris: Seuil, 1981); translated by J. Michael Dash as *Caribbean Discourse* (Charlottesville: University Press of Virginia, 1989).

9. Albert Gérard, "Spécificités de la littérature zaïroise," in Emile van Balberghe et al., eds., *Papier blanc, encre noire: Cent ans de culture francophone en Afrique centrale* (Bruxelles: Editions Labor, 1992), 119.

10. Janice Spleth, "The Political Alienation of the Intellectual in Recent Zairian Fiction," *Studies in Twentieth Century Literature* 15, no. 1 (Winter 1991): 123.

11. V. Y. Mudimbe, *L'écart* (Paris: Présence africaine, 1979); translated by Marjolijn de Jager as *The Rift*. However, since *The Rift* was not available to me at the time of this writing, all translations are mine.

12. Though the country is not named in Mudimbe's narrative, the implication is that it is Zaire, for that is where the Kuba live.

13. Mudimbe, *L'écart*, 67, 68.

14. Ibid., 27.

Célestin Monga, "Cartoons in Cameroon: Anger and Political Derision under Monocracy"

I would like to thank Achille Mbembe for suggesting that I explore some of the issues in this paper, and Marlene Nourbese Philip for her thoughtful comments during presentation of the first draft.

1. I borrow the term "monocracy" from A. Kom, "Writing under Monocracy: Intellectual Poverty in Cameroon," *Research in African Litera-*

ture 22, no. 1 (Spring 1991): 83–92. I also tackle the issue of political derision using the bottom-top approach suggested by Comi Toulabor, that is, a perspective from the people, not from the ruling elites. See Toulabor, "Jeux de mots, jeux de vilains: lexique de la dérision politique au Togo," *Politique Africaine* (September 1981).

2. See Joseph Bucklin Bishop, *Presidential Nominations and Elections: A History of American Conventions, National Campaigns, Inaugurations and Campaign Caricature* (New York: Scribner, 1916).

3. Ibid., 134.

4. From an interview with the director of Messapress, the major company distributing printed media in Cameroon.

5. Following a path initiated by Lemana Louis Marie, a former *Cameroon Tribune* cartoonist who never did political caricature, Popoli and Go'away recently began to draw and compose their caricatures so well that they told their own story, with the aid of a title or a few words of dialogue beneath them.

6. The government-owned *Cameroon Tribune* is the only daily paper in the country.

7. See Achille Mbembe, "La 'chose' et ses doubles dans la caricature camerounaise," manuscript, Department of History, University of Pennsylvania, 1994.

8. For a complete presentation, see A. Koestler, s.v. "Humor and Wit," *Encyclopaedia Britannica* (1994): 683.

9. Henri Bergson, *Laughter: An Essay on the Meaning of the Comic* (New York: Macmillan, 1911), quoted by Koestler.

10. Ibid.

11. Koestler, 684.

12. Ibid., 683.

13. On this issue, see Célestin Monga, *The Anthropology of Anger: Civil Society and Democracy in Africa* (Boulder, Colo., and London: Lynne Rienner Publishers, 1996).

14. See Alvin L. Golman, "Ethics and Cognitive Science," *Ethics* 103 (1993): 337–60.

15. See, e.g., the argument made by D. L. Horowitz, "Democracy in Divided Societies," *Journal of Democracy* 4, no. 4 (October 1993): 18–38.

16. Cf. Jean-François Médart, Communication au colloque, Brazzaville, 50 ans, October 7–8, 1994, at Boston University, Boston, Mass.; see also R. Lemarchand, "African Transitions to Democracy: An Interim (and Mostly Pessimistic) Assessment," *Africa Insight* 22, no. 3 (1994): 178–85.

17. See Célestin Monga, *Measuring Democracy: A Comparative Theory of Political Well-Being*, Working Papers in African Studies no. 206, 2 vols., Boston University, 1996.

18. In 1992, Kuomegni Kontchou, the Cameroonian minister of information, deplored the fact that "no other head of state in the world has been so often insulted as President Biya."

19. Derrick Bell, *Confronting Authority: Reflections of an Ardent Protester* (Boston: Beacon Press, 1994), xii.

20. This is a very popular Cameroonian dictum used by Jean-François Bayart in his book *L'Etat en Afrique: La politique du ventre* (Paris: Fayard, 1989). However, it would be too simplistic to conclude here that money is everything in African politics; as a means of power, it has its limitations. See Célestin Monga, "Le franc CFA, le dollar et la démocratisation." Paper presented at conference: Retour au pluralisme et consolidation de la démocratie, May 5–6, 1995, at Université Laval, Québec.

21. I borrow from Paul Krugman's title *The Age of Diminished Expectations: U. S. Economic Policy in the 1990s* (Cambridge, Mass.: MIT Press, 1990).

22. Cornel West, *Race Matters* (Boston: Beacon Press, 1993), 14, 18.

23. Quoted by Hayden Carruth, *Sitting In: Selected Writings on Jazz, Blues, and Related Topics* (Iowa City: University of Iowa Press, 1993), 118.

M. NOURBESE PHILIP, "EARTH AND SOUND: THE PLACE OF POETRY"

1. Distinction made by Jeremy Hooker, *Poetry of Place: Essays and Reviews, 1970–1981* (Manchester: Carcanet Press, 1982).

2. Terry Eagleton, *Exiles and Emigrés* (London: Chatto and Windus, 1970), 112.

3. George Eliot, *Impressions of Theophrastus Such* (New York: Thomas Y. Crowell & Co., 1880).

4. Marlene Nourbese Philip, "Island Liturgies." Unpublished manuscript.

5. Hooker, *Poetry of Place*, 184.

6. Ned Thomas, *Derek Walcott, Poet of the Islands* (Cardiff: Welsh Arts Council, 1980), 188.

7. Hooker, *Poetry of Place*, 188.

8. Thomas, *Derek Walcott*, 15.

9. Margaret Drabble, *A Writer's Britain: Landscape in Literature* (London: Thames and Hudson, Ltd., 1979), 22.

10. Ezra Pound, *ABC of Reading* (Norfolk, Connecticut: New Directions, 1960), 35.

11. C. L. R. James, "The Artist in the Caribbean," *The Future in the Present: Selected Writings* (London: Allison and Busby, 1977), 183.

12. C. L. R. James, *The Caribbean Revolution,* quoted in *Outlet* (November 18, 1983).

13. Tim Hector, in *Outlet* (November 18, 1983).

14. Les A. Murray, *Persistence in Folly* (Sydney: Angus and Robertson, 1984).

15. Interview with Aimé Césaire in *Présence Africaine,* no. 126 (1985): 33; last emphasis mine.

> Moreover, I am somewhat accustomed to saying that if I wanted to situate myself psychologically—perhaps I can include the people of Martinique in general—I would say that we are a people of Mount Pélée. I feel that my poetry is 'Péléean' because, precisely speaking, my poetry is not at all an effusive poetry, or in other words, a poetry that flows out, perpetually flows out: I believe that speech is *rare*—tenuous—meaning that it builds up over long periods of time; it builds up patiently, finds its way out; no sooner does one believe it to be snuffed out when suddenly the mountainside rips open. This is what gives it its dramatic quality: eruption. Thus is my poetry Péléean. In any case, I think, *it is always in terms of land, or sea, or vegetation that it receives its shape.*

16. Hilary Okam, "Aspects of Imagery and Symbolism in the Poetry of Aimé Césaire," *Yale French Studies* 53 (1976): 185–88.

17. Les A. Murray, *The Peasant Mandarin* (St. Lucia, Australia: University of Queensland Press, 1978).

18. Quoted in Hooker, *Poetry of Place.*

19. Max Dorsinville, *Le Pays Natal* (Dakar, Senegal: Nouvelles Editions africaines, 1983), 21. "The cultural imperative consists in a research of authentic artistry created by a symbiosis among the writer, the country, and the people. . . . In the light of these imperatives predicated on the 'subject' of the Third World, one theme seems central in its literature: the return to one's native land [*retour au pays natal*]."

20. Ibid., 23, 25. [This return, he argues, may be real or symbolic,] "inspired by a double vision made up of contrasts between experiences lived abroad and those emanating from the reality of home." [Return, even the symbolic, implies an acceptance of the *pays natal,* the land of birth, the earth and the body.] "The return to one's native land is equivalent to self-acceptance, but of a collective self inscribed in the biological and ontological time and nature of the land [*pays-nature*]."

21. Marlene Nourbese Philip, *She Tries Her Tongue; Her Silence Softly Breaks* (Charlottetown, Canada: Ragweed Press, 1989).

22. The African-Canadian poet George Eliot Clarke had done impor-

tant work reclaiming for the African-Canadian literary tradition work from nontraditional sources such as sermons. Despite this, however, the point remains that, unlike the United States and Britain, Canada did not have a long-established tradition of a self-consciously literary tradition by Africans.

23. Eagleton, *Exiles and Emigrés*, 184.

M. NOURBESE PHILIP, "WHOSE IDEA WAS IT ANYWAY?"

1. Father Damien Lopez de Haro, Bishop of San Juan. Report to a Diocesan Synod, San Juan, April 30–May 6, 1645.
2. Gomes Eannes de Azurara, Portuguese chronicler (1410–74), "Chronica do descobrimento e conquista de Guine" (Paris, 1841).
3. Fray Thomas Mercado, "Suma de Tratos e Contratos" (Seville, 1587).

ABENA P.A. BUSIA, PREFACE TO *Testimonies of Exile*

1. Abena P.A. Busia, *Testimonies of Exile* (Trenton, N.J.: Africa World Press, 1990). The book did not originally contain a preface; this preface was written after the book had been published.

KOFI ANYIDOHO, "ON OPPRESSION, PRISON, AND EXILE—POEMS"

Selected from Kofi Anyidoho, *AncestralLogic & CaribbeanBlues* (Trenton, N.J.: Africa World Press, 1993).

DENNIS BRUTUS, "THROUGH THE BARS: THE PRISON EXPERIENCE IN POETRY"

1. Frelimo and Renamo are two separate political organizations active in Mozambique. Frelimo (Frente de Libertação de Moçambique) formed in 1962 when three nationalist parties merged. It is currently headed by Joaquim Alberto Chissano, now president of the Republic of Mozambique. Renamo (Resistência Nacional Moçambicana), a former guerrilla group, in conflict with the government between 1976 and October 1992, was registered as a political party in August 1994. The MPLA (People's Movement for the Liberation of Angola) was formed in 1956 as a nationalist group opposing the former Portuguese colonial power in Angola. It has been a governing party since 1975.

DENNIS BRUTUS, "ON PRISON AND EXILE — POEMS"

Selected from Dennis Brutus, *Still the Sirens* (Sante Fe: Pennywhistle Press, 1993), with an introduction by Lamont B. Steptoe.

KEORAPETSE KGOSITSILE, "A SONG OF HOME, A SONG OF EXILE"

Poems read by Keorapetse Kgositsile at the Prison and Exile workshop may be found in his collection *When the Clouds Clear* (Fordsburg: Congress of South African Writers, 1990).

APPENDIX

The Institute for Advanced Study and Research in the African Humanities Northwestern University

1994–95 Seminar on
Powers of Expression and Expression of Power:
Cultural Production under Constraint

Across the humanities and social sciences, increased attention is being devoted to the operations of censorship and to strategies of opposition and resistance. Social scientists examine the conflicting political discourses of human rights and of state intervention into individuals' lives. Humanists scrutinize the ways in which artists seek to resist official pressures, maintain and circulate independent expression, or appear to censor themselves. Under the theme "Powers of Expression and Expression of Power," Institute fellows are examining the varied ways in which artistic and scholarly production in Africa contends with claims of power and authority.

Dr. Kofi Anyidoho, acting director of the School of Performing Arts of the University of Ghana, is a preceptor of the Institute. A prize-winning poet as well as a distinguished scholar specializing in oral and written African literatures, Anyidoho has mapped out a fruitful area of investigation for the year's program, including two major topics for intensive reflection via the workshop mechanism, namely, "The Word Behind Bars and the Paradox of Exile" and "Scholarly Authority and Intellectual Production in African Studies." Through the two workshops, Wednesday seminars held regularly during each academic quarter, and a fellows exchange project with other research centers, we are bringing together a

This text was used to publicize the 1994–95 Institute program and fellowship competition.

group of scholars and artists who, in their discussions and reflections, will map out a number of fresh perspectives on very critical aspects of the arts and humanities in contemporary Africa.

THE INSTITUTE: A BRIEF BACKGROUND

Established in 1989, the Institute for Advanced Study and Research in the African Humanities seeks to give fresh direction and renewed support to the African humanities by examining defined areas of inquiry through year-long seminars under the direction of a preceptor. The product of a research initiative undertaken by the Social Science Research Council and Northwestern University, the Institute is housed at Northwestern under the Program of African Studies (PAS). It benefits from proximity to the Program on International Cooperation in Africa (PICA), which concentrates on medical, social, economic, and political processes transcending national borders, and to the Melville J. Herskovits Library, the largest separate collection of Africana in the world.

The Institute specifically addresses African cultural practices by granting residency fellowships in such fields as oral and written literatures, performance, film and broadcasting, music, and the visual arts. Deploying interdisciplinary approaches that bring together North American, European, and African social science and humanities scholars and arts practitioners, the Institute disseminates the research of its resident fellows through weekly seminar meetings, lectures, conferences, and publications.

The core of the Institute's activities is the weekly Wednesday-evening seminar, attended by Institute fellows, faculty from Northwestern as well as other area institutions, graduate students, and visitors. Fellows as well as other invited scholars circulate their papers in advance to regular participants (approximately thirty) and open the seminar with remarks that offer a frame for the ensuing discussion. Generally, formal discussion lasts for two hours and is followed by an informal social period lasting another forty-five minutes. The weekly seminar is supplemented by occasional Monday-night lectures by visiting scholars and by quarterly "Red Lion" seminars, hosted jointly with University of Chicago anthropologists and historians.

Since its inception, the Institute has addressed three fields of inquiry: In 1991–92 the theme was "The Politics of Representation: Struggles for the Control of Identity," and Dr. Ivan Karp, then of the National Museum of Natural History, served as preceptor. The next year, research clustered around the topic "The Constitution of Knowledge: The Production of History and Culture," with Dr. David William Cohen, former director of Northwestern's Program of African Studies, as preceptor. In 1993–94, the Institute focused on "The Inscription of the Material World," and Dr. Karin Barber of the University of Birmingham served as preceptor. During the 1994–95 academic year, the Institute is studying "Powers of Expression and Expression of Power: Cultural Production under Constraint." Dr. Kofi Anyidoho of the University of Ghana is the 1994–95 preceptor.

In addition, the Institute annually sponsors as many as three workshops (one in each quarter) designed to collectively further research by enabling fellows to concentrate their exchanges on one intellectual subset of the yearlong theme and to solicit the participation of additional faculty who otherwise would be unable to contribute to the Institute's research agenda. For example, under the rubric of "The Inscription of the Material World," the 1993–94 field of inquiry, the Institute hosted one weekend workshop on "Texts in Objects," wherein the preceptor, one fellow, and eight invited scholars examined some of the ways in which both natural and cultural environments are saturated with significance that is specifically textual, that is, taking the forms of narratives, proverbs, poetry, and songs. Some thirty graduate students and faculty from Northwestern, University of Chicago, Loyola University, University of Wisconsin–Parkside, and the Art Institute of Chicago attended. In spring 1994, the Institute sponsored a second workshop on the subject of popular culture and the media in Africa.

Workshop presentations have been edited and published in *Passages,* a sixteen- to twenty-four-page Chronicle of the Humanities inserted twice yearly into the *P.A.S. News & Events* newspaper. Given the newspaper's circulation to over three thousand Africanist scholars and institutions both nationally and internationally, the Institute has been able to disseminate research to a significant public in a timely fashion. Important to note in this respect is the fact that *Passages* circulates free of charge to some five hundred institutions and individuals on the African continent; in the context of scarce foreign exchange, the journal thus constitutes a critical mechanism through which African scholars can remain conversant with emerging lines of inquiry within the field. Given the intellectual acuity of participants and the interdisciplinary, revisionist nature of its research agenda, the Institute is challenging the field of African studies as a whole.

At the level of graduate training, the Institute plays an integral role in revitalizing education in African studies and allied areas of literary and cultural studies. Graduate students consistently attend and participate fully in the weekly seminars. Institute fellows have occasionally offered graduate seminars on such topics as postcolonial literature or women's cultural production in Ghana and regularly consult with dissertation-stage students.

In its first three years of existence, the Institute has hosted forty-nine scholars, selected through an international competition jointly administered by the Social Science Research Council and the Institute's governing board. Those with Rockefeller Foundation and other major funding have typically been in residence from four months up to an entire academic year. In contrast, Zora Neale Hurston fellows, supported by a variety of sources, including sabbatical funds from scholars' home institutions, enjoy an intensive residency, ranging from ten to fifteen days in duration.